DIVERSITY IN
COLLEGE CLASSROOMS

D0171324

Diversity in College Classrooms

PRACTICES FOR TODAY'S CAMPUSES

Edited by
Ann M. Johns
&
Maureen Kelley Sipp

The University of Michigan Press
Ann Arbor

2007 2006 2005 2004   4   3   2   1

A CIP catalog record for this book is available from the British Library.

Library of Congress Cataloging-in-Publication Data

Diversity in college classrooms : practices for today's campuses /
  edited by Ann M. Johns and Maureen Kelley Sipp.
      p.   cm.
  Includes bibliographical references and index.
  ISBN 0-472-08944-7 (pbk. : alk. paper)
    1. Minority college students—United States.   2. Discrimination
in higher education—United States.   3. Educational equalization—
United States.   I. Johns, Ann M.   II. Sipp, Maureen Kelley.
LC212.42.D58   2004
378.1'982—dc22   2003024511

For the many postsecondary faculty who celebrate, and draw from, classroom diversity

Preface

by Isidro Ortiz, Chicana/o Studies
San Diego State University

This scholarly collection represents one of several diversity initiatives undertaken at a four-year, comprehensive public university on the U.S.-Mexican border where, in 1998, people of color became the majority of the state's population. Though in other states, populations may not be as ethnically diverse, almost every college and university seems to be struggling with issues of recruitment, retention, and pedagogy for students who are quite different from those enrolled in earlier periods in our history. Unfortunately, there are faculty, staff, and administrators who oppose various diversity initiatives because they believe in continuing educational practices of the past, because they are offended by "political correctness," or because they think that the pedagogical practices suggested in this volume and elsewhere "dumb down the curriculum" or will fail to enhance student development.

Not surprisingly, the editors and authors of this volume have a very different point of departure. They assume that diversity accrues benefits for all students and that a discussion of appropriate pedagogical practices for learners in higher education enriches theory and research and promotes the scholarship of teaching. The contributors' assumptions are supported by the considerable evidence from the scholarly literature.

Patricia Gurin, in testimony on behalf of the University of Michigan's admissions policy, reviewed extensive literature in demonstrating the importance of diversity to a campus (Gurin 1999). In this effort, she conducted the most comprehensive and original empirical analysis of existing data on racial and ethnic diversity in higher education. Her work confirms that campus diversity directly affects immediate student learning as well as the ways students conduct themselves in postcollege life. Gurin classified campus diversity into three categories: *structural, classroom,* and *informal interactional.* Structural diversity refers primarily to the racial and ethnic composition of the student body. Classroom diversity focuses on "the incorporation of knowledge about diverse groups into the curriculum." Informal, interactional diversity, on the other hand, refers "to the opportunity to interact with students from diverse backgrounds in the broad campus environment."

Given the concerns of this volume, the most relevant of Gurin's findings pertains to the effect of diversity upon learning outcomes. Her research indicates that students "who had experienced the most diversity in classroom settings and in informal interactions with peers showed the greatest engagement in active thinking processes and growth in intellectual and academic skills." Her analyses revealed a consistent positive relationship between student learning in college, classroom diversity, and informal interactional diversity. The results were consistent across racially and ethnically different student populations but were "especially impressive" for White students. The White students "with the most experience with diversity during college" exhibited

> the greatest growth in active thinking processes as indicated by increased scores on a measure of complex thinking and social/historical thinking, growth in motivation in terms of drive to achieve, intellectual self-confidence, goals for creating original work, the highest post-graduate aspirations, and the greatest growth in student values placed on their intellectual and academic skills. (Gurin, 1999, pp. 1–2)

Gurin's case for the educational benefits of diversity is supported by the findings of the first comprehensive investigation of the attitudes toward and experiences with racial and ethnic diversity at Research I universities (Maruyama & Moreno, 2000). In this faculty survey, 69 percent responded that their universities value racial and ethnic diversity; 91 percent believed that "neither the quality of students nor the intellectual standards of class discussions suffer from diversity." Faculty also indicated that ethnic and racial diversity enables "all students to achieve the essential goals of a college education." One-third to one-half of the faculty identified the positive benefits of diversity in the classroom (Maruyama & Moreno, 2000, pp. 13–16).

These findings by Gurin and Maruyama and Moreno underscore the importance of racial and ethnic diversity in enhancing learning and encouraging democratic outcomes and values. However, Patricia King (2000), another researcher, argues that many questions have not been answered, including "What practices work well and poorly in regard to student subgroups that differ by factors such as age, gender, race and ethnicity, sexual orientation, preferred learning styles, and learning or physical disability?" and "What experiences are distinctive for these subgroups that affect students' educational success?"

The literature on diversity and student retention offers preliminary answers to these questions. Regarding the distinctive experiences of Latino and African American students, at least two researchers have found various forms of alienation and marginalization in institutions of higher education (Feagin, Vera, & Imani, 1996; González, 2001). These experiences shape student participation and success on campuses. In the face of such obstacles, some students demonstrate their capability to develop strategies to succeed academically as well as to transform their campuses. Unfortunately, many others give up and drop out.

To promote optimal learning by these, and all, current students, scholars have suggested specific principles to guide institutional policy and practices. Rendón and Garza (1996), for example, have called for a culturally diverse, learning-centered institutional restructuring (pp. 289–308). In terms of the classroom, they have urged faculty to

- focus on active learning,
- validate students' capability for learning,
- identify students' learning needs,
- establish clear learning expectations,
- use teaching practices identified as successful (collaborative learning, learning communities, community-based service learning), and
- employ multiple means of assessment.

College student departure has proven to be a complex puzzle, as noted by Braxton and Mundy (2001). Taking as their point of departure the notion that the reduction of this problem requires "possible solutions derived from the theory and research of several theoretical approaches," Braxton and Mundy offer recommendations for institutional practice. They recommend the practices urged by Rendón and Garza. Those practices and others are discussed in this volume.

The use of these practices can serve as measures of the degree to which student engagement is occurring on a campus. Creating such outcomes can be challenging for institutions where student-faculty ratios are high and where the academic culture tends to reward research over instruction. Nevertheless, even some large doctoral/research universities have become concerned with such learning outcomes, as is shown by their participation in a national study seeking to measure student participation in these kinds of recommended instructional activities (National Survey of Student Engagement, 2002).

Reliance on the pedagogical practices suggested by Rendón and Garza has been identified as being among the conditions that are necessary for maximizing the benefits of a racially and ethnically diverse classroom. These conditions were cited by faculty participants in an in-depth, qualitative, multiple-case study of the multiracial/multiethnic classrooms at the University of Maryland, College Park (Marin, 2000). At this campus, faculty and students concurred that racial and ethnic diversity in the classroom accrued concrete educational benefits. Indeed, they argued that "multi-racial/multi-ethnic classrooms enhance pedagogy and the opportunity to achieve particular educational goals in ways that cannot be replicated by other means" (Marin, 2000). The study participants noted that certain additional conditions were necessary, however. These included

- faculty preparation for teaching in a diverse classroom,
- a learner-centered faculty (and institutional) philosophy, and
- interactive teaching approaches.

Thus, in order to promote optimal student interaction and prevent the loss of significant educational opportunities, institutions of higher education need to offer training to faculty "in how to maximize the educational possibilities of racially and ethnically diverse classes" (Marin, 2000, p. 79).

At the campuses on which the contributors to this volume teach, we are gaining opportunities to promote structural diversity, at the very least. During the 1990s, our campus, like many others throughout the United States, experienced demographic changes that dramatically altered the composition of its student body, particularly its undergraduate population. In the fall of 1993, for example, the undergraduate population broke down as follows: Whites (54.62 percent), Hispanics and Mexican Americans (15.13 percent), Filipinos (5.66 percent), African Americans (5.37 percent), North Asians (4.67 percent), Southeast Asians (3.12 percent), American Indians (0.9 percent), and Pacific Islanders (.55 percent). In the spring of 2001, in contrast, the undergraduate population reflected the following characteristics in terms of ethnic and racial origin: Whites (45 percent), Mexican Americans and other Hispanics (19.7 percent), African Americans (4.5 percent), North Asians (3.6 percent), American Indians (0.8 percent), Pacific Islanders (0.6 percent), and Southeast Asians (3.2 percent). This domestic structural diversity was augmented by international students from eighty different nations and complemented, and complicated, by diversity among dimensions such as gender, age, disability, and sexual orientation.

The growing structural diversity has expressed itself in student life on campus. Already-established student clubs and organizations such as the Movimiento Estudiantil Chicano de Azlan (MEChA) and the Black Student Union have experienced membership growth. New organizations such as the Filipino student organization Samahan, the Association of Chicana Activists (ACHA), and the Lesbian and Gay Student Union have addressed a wide variety of issues on the campus.

At the level of student governance, the growth in structural diversity translated into a shift in the leadership of the Associated Students. In 1993, students of color gained control of the majority of top positions in the organization. Once in office, they initiated transformation in membership of the appointed student government boards. From these positions, the new majority mounted challenges to practices and traditions that they considered culturally insensitive and oppressive, including the university's use of *Aztecs* as a nickname for its sports teams and the accompanying indigenous mascot, "Monty" (Montezuma). The latter stance provoked an ongoing controversy and exposed the existence of deep fissures among students, faculty, staff, and, especially, alumni, often based on ethnicity.

As has been the case in other postsecondary as well as K–12 institutions, the transformation in the undergraduate population has not been paralleled at the faculty level. In spite of sincere efforts to diversify the faculty, instructor ranks have remained largely White, and many of the faculty of color who have been hired are international and have been educated in elite overseas institutions, thus making their living and learning experiences considerably different from those of the first-generation domestic students. The university confronts gaps of student-faculty color and social class. These gaps may be closed with increasing faculty retirements and new recruitments, but for the foreseeable future, they remain a major feature—and a major challenge—of university life. To compound the issue, the campus continues to experience considerable difficulty retaining African American and Latino students at a time when Latinos are well on their way to becoming the majority of the student population, a second challenge for the university and its role in the region.

The increase in structural diversity underscores the importance of the university's commitment to its students. The campus continues to support three separate ethnic studies departments: Africana Studies, Chicana and Chicano Studies, and American Indian Studies. In addition, it has established an Office of Diversity and Equity (ODE), which monitors and encourages diversity in university recruitment and employment and serves as a vehicle for campus sponsorship of diversity-oriented programming such as lectures, film series, and workshops. This office joined the Center for Teaching and Learning in sponsoring this volume and celebrating its contributors.

The university also continues to require all undergraduates to complete two "diversity" courses as part of their undergraduate degree requirements (see Hohm & Venable, this volume). It has created its first Latino Advisory Committee and has begun to write a strategic plan for addressing the diversity concerns of Chicanos and Latinos. Recently, the university president formulated a groundbreaking Compact for Success, an agreement with a local school district with a large Latino enrollment. This agreement furthers teacher-faculty interactions in the various institutions involved, increases students' college preparedness, and guarantees admission to the students who meet the campus admission requirements.

The growth of structural diversity in the undergraduate population has also offered new opportunities for the classroom. The chapters in this anthology document and analyze innovative, creative, resourceful, thoughtful, and replicable responses to the instructional opportunities arising from structural diversity. Discussed here are efforts to enhance the relevance of curricula and pedagogy through multicultural education, the use of portfolios to encourage students to evaluate and analyze their experiences with diversity, and experiential learning alternatives such as a "cultural plunge" and community-based service learning, as well as collaborative and group activities in the classroom.

The volume's authors are themselves diverse, representing various racial and ethnic groups and variety in gender, sexual orientation, and academic ranks. They speak of their experiences as diverse students and, in one case, as a new, diverse instructor. Fully as important, they demonstrate that classroom approaches that address diversity should not be confined to one discipline or college; they can be reflected in any subject matter, from business to mathematics to social work.

According to Gurin (1999, p. 1), "for new learning to occur, institutions of higher education have to make appropriate uses of structural diversity." The chapters of this anthology argue for such uses. At a time when structural diversity continues to grow in colleges and universities in North America, their insights are timely. Together, they advance our understanding of effective instructional practices in this new academic world.

Acknowledgments

A project like this requires cooperation and support; and fortunately, the staff at San Diego State University's Center for Teaching and Learning benefited from both. First of all, we would like to thank the Office of Diversity and Equity and the President's Office on our campus for providing a grant to commission the chapters, for celebrating the authors at a lovely reception at University House, and for funding some of the initial production costs. Provost Nancy Marlin and Vice President for Student Affairs James Kitchen have been supportive not only of this project but of several of the diversity workshops and conferences initiated by the center. Isidro Ortiz (Chicana/Chicano Studies) and Shirley Weber (Africana Studies) have contributed not only to this volume but to campus understanding of issues relating to diversity and social justice. The undergraduate deans Carole Scott and then Geoffrey Chase sustained the project for more than two years, providing both secretarial and administrative assistance. Within the Office of Undergraduate Studies, Jose Preciado and the College Readiness staff were consistently encouraging and helpful. And a very special thanks goes to Lorraine Ulanicki, the center's program coordinator, who organized our materials, interacted with the authors, managed student staff, and buoyed us throughout with her enthusiasm and grace.

We are also very appreciative of Kelly Sippell and the editorial board of the University of Michigan Press, who immediately understood the value of this collection for and by classroom teachers at the postsecondary level, many of whom are themselves diverse. We have strived to assemble a volume that is worthy of their confidence.

Finally, we thank the authors, whose commitment to diversity and good teaching shines through these chapters in ways that are both unusual and uplifting.

Contents

OUTSIDE THE CLASSROOM: INVOLVING STUDENTS IN THE CAMPUS AND COMMUNITY

1
Introduction

Ann M. Johns and Maureen Kelley Sipp

All across the United States, college and university classrooms are becoming increasingly diverse. Students are more varied ethnically and linguistically; they are often older than the traditional student; they may have disabilities or be in need of special assistance. As Venable (in this volume) notes, "only about one-sixth of undergraduate students meet the traditional characterization of being full-time students between ages 18 and 22 living on campus." These changes in postsecondary demographics, occurring, in many cases, without comparable changes in the demographics of college and university faculty, have led to a variety of concerns on the part of campus administrations and to faculty discussions of diversity in the classroom. San Diego State University (SDSU), like many public (and private) institutions, is exploring pedagogical approaches that must, by necessity, vary considerably from those that were in place when many of its faculty were undergraduates, initiatives that are designed to enhance the experience and increase the retention of all currently enrolled students regardless of ethnicity, age, gender preference, or disability.

Funded by a grant from the campus Office of Diversity and Equity, SDSU's Center for Teaching and Learning commissioned chapters on diversity and pedagogy from a faculty that is itself quite diverse, individuals whose own campus experiences have led them to make creative decisions about pedagogy. The result was this volume, in which research and theory—and their applications to culturally responsible pedagogies—are discussed.

Though all of the chapter authors are from the same campus, they focus on issues that are being discussed throughout North America. This volume can be described as follows:

- **Inclusive:** "Diversity" is discussed in terms of ethnicity, culture, dialect and second language variation, sexual preference, age, and disability.
- **Written by faculty who are themselves diverse, about their own work in the classroom**
- **Varied in terms of approach:** Chapters focus on research (e.g., Hohm & Venable; Branch), explore assessment approaches across the curriculum (Jones; Zuniga; Venable), discuss diversity among faculty (Wang & Folger) and students (Fielden; Johns), address pedagogy in low-paradigm disciplines (e.g., education, social work) as well as in the high-paradigm disciplines of mathematics and sciences (Yerrick; Mukhopadhyay & Greer), and provide guidance in assigning out-of-classroom experiences, including service learning, experiential learning, and community action (Washington; Young; Weber).
- **Varied in terms of chapter purpose:** Some of the chapters are organized as research studies; some integrate research, theory, and pedagogy; and others combine narratives, pedagogical experiences, and advice to colleagues.

Thus, diversity is here broadly defined and variously constructed—as it should be, considering our current student and faculty populations.

Following the introduction (chap. 1) are two chapters in which "diversity" is described and assessed. In chapter 2, Hohm and Venable present their (replicable) survey of student responses to cultural diversity requirements on this large campus, a study that has been used as evidence for the importance of these classes to the students' liberal education. In chapter 3, Branch explains at some length a framework for measuring the intensity and type of multicultural education practices; then he applies that framework to classrooms across the curriculum.

In chapter 4, Jones synthesizes two theoretical perspectives on culturally responsive teaching, applies one to her own classroom, and presents four general pedagogical goals for all teachers. In chapter 5, Zuniga advocates the use of portfolios in diverse classrooms, an approach to curriculum and assessment that has had positive effects in many classrooms. Venable (chap. 6) then takes up the issue of cooperative learning, an approach that emphasizes process and group dynamics. She walks the reader through a collaborative learning assignment, from objectives to assessment. Since diversity also refers to disability, Fielden (chap. 7) provides instructors with specific examples of law and accommodation that are important to our understanding and teaching of students with disabilities. In chapter 8, Johns turns to linguistic diversity among students, discussing both who our students are and how we might approach students' prior knowledge, errors, plagiarism, and literacy. In chapter 9, Wang and Folger turn to faculty diversity and the ways in which diversity, expertise, student expectations, and technology can influence the classroom atmosphere.

The next two chapters focus on what some have termed as high-paradigm disciplines, mathematics and science, which do not attract a significant number of diverse students. In chapter 10, Yerrick takes a constructivist approach, explaining how science can be made accessible to diverse postsecondary students. Mukhopadhyay and Greer (chap. 11) address accessibility in terms of mathematics, and like Yerrick, they provide practical advice for developing accessible curricula and pedagogical practices.

The final section of the volume turns to the students' involvement in the community, presenting classroom-related experiences for diverse (and all) students through tested pedagogies. In chapter 12, Washington provides an overview of community-based service learning and then discusses how she relates her pedagogical objectives to student involvement in their local communities. Young (chap. 13) describes community activities based upon experiential learning. Finally, Weber (chap. 14) advocates community action—how students can become change agents within their own ethnic communities and within the community at large.

What we have here, then, is a volume that combines theory and research, presenting the work of *practitioners,* a diverse group of faculty who speak not only from theory and research but also from classroom practice. We hope that faculty readers of this text will share in our enthusiasm for creating new classroom strategies that adapt to the changing nature of college campuses across the United States.

GENERAL ISSUES AND QUESTIONS

2

Cultural Diversity Courses: The Students' Perspectives

Charles F. Hohm and Carol F. Venable

Faculty, staff, and administration in academia are aware of the fact that courses dealing with diversity are increasingly being instituted as requirements for graduation. How widespread is such a requirement among U.S. colleges and universities? A report published by the National Association of Scholars (1996) found that one-half of the fifty top-ranked liberal arts colleges and universities in the United States had diversity course requirements.

The first national survey to examine the trend of U.S. colleges and universities to require a diversity course for undergraduates was conducted by the Association of American Colleges and Universities in 2000 (Humphreys, 2000). Funded by the James Irvine Foundation and sent to every accredited university and college in the United States, the study resulted in 543 completions, representing a wide array of institutional types and every region of the country. The main finding was that over half (54 percent) of the institutions had diversity requirements in place and that an additional 8 percent were in the process of developing diversity courses (Humphreys, 2000). Only one-quarter of the institutions having diversity requirements have had them in place for more than ten years (Humphreys, 2000). Humphreys (2000, p. 2) reports that

> forty-five percent had put them in place in the past five to ten years and another 30 percent reported having their requirements in place for less than five years. A majority of those schools with requirements (58 percent) require only one course, while 42 percent require two or more diversity course.

The survey showed that there was variation among the institutions with regard to how they defined diversity: "Of those schools with requirements, 83% offer one or more courses addressing diversity in the U.S.; 65% offer one or more courses addressing diversity outside of the U.S.; and 76 percent offer one or more non-Western cultures courses" (Humphreys, 2000, p. 2).

In a follow-up article dealing with the survey, Schneider (2001, p. 1) points out that of the 434 responding four-year campuses, 60 percent report that they have the diversity requirement in place. On the west coast, the percentage increases to 78 percent.

Reviews of the Literature

Given the growth in the number of diversity courses, the question arises as to how we should measure the effects of these courses. In the curriculum development process, assessment of learning outcomes is a critical step. Often, an overlooked source of information about the effects of courses is the student.

Students as Course and Program Evaluators

Assessment of learning outcomes occurs on various levels. While we often think of direct measurement of content learning (see Walvoord & Anderson, 1998; Angelo & Cross, 1993), perceptions of value also yield important information. Researchers have used students' perception of learning in various situations. For example, at Virginia Tech, Riess and Muffo (1996) used group interviews of senior mathematics majors to test analytical and oral presentation skills and knowledge of basic math principles as well as to gather opinions about student experiences. Staik and Rogers (1996) report that on their campus (University of Montevallo), the use of periodic reports by a student advisory council in psychology led to changes in curriculum, instruction, and ethical behavior expectations for psychology majors. Walker and Muffo (1996) report that the alumni advisory board of the civil engineering department at Virginia Tech hosted a dinner for current student representatives during which a candid, structured discussion of the civil engineering major took place. The alumni summarized the results of the discussion for the faculty. As a result of this assessment, a number of changes were made in computing resources, laboratory facilities, and the teaching of writing and speaking.

At Ohio University, Williford and Moden (1996) report that a freshman satisfaction survey conducted since 1978 has produced improvements in advising, registration, and staff training and that, as a result, freshman-to-sophomore retention has increased by 20 percent since 1978. Muffo and Bunda (1993) summarize the experiences of a number of universities that have used student attitude and opinion data as valid indicators of existing problems or successes. The authors suggest that such data can point to potential solutions if used in a thoughtful and deliberate manner. Finally, Waluconis (1993), in an essay on student self-evaluations, points out the many ways in which these evaluations can be used to further student learning. In short, our students should be viewed as an important source of information regarding curricular and departmental issues.

Research on the Effects of Cultural Diversity Courses

Research provides evidence of positive learning outcomes associated with having cultural diversity courses. In a large-scale study, Astin (1993a, 1993b, 1999) found that five specific student diversity experiences have positive effects on two value outcomes: (a) cultural awareness and (b) commitment to promoting racial understanding. These experiences include taking an ethnic studies course, taking a women's studies course, attending racial/cultural awareness workshops, discussing racial or ethnic issues, and socializing with someone of another racial/ethnic group. In addition, these student diversity experiences positively affect the levels of students' overall satisfaction with college and student life.

What do students think about the diversity requirement? There does not appear to be much literature on the topic. Gold's (2001) case study reports on the attitudes of five students at Hamilton College, a small liberal arts college in upstate New York (pp. 1–4). Her report shows that "in general, these students affirmed that the ongoing diversification of Hamilton's curriculum was having a positive impact, but expressed reservations about other areas of college life that remained less affected by attention to diversity" (Gold, 2001, p. 1). Also, these students felt that a separate diversity course should not be needed, because diversity should be embedded in all courses (Gold, 2001, p. 2). While the input of five students from a small liberal arts college on the topic of diversity is interesting, additional attitudinal information from a more representative sample of college students is needed.

The Context of This Study: The Campus and the Cultural Diversity Requirement

San Diego State University is part of the twenty-three-campus California State University System and is designated a "Doctoral/Research

University—Intensive" by the Carnegie Foundation. The diverse student body of over thirty-two thousand makes the university one of the largest institutions in the country. Being an urban university with a large commuter population, the student body is similar to the population of southern California, with more than 50 percent of the students classified as non-Caucasian. In 1981, San Diego State University established a requirement for each student to complete a three-unit upper-division "cross cultural" general education course. In 1992–1993, the term *cultural diversity* was substituted for the term *cross cultural* (San Diego State University, 1992a).

Census data for 2000 show that the university is located in a city whose ethnic diversity has increased considerably in the last ten years (see "Despite Gains, County Slips," 2001; "State's Latino, Asian Populations Soar," 2001; "San Diego's Melting Pot," 2001). In 1990, Whites made up 59 percent of the population. By 2000, that figure had dropped to 49 percent. Latinos increased their share from 21 percent in 1990 to 25 percent in 2000. Asians also increased their percentage in the population of the city (from 11 percent to 13 percent), while the percentage of Blacks and Native Americans declined a bit (9 percent to 8 percent and 0.5 percent to 0.3 percent, respectively). The category of multiracial did not exist on the 1990 census form but did appear on the form in 2000, when 4 percent of the city's population identified themselves as multiracial. Data for the county of San Diego and the state of California show an even greater degree of ethnic and racial diversity than exists in the city of San Diego ("State's Latino, Asian Populations Soar," 2001). While this increased diversity may suggest, to some, that because of the multicultural environment in southern California, diversity courses are no longer necessary, a survey shows that students believe the diversity course should be continued because it is a valuable part of their educational program.

The following sections provide a brief history of the requirement to take a diversity course and the results of a survey of students who were in the process of completing their requirement.

History of the Cultural Diversity Requirement at the University

In the fall of 1981, the university's general catalog started to include a cross cultural general education requirement. According to the 2000–2001 general catalog, each student "must have at least one three unit cross cultural course in either Social and Behavioral Science or

Humanities" (San Diego State University, 2000b, p. 105). Forty-four courses were offered as cross-cultural general education courses in 1981.[1]

Each campus in the California State University System was free to structure its general education requirements, including the cultural diversity requirement, in a manner best suited to that particular campus, as long as the main CSU requirements were adhered to. San Diego State University opted for the requirement of one three-unit course in cultural diversity. It should be noted that there was not a great deal of discussion about this issue in the University Senate. A perusal of the Senate minutes in the years prior to the 1981 "cross cultural" requirement and the 1992 "cultural diversity" requirement shows very little discussion or debate on this topic, because most of the faculty viewed the cultural diversity requirement as a positive thing.

While it may have been relatively easy to distinguish a "cross cultural" course in 1981, changes in population patterns, multicultural experiences, and changes in communication and technology have made distinguishing of a "cultural diversity" course more difficult. Advances over the past twenty years have brought more diverse groups together, and the acknowledgement of what is "diverse" appears to have evolved as courses have been proposed over the years.

Officially, the criteria for a diversity course have not changed from the initial designation in 1992 (San Diego State University, 1992b, p. 85). The curriculum guide states that the upper-division cultural diversity courses must meet two main criteria: first, that the "primary focus [be] on alternative perspectives to those prevalent in the traditional introduction to or survey of a discipline"; second, that the "primary emphasis [be] on non-Western or nondominant cultures, views, or traditions" (San Diego State University, 2000b, p. 89).

The initial application of these criteria resulted in seventy-nine courses, as shown in the 1992–1993 catalog (San Diego State University, 1992a). There are now ninety-seven courses having this designation (San Diego State University, 2000b). Over time, as the courses grew in number and as the content of material in other courses expanded to include diversity issues, discussions would arise as to whether there was still a need for a special designation. Sometimes the question would arise as to whether students perceived the value of these courses (i.e., are the courses accomplishing what was intended?). Conflicting anecdotal evidence was offered saying that "students don't care about diversity courses," "students love these courses," "students only want to take courses in their major," "students feel that diversity courses are important," and so on. As a result, the General Education Committee undertook a brief survey of students to assess what students felt about their diversity courses.

Methodology

In the spring of 1996, the General Education Committee undertook an assessment of the beliefs that students held after completing their diversity course requirement. Faculty in these courses were asked to administer a brief anonymous survey during the last two weeks of the semester. Participation in the survey by faculty and students was voluntary. There were ninety-three course sections representing seventeen departments.

Several graduate students from a technical field unrelated to any of the departments offering diversity courses were interviewed, and they assisted in developing the survey. These students had attended the undergraduate program. They were questioned about their reasons for registering for particular courses. While these students demonstrated their interest in furthering their education, they reported that they were pragmatic as undergraduates in obtaining access to required courses to ensure graduation on a timely basis. They indicated that for general education courses, they took what fit into their schedule after first obtaining the courses in their major and after meeting other outside commitments. Nonetheless, they reported receiving much value from their diversity courses. As a result of their input, the survey was designed to include whether students primarily took a diversity course to meet requirements or to learn about diversity issues.

Survey Results

One thousand seven hundred and twenty students completed the survey. In addition to being asked multiple-choice questions, students were allowed to provide optional comments to support their position on whether there should be a requirement for a diversity course. Optional comments were provided by over 50 percent (881) of those responding. In the following sections, we discuss both the quantitative and the qualitative results.

Quantitative Results

The survey instrument used in this research project posed a number of questions. The first question was, "What was your main reason for choosing this particular course?" Figure 1 shows the question, the dif-

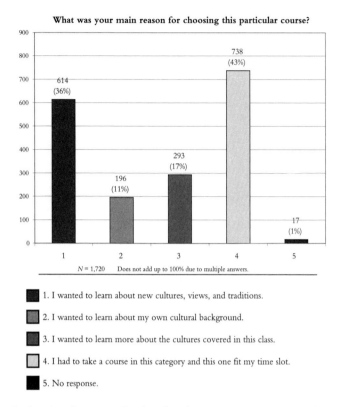

What was your main reason for choosing this particular course?

N = 1,720   Does not add up to 100% due to multiple answers.

1. I wanted to learn about new cultures, views, and traditions.

2. I wanted to learn about my own cultural background.

3. I wanted to learn more about the cultures covered in this class.

4. I had to take a course in this category and this one fit my time slot.

5. No response.

Fig. 1. Students' main reasons for choosing the course: response categories and absolute and percentage breakdowns of responses

ferent response categories, and both the absolute and percentage breakdowns. The most popular response (43 percent of the total) was, "I had to take a course in this category and this one fit my time slot." The second most popular response (36 percent of the total) was, "I wanted to learn about new cultures, views, and traditions." The response "I wanted to learn more about the cultures covered in this class" was the third most popular response (17 percent of the total), while the least popular response (11 percent of the total) was, "I wanted to learn about my own cultural background." In short, the modal response to why students were taking a diversity course was because it is a requirement and it fit a student's schedule. However, 64 percent of the students were taking the diversity courses to learn about other cultures or their own culture.

The second question asked was, "Which statement best represents your experiences in this course?" Figure 2 shows the question, the different response categories, and both the absolute and percentage break-

Which statement best represents your experiences in this course?

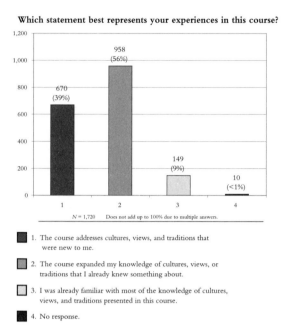

1. The course addresses cultures, views, and traditions that
   were new to me.

2. The course expanded my knowledge of cultures, views, or
   traditions that I already knew something about.

3. I was already familiar with most of the knowledge of cultures,
   views, and traditions presented in this course.

4. No response.

**Fig. 2. Students' assessments of their experiences in the course: response categories
and absolute and percentage breakdowns of responses**

downs. The most popular response (56 percent of the total) was, "The
course expanded my knowledge of cultures, views, or traditions that I
already knew something about," while the second most popular
response (39 percent of the total) was, "The course addresses cultures,
views, and traditions that were new to me." The response that was least
voiced (9 percent of the total) was, "I was already familiar with most of
the knowledge of cultures, views, and traditions presented in this
course." Clearly, the lion's share of these students saw the diversity
courses as adding either new or supplementary information on cultures, views, or traditions.

The third question posed to the students was, "Would you recommend this course to a friend?" Figure 3 presents a pie chart showing the
distribution on this question. It is gratifying to see that 91 percent of
the students answered in the affirmative. The students were then asked,
"If yes, check all that apply." The bar chart in figure 3 shows that the
primary reason they would recommend the course to a friend was that
"the course was interesting" (82 percent), followed by "the instructor
made this material relevant to me" (58 percent) and "the course information will be useful in my daily life" (49 percent). Only 18 percent

Would you recommend this course to a friend? Is so, why?

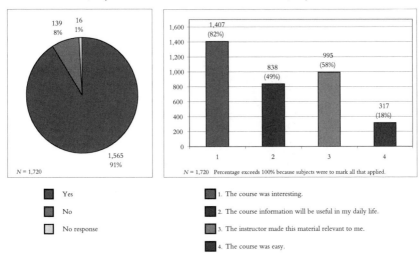

Fig. 3. *Left panel:* **Percentage and numerical breakdowns of affirmative and negative responses.** *Right panel:* **Primary reasons for affirmative responses.**

said they would recommend the course because "the course was easy." In short, students who have taken cultural diversity courses are very likely to recommend these courses to their friends, but not because the courses are easy. Rather, the courses would be recommended because they are interesting, informative, and taught by instructors who make the material relevant.

Finally, the students were asked, "Should there be a requirement to take a diversity course?" Figure 4 shows that 79 percent of students answered in the affirmative. To gain insight into why students do or do not think there should be a diversity requirement, a follow-up question asked, "Briefly give your reasons for answering yes or no." The students' written responses to this follow-up question resulted in thirty pages of typed (single-spaced) responses. The next section of this chapter deals with these comments.

Qualitative Results

Students were asked to provide a brief optional comment on why they felt there should or should not be a diversity course requirement. Over 86 percent of the 881 comments provided positive statements about the requirement. An analysis of the negative responses, however, indicated not a strong objection to diversity issues but, instead, a variety of more pragmatic items related to completion of requirements.

Positive Statements. A perusal of the 754 positive statements suggested

Should there be a requirement to take a diversity course?

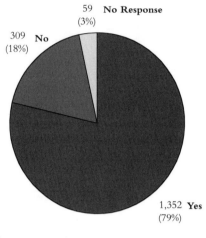

59   No Response
(3%)

309   No
(18%)

1,352   **Yes**
(79%)

N = 1,720

Fig. 4. Percentage and numerical breakdowns of affirmative and negative responses

a number of themes. These themes and a few representative comments accompanying each theme are presented here. (The statements are written in the students' own prose and have not been edited.)

> *Theme 1.* Our world (the university, city, nation, and planet) is becoming more diverse, and students need to be made aware of this diversity in order to be thoughtful and successful citizens.
>
> "I definitely feel all students should be familiar with cultures aside from their own. We live in a city where there are hundreds of cultures and to ignore those aside from your own would be cheating yourself."
>
> "It's important to learn about other cultures because we live in a society that is so diverse. By taking these types of classes we can better understand and respect another's viewpoint."
>
> "I think that if more people take diversity courses, they will not only be able to better see where people are coming from, they will notice that most ideas and thoughts transcend cultures and are thought about everywhere. Appreciation of the differences and the recognition of similarities."

"People, especially Americans, know too little about other cultures. Diversity is as important as salt; it's not a food but you can't live without it."

Theme 2. Diversity courses enrich the lives of students, make them well-rounded, and give them the knowledge and skills they need to compete in an increasingly diverse world.
"Our world is a diverse place filled with people of every culture. Students should have some introduction to other cultures before they enter the workforce."
"Because an educated person is one who is culturally sensitive to all."
"Learning about other cultures other than your own, enriches your life, and changes the way you think of people different from you (in a positive way)."
"It is important to get different views, as to form personal opinions. It helps one to be a more well rounded person."
"Although I would not have taken this course without the absolute need to fill a category in my G.E., I think that it helps a student graduate with a more well rounded education."

Theme 3. Diversity courses reduce ignorance and hence hatred, intolerance, and racial/cultural conflict.
"I think it helps reduce racism and bias. If people learn and understand other cultures it helps them get along better with those other cultures because it helps get rid of ignorance."
"The more that a person knows about another culture, the less likely he is to be racist toward that culture."

Theme 4. Diversity courses result in a decrease in ethnocentrism.
"Most of our academic career we learn only of the dominant groups in history, tradition, and politics. It should be an academic institution's right to make students less ethnocentric (less narrow-minded)."
"We as Americans need to be aware of different cultures and realize that we are not necessarily a better society. There is much we can learn from other cultures."

Theme 5. Diversity courses reduce students' reliance on stereotypes, prejudices, and biases.

"Some people don't want to know about others and have set attitudes and stereotypes about people that are different. A diversity class may untangle or eliminate these one-sided views that some people have."

"The world should have to take this course! It would be wonderful if we could stop discrimination."

"Many of the problems that we have in the world revolve around lack of knowledge. I don't think that racism or prejudice could exist in an educated society."

Theme 6. Diversity courses help students learn more about themselves.

"How can we grow as people if we keep to ourselves? To know other ways is to know yourself."

"I think that people should be made to acquire some understanding of other cultures. It betters relations between ethnic groups and give you insight into your own background."

Theme 7. Diversity courses help broaden students' worldviews.

"Because cultural diversity is important to understand. The saying 'expand your horizon' comes to mind."

"There are a lot of sheltered people in the world today that are unexposed to classes, races, and societies other than their own."

Theme 8. Many students would not take diversity courses if they were not required.

"We are increasingly specialized in our college departments. I believe that a diversity course benefits students who would not seek a diversity course on their own because the person who wouldn't actively seek the understanding of other cultures on their own is generally the one who needs it the most (If you aren't interested in other cultures, its probably because you are ignorant of them)."

"Students, including me, tend to take courses just to graduate and they don't take chances. There is more to college than basic requirements. This class and others like it bring people together."

"Yes, most people including myself think they know all they need to know about other societies and cultures. Its not till you're forced to take a class that you realize how much you didn't know and you learn so many interesting things."

Theme 9. More than one diversity course should be required.
"Knowledge about other people and cultures (besides ourselves) is the key to understanding and accepting others. There should be more required multicultural courses."
"It seems like the whole notion of college/university is to expand your horizons. In fact, I think there should be more."

Negative Statements. Of the written comments to the question "Should there be a requirement to take a diversity course? Briefly give your reasons for answering yes or no," only 14 percent of the comments (120 out of 881) were negative. A perusal of the 120 negative statements suggested a few themes. These themes and a few representative comments accompanying each theme are presented here. (The statements are written in the students' own prose and have not been edited.)

Theme 1. Students are already exposed to diversity at the university. The requirement is redundant.
"With the proximity to the border, and the diverse representation of cultures in the classroom, the requirement becomes redundant."
"The diversity requirement doesn't take into account people who have already had cultural exposure. Like the upper division writing requirement exam, there should be a similar exemption for the cultural diversity requirement so that we don't have to waste an entire semester fulfilling a superfluous requirement."
"By now we've faced so much diversity in our lives, one class isn't going to have much impact positively or negatively."
"I believe that just by living here and attending this school you are exposed to many different cultures."

Theme 2. Students are already interested in taking such courses. You do not need to make it a requirement.

"I think a lot of people are already interested in this type of course so there is no need to make it a requirement."

"It should be left up to the individual. I have chosen several of these type courses on my own, (i.e., Latin America hist, SE ASIA hist, Africana hist, etc.), without being forced to take them."

Theme 3. No one should be forced to take a diversity course.

"People shouldn't be forced to take classes not relevant to their major."

"Should be optional, not required."

"No, although I think it is important to learn of other cultures, etc. Often these courses are offered at odd times or are hard to fit in rigorous schedules. They should be optional."

"If you force people to take cultural diversity courses, the purpose of educating the individual might be defeated. Human nature rebels against being forced to do something. There would probably be a lack of interest, enthusiasm, and learning."

Theme 4. This requirement should be at a lower-division level, not an upper-division one.

"Not once all lower division GE is met. When upper division should concentrate on your major."

"I understand and appreciate the need for students to learn about other cultures, however it should not be Upper Division, as I have taken classes at community college that are equivalent and do not count."

"This sort of material is covered in lower division General Education."

Theme 5. There are already too many required courses that are not connected to the major.

"There are too many required courses already. Especially for engineers."

"There are too many requirements that have nothing to do with my major. This course was a waste of time."

"Many diversity courses offered are a waste of time, when students have the need to concentrate on subject matter dealing with the major."

"I don't think the GE requirement should be anymore

specific than they already are. It makes it *really* difficult
to get through your major while taking a lot of classes
you already don't want. This makes it even more
difficult for those [who] find it very *uninteresting*."

Theme 6. Members of a particular group tend to take classes with
their own group.
"Because it is supposed to show diversity but Mexicans take
Mexican American and African Americans take African
Americans and women take Women Studies. White
males don't get a cultural choice like others."
"I don't feel there should be a requirement to take diversity
courses since people tend to take those courses familiar
to them (example mostly black students in Afro-Amer-
ican classes.)"

Concluding Remarks

Assessment of student learning outcomes can be done in a number of
ways. Sometimes, a direct assessment of what the student has learned is
called for. For example, a standardized, nationally normed examination
on a particular subject area could be utilized to ascertain the level of
learning taking place in an institution. However, assessment can also be
accomplished by asking students their opinions about what they have
learned. That is the approach taken here, and we feel it has been productive.

We have learned that students, after having taken a required cultural
diversity course, overwhelmingly view such a requirement as a sensible
one. They seem to understand that just because our society is becoming multicultural, that does not mean that we automatically soak up
knowledge about multiculturalism and diversity. Also, diverse groups
coexisting and living side by side do not necessarily have knowledge
and tolerance of other groups. We need to be informed about these
differences, and one means to that end is the required cultural diversity
general education course. Our students, who have taken diversity
courses, seem to understand this.

Some might question the utility of a student taking a diversity course
that deals with his or her own culture. Again, just because a student has
a particular cultural heritage does not mean that the student is knowledgeable about his or her culture. A diversity course can provide students with knowledge about the history and traditions of their background.

Finally, faculty are often bothered by the occasional statement that the university is forcing students to take diversity courses and that this is being done because the university is advancing a liberal or politically correct agenda. This research project shows that, by and large, our students do not feel this way. To the contrary, they most definitely see the importance and utility of learning about diverse cultures and groups.

Note

1. The impetus for the inclusion of a cross-cultural course came from the Office of the Chancellor at California State University in 1980 and 1981 in the form of Executive Order Number 338 (California State University, Office of the Chancellor, 1980) and Executive Order Number 342 (California State University, Office of the Chancellor, 1981), both of which delineated general education breadth requirements, and Executive Order Number 595, which was issued in 1992 (California State University, Office of the Chancellor, 1992).

Before addressing general education requirements, Executive Order Number 338 states, "Instruction approved to fulfill the following requirements should recognize the contributions to knowledge and civilization that have been made by members of various cultural groups and by women" (California State University, Office of the Chancellor, 1980, p. 3). Then the document lists the distribution of general education requirements. Section C asserts "[a] minimum of twelve semester units among the arts, literature, philosophy and foreign languages," and part of the narrative reads as follows: "Studies in these areas should include exposure to both Western cultures and non-Western Cultures" (California State University, Office of the Chancellor, 1980, p. 4). Section D asserts "[a] minimum of twelve semester units dealing with human social, political, and economic institutions and behavior and their historical background," and part of the narrative reads as follows: "Problems and issues in these areas should be examined in their contemporary as well as historical setting, including both Western and non-Western contexts." The wording on this topic in Executive Order Number 342 (California State University, Office of the Chancellor, 1981, Attachment A, pages 1–3) is essentially the same as that in Executive Order Number 338. In 1992, Executive Order Number 595 was issued from the Office of the Chancellor (California State University, Office of the Chancellor, 1992). This executive order substituted *diverse* for *various* in the wording. Before addressing general education requirements, Executive Order Number 595 states, "Instruction approved to fulfill the following requirements should recognize the contributions to knowledge and civilization that have been made by members of diverse cultural groups and by women" (California State University, Office of the Chancellor, 1992, p. 3). The wording in Sections C and D remained the same as in Executive Order Number 342.

Additional Resources

Assessment Books/Monographs

Allen, M., Berube, E., McMillin, J. D., Noel, R. C., & Rienzi, B. M. (Program Assessment Consultation Team [PACT]). (2000). *PACT Outcomes Assessment Handbook*. Bakersfield: California State University, Bakersfield.

This may be the single most useful assessment guide in the country. It is relatively short (sixty-four pages of main text) but is chock-full of extremely useful and pragmatic tips. It defines assessment of student learning and covers the many assessment techniques available to us. Most important, it gives us the pros and cons of each of these techniques. This handbook is not published and is not on the Web, because the Bakersfield folks like to continually update the work. However, they are more than happy to provide a free hard copy of this very helpful compendium. Just call them at (661) 664–2084 or write to 9001 Stockdale Highway, Bakersfield, CA 93311–1099.

Angelo, T. A., & Cross, K. P. (1993). *Classroom assessment techniques: A handbook for college teachers* (2nd ed.). San Francisco: Jossey-Bass.

This book is famous for helping college instructors with actually doing assessment in the classroom. The book has three sections: (1) "Getting Started" (2) "Classroom Assessment Techniques," and (3) "Building on What We Have Learned." More than most books, this monograph offers "hands-on" examples that instructors can utilize in their assessment work.

Banta, T. (Ed.). (1993). *Making a difference: Outcomes of a decade of assessment in higher education*. San Franciso: Jossey-Bass.

Though this book is nearly a decade old, it is still worth reading. This book of twenty-four chapters written by internationally respected assessment experts is comprised of five parts: (1) "Transforming Campus Cultures through Assessment," (2) "Adapting Assessment to Diverse Settings and Populations," (3) "Outcomes Assessment Methods That Work," (4) "Approaches with Promise for Improving Programs and Services," and (5) "State-Level Approaches to Assessment."

Hohm, C. F., & Johnson, W. S. (Eds.). (2001). *Assessing student learning in sociology* (2nd ed.). Washington, DC: American Sociological Association.

Though this monograph was produced with the expressed purpose of helping sociology departments with assessment of student learning outcomes, it will be useful to colleagues in other disciplines. The monograph has five sections. The first section provides an overview of assessment, including the need for this activity. The second section presents assessment in various venues—a community college, a private university, a system (the California State University System of twenty-three campuses), and student views in departmental assessment. The third section presents various methodologies, from electronic assessment portfolios, to focus groups, to the capstone course. The fourth section gives numerous previously published assessment articles. The last section includes various things such as the American Association for Higher Education's nine principles of good practice for assessing student learning and assessment resources on the Web. (The mailing address and telephone number for the American Sociological Assocation are as follows: 1307 New York Avenue NW #700, Washington, DC 20005; (202) 383–9005.)

Nichols, J. O. (1995). *The departmental guide and record book for student outcomes assessment and institutional effectiveness.* New York: Agathon Press.

The main text of this book is only sixty-eight pages, but it is a very useful sixty-eight pages. This is yet another very pragmatic and useful book that department chairs will find very beneficial. Nichols has two other companion books by the same publisher: *Assessment Case Studies: Common Issues in Implementation with Various Campus Approaches to Resolution* (1995) and *A Practitioner's Handbook for Institutional Effectiveness and Student Outcomes Assessment Implementation* (3rd ed., 1995).

Walvoord, B. E., & Anderson, V. J. (1998). *Effective grading: A tool for learning and assessment.* San Francisco: Jossey-Bass.

Like Angelo and Cross's book, this monograph offers "hands-on" examples that will be very helpful to instructors. Its key contribution is to show how the grading of students' course work can be effectively utilized to assess and improve teaching and student learning.

Web Sites

<http://www.aahe.org>. The American Association for Higher Education (AAHE) Assessment Forum (<http://www.aahe.org/assessment>) is the primary national network connecting and supporting higher education stakeholders involved in assessment.

<http://www.ericae.net>. The Web site of the Educational Resources Information Center (ERIC) Clearinghouse on Assessment and Evaluation contains a full text Internet Library on Assessment, an online refereed journal, and numerous listings of assessment and evaluation resources.

<http://www.iea-nich.com>. The Web site of Institutional Effectiveness Associates, an organization that provides consulting and materials on outcomes assessment, offers a publication on assessment of general education and provides blank forms that can be used to document assessment efforts.

3
Cross-Cultural Curricula: Four Case Studies

André J. Branch

Although college and university classrooms are becoming increasingly diverse culturally and linguistically, curricula and pedagogy on many campuses have remained relatively unchanged since the 1960s. Garcia and Smith (1996, p. 266) note, "While it may seem obvious that students' backgrounds should have a relationship to what is taught, this has not been a prevailing assumption of curricular development in higher education." College and university professors, in large part, do not make connections between their disciplines and the cultures of their students. This is unfortunate for all concerned—and for the diverse society in which we live.

In fact, campus curricula and pedagogies should be completely reconsidered, and, in many cases, revised, in light of the demographic changes on our campuses. Rendón and Hope (1996, p. 26) have written, "Educating a new student majority requires rethinking the way instruction is delivered." Not surprisingly, a growing body of research indicates that culturally relevant curricula and pedagogies are effective in helping to increase the academic achievement of all students, but especially those who are diverse. (Au, 1980; Bell & Clark, 1998; Cazden & John, 1971; Ladson-Billings, 1995; Norment, 1997).

Fully as interesting as the resistance to curricular change are the efforts by some faculty to respond to students' needs and cultures in their classrooms. Thus, in this chapter, I will report on the findings of a research study of four university professors, in mathematics, English, science, and history, as they attempted to approach teaching and learning from multicultural perspectives.

Before launching into a discussion of the research, it is important that I situate myself as researcher (Collins, 1991; Ladson-Billings,

1995). All research is influenced by the researcher's positionality, specifically the race, socioeconomic class, and gender of the researcher. I want to acknowledge at the outset the subjective factors that have undoubtedly influenced the design of this study, the method of the data collection, and the interpretation of the data (Code, 1991). I am an African American male, an assistant professor in the School of Teacher Education at a large, comprehensive public university. As a scientist and teacher educator in the area of curriculum and instruction, I am particularly interested in the development of effective multicultural education curricula and pedagogies. Of great concern to me is the persistent gap in achievement that leaves African American and other students of color far behind White students in college classrooms. Multicultural education appears to be the most promising of the school reform movements, because, among other things, it affirms the cultural capital that students of color bring to the teaching/learning process. Therefore, I have chosen to situate my work in this area.

Conceptual Framework for the Research

The conceptual framework I used for the design of this study was created by James Banks (1997a), who organizes our understanding of multicultural education into five dimensions. At the heart of multicultural education is the goal of increasing academic achievement through curriculum and pedagogy for all students, specifically students of color and from underachieving groups. In the remainder of this section, I will discuss Banks's dimensions of multicultural education and a few of the ways that they can be applied across the curriculum. All five dimensions of the conceptual framework explained here are displayed in figure 1.

Dimension One: Content Integration

Level One: The Contributions Approach

The most common way to practice multicultural education within the framework created by Banks (1997a) is to integrate cultural/ethnic content into lessons, lectures, or other classroom activities in order to illustrate key concepts in the discipline or subject matter. In his handbook on research on multicultural education, Banks (1995) explains that there are four levels at which teachers can integrate cultural/ethnic content. At the first level, teachers mention some of the "contributions" to the subject matter of some ethnic heroes from selected ethnic groups. At this level, teachers focus on ethnic heroes, holidays, foods,

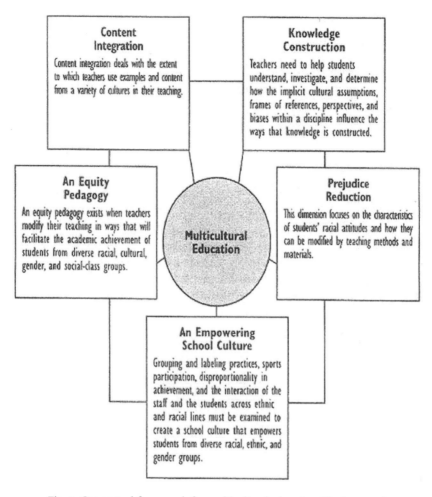

Content Integration

Content integration deals with the extent to which teachers use examples and content from a variety of cultures in their teaching.

Knowledge Construction

Teachers need to help students understand, investigate, and determine how the implicit cultural assumptions, frames of references, perspectives, and biases within a discipline influence the ways that knowledge is constructed.

An Equity Pedagogy

An equity pedagogy exists when teachers modify their teaching in ways that will facilitate the academic achievement of students from diverse racial, cultural, gender, and social-class groups.

Multicultural Education

Prejudice Reduction

This dimension focuses on the characteristics of students' racial attitudes and how they can be modified by teaching methods and materials.

An Empowering School Culture

Grouping and labeling practices, sports participation, disproportionality in achievement, and the interaction of the staff and the students across ethnic and racial lines must be examined to create a school culture that empowers students from diverse racial, ethnic, and gender groups.

Fig. 1. Conceptual framework for multicultural education (Banks, 1997a)

and festivals (Banks, 1995). Mentioning to a college class of biology students that George Washington Carver was a famous African American agronomist who found hundreds of uses for the peanut would be an example of the contributions' approach to content integration.

Level Two: The Additive Approach

At the second level, called "additive," teachers add significantly more ethnic content to the curriculum. For example, a teacher of comparative literature may add Luis Valdez's play *Zoot Suit* to the course reading list. This play might be the only play by a Mexican American assigned to the class, and it could be the only assigned play written by a person of color. In both the contributions and additive levels of content integration, the structure, purpose, and goals of the curriculum do not change at all. Examples of people of color are simply added as appendages. College professors who only use these levels of content integration could very well hear an aware student ask, "What other contributions were made by African Americans to the understanding of agriculture?" or, "Was there only one Mexican American play?"

Level Three: The Transformation Approach

The third level of content integration, "transformation," encourages students to view subject matter and central concepts from different cultural perspectives. Often, new concepts appropriate to multicultural education are added to the curriculum. Thus the nature and purpose of the curriculum is transformed. College students in more traditional U.S. history classes typically learn about the cross-country movement of the earliest immigrants to the United States. This movement is commonly called the "Westward Movement" or "Westward Expansion." When college and university professors label this movement of human beings as such, without deconstructing the terminology, they leave students with the perspective of the Europeans who were moving or expanding westward. Moreover, the teaching of related concepts, such as "pioneers," "settlers," "founders," and "taming the land," focuses on the Europeans who moved West. Furthermore, using these terms without deconstructing them perpetuates the misconception that before the arrival of the Europeans, no one lived in what is now called the United States.

However, with a transformation of the curriculum, students get a different perspective. It is known that other cultural groups—the American Indians, African Americans, and Chinese—played significant roles in this Westward movement and its consequences. For example, groups of American Indians were destabilized; some were killed, and others, like the Cherokee during the Trail of Tears, died trying to get out of the way of Europeans. When American Indian perspectives are included in the teaching of this part of U.S. history, concepts like "pioneer," "settler," and "frontier" must be deconstructed; and other concepts such as "invasion," "occupation," "oppression," and "displacement" are added to the curriculum.

Level Four: The Social Action Approach

Practicing multicultural education at the fourth level of content integration, "social action," provides students with opportunities to "make decisions on important social issues and take actions to help solve them" (Banks, 1997b, p. 26). Tate (1995) studied a mathematics teacher who worked at this level. The teacher designed a mathematics unit in which students studied the number of liquor stores in their low-income community. Their study included the revenue that was earned and spent on alcohol, the physical space taken by these establishments, and the loss of family income because of time spent in and around the liquor stores by its drunk patrons. After their study, the students brain-stormed what they could and would do to address this deleterious sit-uation. They then decided to write letters to the city council demand-ing that these liquor stores be removed from their neighborhood. And they were! Thus, at this level, efforts are made to both transform the curriculum and encourage student action. (See, e.g., Weber, in this volume, for a curriculum at this level.)

Dimension Two: The Knowledge Construction Process

Practicing multicultural education can also take the form of "helping students to understand, investigate, and determine how the implicit cultural assumptions, frames of references, perspectives, and biases within a discipline influence the ways in which knowledge is con-structed within it" (Banks, 1997a, p. 21). Banks calls this dimension of multicultural education "the knowledge construction process" (p. 21). Having its roots in epistemology, this process assumes that all school knowledge is socially constructed and that this knowledge is mediated by subjective factors (Code, 1991) including race, socioeconomic class, and gender. There are many examples in the literature of how knowl-edge construction can take place. Banks (1997a, p. 21) writes, for example, "Students can analyze the knowledge construction process in science by studying how racism has been perpetuated in science by genetic theories of intelligence, Darwinism, and eugenics."

An example from philosophy illustrates how university instructors might practice this dimension of multicultural education. In an intro-ductory philosophy course, students are usually introduced to the var-ious branches of philosophy—epistemology, ontology, existentialism, and so on. Plato, Aristotle, Rousseau, and Kierkegaard are just a few of the writers whose works are included. To practice multicultural edu-cation using the knowledge construction dimension, the instructor of an introductory philosophy course could investigate some reasons for the absence of women writers in the traditional representative literature of this discipline. In so doing, students would learn that knowledge is constructed to serve the interests of those who have the power to con-struct it. Moreover, students will learn that knowledge is not objective or objectively produced within a specific historical context. There is a combination of objective and subjective factors that influence the creation of knowledge (Code, 1991; Collins, 1991).

Dimension Three: Equity Pedagogy

Teachers may also practice multicultural education by using an equity pedagogy, the third dimension of multicultural education. Practicing multicultural education in this way, "teachers modify their teaching in ways that will facilitate the academic achievement of students from diverse racial, cultural, gender, and social-class groups" (Banks, 1997a, p. 22). Such strategies are said to be "culturally responsive" (Irvine & Armento, 2001), yielding significant academic gains for students. Since calling attention to oneself independent of one's group is inconsistent with many American Indian cultures, an instructor who does not single out American Indian students for oral recitation or independent work at the board can be said to be using an equity pedagogy.

Equity pedagogy, like all the dimensions of multicultural education, addresses students' academic achievement. Ladson-Billings (1995) argues that such an approach should also teach students to recognize and critique social inequities and should help students to become culturally competent in a number of contexts. Facilitating students' ethnic identity development is one way to address these issues. Branch (1999) found that one way to facilitate ethnic identity development in students is to provide them with positive ethnic content knowledge (i.e., positive information about their ethnic groups) throughout the curriculum.

Dimension Four: Prejudice Reduction

Practicing multicultural education can also take the form of reducing prejudice among students. Banks (1997a, p. 22) writes that curricula should assist students in developing "positive attitudes toward different racial, ethnic, and cultural groups." By using multicultural learning materials (Katz & Zalk, 1978) and cooperative learning strategies as described by Slavin (1979), college teachers can help students develop these attitudes. When using cooperative learning strategies, teachers should remember Allport's (1954) ingredients for harmonious interracial interaction. He writes that the task on which students work should

- be sanctioned by an authority figure,
- give students equal status within the group,
- promote work cooperation instead of competition, and
- have a shared goal.

Dimension Five: An Empowering School Culture

The fifth dimension of multicultural education represents a total school effort to engender a "school culture and organization that promotes gender, racial, and social-class equity" (Banks, 1997a, p. 23). Implementing an effective empowering school culture requires that all of those working at the university assist in rethinking the goals and direction of a campus. Isolated actions by individual faculty members are not likely to effect total university change. Nonetheless, individual faculty members can employ classroom strategies that empower, on an individual basis, students from diverse racial, ethnic, and gender groups.

Participants and Methodology

As is the case on many campuses, my campus has a number of faculty who have attempted to make their classrooms and curricula appropriate to the diverse student populations whom we serve. To explore this issue, I designed some research using a modified case study approach (Miles & Huberman, 1994). The principal research question to be answered was, "How do instructors in colleges and university in various disciplines practice multicultural education?" A secondary question was, "Which levels are most common in multicultural approaches?"

To identify potential participants, I used a nomination strategy that is common to qualitative research (Howard, 1998; Ladson-Billings, 1995). I asked the faculty development coordinator for the campus, the director of the Center for Teaching and Learning, to nominate exemplary professors who might be willing to participate in this case study. Four of those professors, representing the Departments of English and Comparative Literature, History, Mathematics, and Physical Science agreed to participate.

Interviews

Each of the professors was interviewed twice for a maximum of ninety minutes. The interviews took place on the campus or in the homes of the participating professors. The first interview was semistructured and began with the questions in the interview protocol in appendix A. The purpose of the first interview was to investigate the professors' understanding and commitment to multicultural education. After reviewing Banks's framework and hearing from me an explanation of each of the dimensions of multicultural education, these faculty explained how they implemented a multicultural dimension in their classes. In the second interview, which followed the observations of their classes, I posed questions whose answers helped to clarify seeming contradictions between the first interviews and the observations.

Observations

To triangulate the interview data (Miles & Huberman, 1994), I made at least one observation of each instructor's classes and collected relevant artifacts such as syllabi, examinations, and handouts. During the observations, I looked for consistencies, or the lack thereof, between Banks's framework, the instructors' conceptions of multicultural education as stated in their interviews, and what actually happened in their classes.

Results

In this section, I will introduce at some depth each of the four faculty who agreed to participate in the study. Under "Background Information," I mention their areas of specialty within their disciplines, present the structures and procedures for their classes, and discuss the primary focus in each course observed. Under "Multicultural Education Practices," I show how these professors practiced multicultural education.

Maria Santa Cruz: Making the Authors Human

Background Information

Dr. Maria Santa Cruz, a specialist in nineteenth-century American literature, is an assistant professor of English and comparative literature. She has been teaching for six years, two of which have been on our campus. A Latina, Santa Cruz believes her ethnicity serves an important function in her approach. She explained its relevance this way:

> It works to dispel the perception that knowledge belongs to certain groups, or that certain types of knowledge belong to certain groups. Some people are very surprised to find a Latina interested in people like Emerson and Hawthorne, which is a way of saying that Emerson and Hawthorne don't belong to Mexican people. Literature belongs to anyone who reads it, and since I read three languages, there's a hell of a lot of literature that belongs to me.

Discussion is the primary mode of instruction in her class on American literature from 1800 to 1860. A question that permeates this discussion throughout the term is, Who is in charge of determining what constitutes great works of art? Santa Cruz believes Shakespeare, Milton, and Chaucer were called great writers because in the 1900s the United States was being run by wealthy White men. She explains, "I help the students figure out in terms of history where power resides."

What seems to be most important to Santa Cruz is making human the authors whom her students read. She does this by putting the authors and their writings in context. She explains to students the personal background of the writers and what was going on in their world when they wrote the work being read. At our first interview, she said, "Just like I have to explain Frederick Douglass's world, I have to explain Emerson's world. Explaining the context of writers puts them all on a level playing field. No author is inherently great. He or she is great because someone in power determined that she or he was great." When I observed her class, she introduced *The House of Seven Gables* with background information about Hawthorne and his world. Students learned that he was the son of a minister in a long line of family ministers. In addition to learning that the novel, as a genre, was not highly regarded in the nineteenth century, students also learned of the class distinctions that prevailed in the United States in the nineteenth century and that undoubtedly influenced Hawthorne's writing.

In addition to classroom discussions, Santa Cruz provides students with opportunities to express themselves through weekly response papers. She believes that if students are required to write, they will read the assignment. At our first interview, she also said that the response paper "gives them a way to explore ideas, say what they think, and express themselves to me without worrying about other students."

Multicultural Education Practices

Content Integration. "Telling Stories about 'America'" is the theme of Santa Cruz's course in American literature from 1800 to 1860. Santa Cruz has been careful to include literature from various ethnic groups in order to answer two of the questions from her syllabus, "What types of stories did the early U.S. like to tell about itself and to itself?" and "How can we see the image of America, and Americanness, developing in our early literature?" Native American, African American, and European American authors are represented in the required readings for this course. By using this ethnically diverse literature to see the image of America and Americanness, Santa Cruz is practicing the content integration dimension of multicultural education. Key concepts are taught using examples from different cultural groups, and new concepts have been added to the curriculum because of the presence of these groups.

Knowledge Construction. When Maria Santa Cruz explains to students that the people in power (sociopolitically and economically) determine what constitutes great literature, she is practicing the knowledge construction dimension of multicultural education. Santa Cruz assists students in understanding that in the nineteenth century, just as today, people of privileged socioeconomic status decided the aesthetic standards as well as the political standards. She explained in our first interview: "A small proportion of people knew how to read in the nineteenth century. A large percentage of wealthy White women could not write their names." Not surprisingly, then, it was wealthy White individuals (primarily male landowners) who decided what was good literature. Teaching her students this literary reality, she illustrates the social construction of knowledge—how race, socioeconomic class, and gender mediate the knowledge construction process.

Equity Pedagogy. This professor taps into the different learning styles of her students in at least two ways that were readily visible in the classroom. She does not require all students to read aloud in class, but she provides this opportunity to those who feel comfortable reading aloud. When I observed her, the African American, Latino, and Latina students readily took turns reading aloud. In their review of learning styles research, Irvine and York (1995) found that these cultural groups preferred group learning situations and that they "learn by doing" (p. 490). While the weekly response paper may be preferred by many of the shy students, this mode of expression also allows the American Indian students to learn in a way that they prefer. Irvine and York write that American Indians prefer to "learn privately rather than in public" (p. 490). Santa Cruz admits that learning styles research does not necessarily guide her pedagogy; nonetheless, these particular strategies are consistent with a summary of findings regarding preferred learning styles of Latinos, American Indians, and African Americans.

Prejudice Reduction. Of the four professors interviewed for this study, Dr. Santa Cruz alone reported that she was aware of prejudice in her students because of comments they made in class in connection with the literature they read. At our second interview, Santa Cruz said this about one of her twentieth-century literature classes: "After reading Maxine Hong Kingston's *The Woman Warrior,* I've consistently had students make comments like 'This is an example of how the Chinese do not value women.'" Santa Cruz explained her understanding of the students and her response this way:

> For many reasons, all of which have to do with her narrative style, the book shouldn't be interpreted as *the Whole Truth* [Santa Cruz's emphasis]! Demonizing China is not an object of any of my classes!

I try to get students to complicate their ideas by pointing out passages or lines that contradict their statements. I also remind them that we are scholars of literature, and if they want *the Whole Truth* [Santa Cruz's emphasis], they belong in either philosophy or religion, and if they want statistical data, they belong in sociology. Many of my students are willing to have their ideas complicated. Those who aren't go on their merry way.

Discussion

In the classes taught by this Latina with expertise in nineteenth- and twentieth-century American literature, there are examples of a number of the multicultural approaches found in Banks's framework. Santa Cruz's choice of readings by diverse authors, often authors who went unrecognized in their time, shows her interest in *content integration*. She works on the *knowledge construction* concept when assisting students in understanding how decisions about the literary canon are made. *Equity pedagogy* is evident when she provides a variety of assessment types, encouraging some students for whom it is culturally appropriate to read aloud and promoting the use of journals for students whose cultures may not promote performance. Finally, she encourages *prejudice reduction* by asking students to interrogate their own stereotypes of particular groups of people who live in this country.

John Franklin: Beyond the Elites of History

Background Information

Dr. John Franklin is a pre-Columbianist, a specialist in pre-European/Latin American cultures. He teaches "United States History for Teachers" and has been teaching in the History Department for ten years. Although many teachers of U.S. history begin this journey on the east coast of the United States and work their way west, Franklin starts in Mexico and works his way north. During our interview, he told me that this approach "has a certain resonance" with his Mexican American students. Of the thirty-eight students I counted while observing his class, eleven appeared to be Latinos. Fluent in Spanish, Dr. Franklin periodically spoke in this language during his lecture and slide presentation.

It is important to this instructor that students understand and can relate to the course. To facilitate this cultural connection, he has chosen a two-volume text called *A History of Us*, by Joy Hakim. He describes the text as "culturally balanced" and says of the author, "she brings in more than elite history; she brings in non-elites." In addition to Dr. Franklin's lecture, other activities during the class session were his slide presentation and students' oral presentations of their lesson plan prospectus.

Multicultural Education Practices

Content Integration. As noted, John Franklin begins his teaching of U.S. history in the south and works his way north. This course not only includes Mexican American students, who may be alienated altogether in other U.S. history courses, but gives their cultural group primacy. It is not surprising, then, that the professor finds this strategy motivating among Mexican American students. Dr. Franklin also interjects Spanish words and phrases into his lectures. This practice affirms the culture and language of Mexican American students, while enhancing the content of the class for all students. In our second interview, Dr. Franklin told me that he has "competency" in the Spanish language. He said further:

> I use terms that are appropriate only in the Spanish language—certain institutions, like *encomienda* and *repartimiento,* things of that sort that I do expect the students to use and to know. It is important to understand cultures as much as we can, and terminology appropriate to that culture.

Latino students in this class hear their language—which has been historically demeaned in educational circles in this part of the country—spoken by their professor to explain essential concepts and knowledge for the course.

Knowledge Construction. Dr. Franklin returns to the Latin root of the word *facts* in order to teach students that knowledge is socially constructed. "*Facts,*" he informed me at our first interview, "comes from the Latin root *facere,* meaning 'to make.' Facts are made by people." He often asks students, "Who made the facts?" This question is incisive and central to an appreciation of all school knowledge, as is the understanding that the subjective factors of race, socioeconomic class, and gender influence the construction of knowledge. Dr. Franklin understands this principle and applies it in his treatment of Spanish and British colonialism. At our second interview, Dr. Franklin informed me that he offers alternative perspectives to those of the Europeans who looked at the American West in terms of manifest destiny and the frontier. He said he makes it clear that "there were other people here, particularly Native American people who saw it entirely differently and who resisted the notion of frontier—the expansion westward of the

Europeans." He also discusses Mexico and California in the 1840s and the resistance of Spanish-speaking people in the Americas.

Historians make a distinction between "moral empathy" and "historical empathy" to avoid judging past actions and behaviors using present-day values. When I observed Dr. Franklin's class, he reminded students of these distinctions, saying, "twentieth-century people would be appalled at the treatment of the Indians by the Spanish—moral empathy. The Spanish saw their treatment of the Indians as instrumental in saving their souls—historical empathy."

I must note here that I have difficulty, as a person of color, with this distinction, which is European in perspective. Using these same empathic distinctions, one might ask, "Did the Indians see their treatment by the Spanish as instrumental in saving their souls, or were the Indians of that day themselves appalled by their own enslavement, rape, and murder at the hand of the Spanish?" At our second interview, I asked Dr. Franklin these questions. He responded that many of the American Indians did not believe the Spanish to be saving their souls and that the former often rebelled. More important, he said a discussion among those who disagreed with the historians' distinction had taken place in his classroom the day before. He said the following to his students.

> Indeed, many Native Americans did not feel that the Europeans were justified "saving their souls," but as I stressed, the missionaries were often backed with the Spanish military, so it was a coercive element there and the Indians in fact had resisted. You also have to look at other forms of resistance. The Native American's assertive pre-European symbolic art in the mission system under the noses and eyes of the watchful padres was a form of cultural resistance.

Discussion

In this second case study, we can again see evidence of Banks's framework. Dr. Franklin approaches content integration in a variety of ways. He makes major efforts in terms of *content integration* for his students, most of whom will be future teachers in the public schools. His textbook has been chosen because it interrogates traditional interpretations and takes a multicultural stand. He uses Spanish in important ways—to delineate essential concepts. He is determined that the students will understand the *knowledge construction* aspects of history, and he teaches the juxtaposition of moral and historical empathy as relevant to the constructions of what we understand and believe about history.

Though other elements of Banks's framework are not as evident, these two, content integration and knowledge construction, are basic to course goals and student learning.

Allan Reimer: Mathematics Is Not A-Cultural

Background Information

Dr. Allan Reimer is an associate professor of mathematics. He received his mathematics training in Ireland and taught for a number of years in Europe. At the time of this writing, he was completing his first year of teaching on the campus. Like Dr. Franklin's students, many of Dr. Reimer's students are future teachers. One of the many pedagogical principles he has adopted relates to his understanding that students employ a variety of learning styles. On this topic, he says, "I approach [math] problems in many different ways: trial and error, algebraic, pictorial, physically acted out." He told me: "Understanding different methods of solution is very powerful. I think my students will differ and their students will differ."

Dr. Reimer believes strongly that mathematics is cultural and must be connected to mathematical content in students' lives. Very often, this means that the curriculum is enriched, reflecting the cultural experiences of the students.

Multicultural Education Practices

Content Integration. This instructor believes that math is "one tool for describing what happens in a context." In order to provide an appropriate context, he asks students to collaborate on the creation of a poster that tells the story of the California energy crisis. With this activity, students bring in their own particular stories about the effect of the energy crisis on their lives, and then the mathematics of this important issue is approached. The students' different cultural backgrounds, as well as their different experiences with energy, create their poster's story and contribute to the cultural content of the course. Incorporating students' stories into the curriculum, Reimer makes reasoning about the mathematical science of the energy crisis relevant to their own lived experiences. Because students' experiences are incorporated into the curriculum, they are more engaged and gain a better understanding of the concepts being taught to them. Because many of his students are teachers, they take this "lived experience" approach to their own classrooms.

Equity Pedagogy. Dr. Allan Reimer's understanding that "students will differ" is at the very heart of equity pedagogy. This understanding guides his use of different methods of instruction and his consistent search for, and use of, cultural connections to help students understand math concepts. Reimer says: "Math is not just numbers. I ask my students, 'How does context and culture enter into math?'" When I observed his class, he used references to sand in the park, waiting for buses, energy, and water to help students understand mathematical concepts. Everyday experience in all of their lives became central to their understanding of math concepts and how they can be taught.

Discussion

In Dr. Reimer's class, lived experience becomes the backdrop for understanding the abstractions of mathematics. He claims, "math is an everyday experience; we all use math in important ways in our lives." Through his *content integration* and *equity pedagogy* approaches, he decreases the students' fear of math and assists them in understanding how this subject is integral to their lives and the lives of their current or future students.

Marilyn Rayburn: Encouraging Students to Think Like Scientists

Background Information

Marilyn Rayburn directs the campus program for K–12 teacher education in addition to teaching a natural science course. When I observed Dr. Rayburn's class, I wrote, "Marilyn seems absolutely enthralled with watching the critical thinking of her students." At our second interview, I showed Dr. Rayburn this comment. She responded with apparent glee: "I am enthralled. I love teaching and watching my students think. Some people say I am crazy for teaching in addition to being an administrator, but I would not give up my teaching."

Her natural science curriculum has a three-unit focus: light and color, magnetism, and current electricity. From the interview, observation, and significant artifact data, it is clear that the ability to think like a scientist is important to a student's success in this course. Thinking like a scientist, according to Dr. Rayburn, involves "making observations, inferences, and predictions and doing experiments to test one's predictions." In the "pedagogy" section of her syllabus, Dr. Rayburn writes that "students will always provide evidence (usually from experiments) to support their ideas."

Group work is the major component in Dr. Rayburn's class; each group of three is composed of a low-, middle-, and high-performing student. Every lab table consists of one fast-moving group and one slower-moving group. A typical class is organized as follows:

- students work independently to generate ideas that explain some set of phenomena;
- they then share their ideas with their group members and perform experiments testing their ideas;
- next, they present their explanations to the entire class;
- finally, Dr. Rayburn leads a class discussion, "whose purpose is to develop a single set of consensus ideas . . . that the class agrees is reasonable and can be supported with evidence."

Multicultural Education Practices

Content Integration. Dr. Rayburn reported that it is the students, not the teacher, who bring cultural content knowledge into classroom discussions. At our first interview, she said: "Students are making observations, inferences, and predictions. If they bring in something cultural, that's them, not me." Each cycle of Rayburn's class begins with an elicitation phase. In this phase, students "are asked to draw on prior experience to invent an initial explanation for groups and as a whole class." Rayburn explains, "The purpose of the activity is to raise relevant issues regarding the phenomenon and to encourage the class to offer some initial ideas that could be starting points to address the issues." The elicitation phase appears to present an appropriate opportunity to make use of ethnic content knowledge from the various groups represented in the class.

A number of times, I heard students describe the flow of electricity in terms of carrots and gremlins, with little gremlins (conductors) carrying the carrots (units of electricity). Rayburn informed me that the carrots-and-gremlins idea was instituted because the course designers wanted something with which all students could identify to explain the flow of electricity. This is precisely the rationale for content integration—using examples from the lived experience of students to elucidate key subject matter concepts.

Knowledge Construction. When Dr. Rayburn's students make observations, inferences, and predictions based on a working hypothesis and subsequently make generalizations, they are constructing knowledge. The students may not realize that the subjective factors of race, socioeconomic class, and gender influenced the scientists whose working hypotheses they are testing. In the same way, the race, socioeconomic class, and gender of these students influence the hypotheses and generalizations that they make and share with their classmates. The subjectivity that students, like the scientists before them, bring to their analyses constructs their claims. Code (1991) reminds us that all knowledge construction is a combination of subjective and objective factors.

Equity Pedagogy. Rayburn also evaluates the learning of her students in various ways. On a daily basis, students volunteer to explain to the entire class their own or their group's understanding of the phenomenon under investigation for the day. Dr. Rayburn collects from students completed work sheets of the day's activities, as well as drawings and narratives of students, which explain their understanding of the concepts being taught. Dr. Rayburn seems aware in some sense of learning style differences. In the section "Journal Reflections" in her course syllabus, she writes:

> Because many of you are prospective teachers, we believe it is particularly important for you to monitor your own learning. You should be aware of how your own initial ideas are challenged and (perhaps) changed and how you came to understand and to believe *certain alternative ideas* [my emphasis]. We believe that monitoring your own learning will help you become more aware of the learning of your future pupils and should therefore make you a more effective teacher.

Discussion

We see here another instructor who has adapted her classroom to the current student demographics. In the area of *content integration,* she relies heavily on the lived experiences of all her students to interpret the phenomena being studied. Though, of course, the students use science textbooks, they apply the concepts from these texts to what they know. *Knowledge construction* takes place as students work through the scientific method, using evidence to draw conclusions about the data they have studied. One particularly strong element in her classroom is the use of groups, and it is in this area that *equity pedagogies* can be identified. The group work is assessed in a variety of ways, demonstrating the instructor's understanding of student preferences for assessment and of their need to work through their learning socially as well as individually.

From this study, it can certainly be concluded that a multicultural curriculum can be instituted in disciplines across the campus. Most interesting to us as faculty should be the different ways in which Banks's framework is realized, depending upon the discipline, student level, and student goals. In several cases, the class was composed principally of current and future teachers; this, of course, makes the pedagogical approaches even more central to the success of the class. I will here discuss at more length some of the concepts from Banks and, in some cases, critique these instructors' approaches, making suggestions for even more infusion of multiculturalism.

Content Integration: Some Comments on Terms

When I observed Dr. Franklin's history class, the term *frontier* was used by students and the instructor to identify the territories the Spaniards invaded and occupied in the southwest of the United States and the territory the British occupied as they moved west from the eastern United States. *Frontier,* as well as the term *manifest destiny,* is also used in the course syllabus.

As this instructor acknowledged, future teachers, and citizens, need to know that such terms are evidence of the European perspective in U.S. history. Transforming the curriculum, at the very least, means teaching U.S. history from the various perspectives of the people who made this history, using the terms that these people used. Certainly, the Native Americans who met the arriving European explorers and colonists in the southwest and east and midwest did not consider their land "frontier." Dr. Franklin reported that he explains in the first meeting of the course that the term *frontier* is evidence of a European perspective and that it is used because it is the terminology of American history textbooks. He explained that he provides other perspectives on the term *frontier* by noting both the Americans' resistance to it and the resulting physical conflict.

Concerning Dr. Rayburn's approach, gremlins and carrots are probably appropriate examples from popular culture to help students understand the flow of electricity. Dr. Rayburn could advance her practice of multicultural education, and likely further motivate her students, if the examples for students of color were also representative of their ethnic experiences.

Knowledge Construction

Dr. Franklin knows that critically important for all students, particularly future teachers, is an understanding that textbooks are not neutral and that they perpetuate the bias that exists in their subject matter disciplines. Textbooks that speak of "manifest destiny" and "frontiers" without deconstructing these concepts are perpetuating knowledge from a Eurocentric perspective. In order to be competent instructional leaders in public schools, teachers need to know how to deconstruct these terms and correct other misconceptions, by using texts such as Takaki's *A Different Mirror: A History of Multicultural America* (1993), Zinn's *A People's History of the United States, 1492 to Present* (1995), and Loewen's *Lies My Teacher Told Me: Everything Your American History Textbook Got Wrong* (1995). Introducing these texts in the class would perhaps give students a fuller perspective on knowledge construction.

At our second interview, Dr. Rayburn said that the scientific method she teaches her students is Western and Eurocentric. She wondered aloud about the extent to which successful scientists of color, specifically African Americans, have compromised their own cultural ways of thinking in order to think like and succeed under the current scientific hegemony. Scientists of color have written about these compromising experiences. Michelle Cliff (1988, 57) writes:

> My dissertation was produced at the Warburg Institute, University of London, and was responsible for giving me an intellectual belief in myself that I had not had before, while at the same time distancing me from who I am, almost rendering me speechless about who I am. At least I believed in the young woman who wrote the dissertation—still, I wondered who she was and where she had come from.

For some individuals, the distancing of which Cliff speaks begins much earlier than the dissertation stage of professional development. Researchers have documented the phenomenon of students caught between minimizing their ethnicity in order to achieve academically or maintaining their ethnic connections at the peril of their academic success (Fordham, 1988). When confronted with this destructive dichotomy, some students have opted for "racelessness." Fordham, who studied this issue, asks, "[I]s racelessness a pragmatic strategy or pyrrhic victory?" (p. 54). Making connections between culture and academic success is one of the effective resolutions Fordham offers to this unhealthy choice with which students of color are confronted.

Throughout this chapter, I have implied that teaching and learning occurs within cultural contexts. Irvine and York (1995, p. 494) note:

> Cultural variables are powerful, yet often overlooked, explanatory factors in the school failure of children of color. African American, Hispanic, and Indian students bring to the school setting a distinctive set of cultural forms and behaviors, including their group's history, language, values, norms, rituals, and symbols.

Students in Dr. Rayburn's class are participating daily in the knowledge construction process. They are likely to excel—without loss of themselves—if they are encouraged to think like scientists while using their own culturally appropriate ways of thinking to inform the way Western Eurocentric scientists think.

Equity Pedagogy

The form of equity pedagogy practiced most often by professors in this study was that of attending to different learning styles of students. Although they were not necessarily aware that students of color tend to perform better when teaching styles vary to accommodate their learning styles (Hale-Benson, 1986; Ramírez & Castañeda, 1974; Swisher & Deyhle, 1989), these professors consistently used various teaching strategies to facilitate learning. This respect of different learning styles was especially evident in the assessment processes and in the use of group work.

Small-group work has been found to be consistent with the learning styles of African Americans, Latinos, and American Indians (Irvine & York, 1995). Although she believes that her class is too large for small-group work, Santa Cruz might improve her practice of multicultural education, particularly the implementation of equity pedagogy, by finding ways to incorporate small-group strategies into her pedagogy. Seven of the sixteen students in her class were students of color, and such students would likely benefit from small-group strategies.

Drs. Rayburn, Franklin, and Reimer said they did not address prejudice reduction because they were not aware of any racial conflicts in their classes. The absence of open conflict between individuals or groups of different racial groups is not necessarily proof that prejudice, or conflict, does not exist. It is reasonable that university students, like their adult counterparts inside and outside the university setting, have learned sophisticated ways of covering up their prejudices. Given the racial crisis in the United States, it is likely that university students mirror the larger society in their harboring of racial prejudices. Like most Americans, they need to develop more democratic, affirming, and accepting attitudes toward those in racial groups different from their own. By using a combination of cooperative learning strategies (Slavin, 1979), Allport's (1954) ingredients for harmonious interracial interaction, and opportunities for out-of-class experiences and reflections (see Weber, Washington, & Young, this volume), university teachers across the curriculum are likely to foster in their students a desire to value individuals of different racial groups.

Professors Santa Cruz, Rayburn, and Reimer are likely to reduce prejudice in students by incorporating Allport's (1954) ingredients when they use cooperative learning strategies in mixed-race groups (Slavin, 1979). Additionally, all instructors should remind students that they each have significant and unique contributions to make to the group work because of their racial and ethnic differences. Leveling the playing field in this way forestalls what Elizabeth Cohen (1972) calls "the interracial interaction disability." Cohen found that when students do not believe that group members of all racial groups have essential contributions to make, both White students and students of color expect White students to take over and do the work of the group.

University professors can also use the proven effective strategies of Katz and Zalk (1978) in the public schools to reduce prejudice in their students. These practitioners were able to reduce prejudice in children by

- teaching them to distinguish between the faces of people of color in the same racial group,
- increasing their positive interracial contact,
- providing vicarious interracial contact, and
- positively reinforcing the color black.

Assigning tasks to mixed-race groups of students and using multicultural literature are two of the most common ways that teachers may use to increase students' positive interracial contact and to provide them with vicarious interracial contact. Content integration in the classroom may not suffice. The work of Schofield (1997) and Tomlinson (1996) reminds teachers that without additional pedagogical work, students may not make the positive connections that teachers intend them to make between multicultural literature and individuals in their racial outgroups.

Student Empowerment

The atmosphere of Dr. Rayburn's class was generally empowering. I found her to be affirming to all of her students, men and women alike. As any good teacher does when students are asked to work in groups, she dutifully visited groups numerous times to answer questions, provide expert knowledge, and generally check their progress on the assigned tasks. She seemed equitable in the way she called on students to work at the board. As there were far more women in the class (there were twenty-five women and six men), she called on women with more frequency. However, when I asked her if students of color seemed to benefit more than White students from the group configuration and group analysis of ideas in the class, she said no and added:

"Females tend to be less sophisticated than the males. The males seem to have paid attention in their previous science course" (first interview).

It is possible that males perform better in this science class because, unlike their female counterparts, they have been encouraged and expected to do well in science in their previous K–12 schooling. (See Mukhopadhyay & Greer, this volume.) Rayburn could advance her practice of multicultural education in her physical science course by investigating the bias that exists in science that empowers men to excel and sometimes leaves women behind. Moreover, having a discussion with her entire class about the differences in achievement in science between females and males, as well as between students of color and White students, would be beneficial. An investigation by Rayburn and her students of the different ways that boys versus girls and students of color versus White students are socialized related to science knowledge may interrupt negative messages that females and students of color receive regarding their own achievement in science.

Implications for Research and Practice

Though revealing in a number of ways, this is a very small study of only four faculty. Research studies and analyses of all academic disciplines are needed to investigate how faculty across the United States might implement multicultural education in their classrooms. Campuses are likely to benefit from additional qualitative research studies that include more observations of university classroom teaching.

The interviews and observations in this study suggest that students' cultures and everyday, lived experiences not only were relevant to the content under investigation but in many ways facilitated the understanding of the content being studied. Faculty who use approaches that benefit all students, such as group work and community-based service learning, will certainly serve their ethnically diverse students more effectively.

Faculty interested in practicing multicultural education in their classrooms are likely to make great progress by asking and answering the following questions related to implementing multicultural education in their university classrooms.

- What information from students' cultures might I use to illustrate key concepts in my discipline? (Content Integration)
- What are the appropriate ways for me to show students how

race, socioeconomic class, and gender influence how knowledge is constructed in my discipline? (Knowledge Construction)
- What strategies might I use to develop in students' cultural competence through curriculum? (Equity Pedagogy)
- In what ways might I vary my teaching style and pedagogies to be consistent with the learning styles of my students? (Equity Pedagogy)
- At what junctures in my course(s) might I use cooperative learning strategies that are proven to create in students more democratic values? (Prejudice Reduction)
- What classroom strategies might I use to help create and support a school culture that ensures that all of my students are empowered to achieve academically at their university? (Empowering School Culture)

Appendix A: Interview Protocol

Tell me your area of expertise.
How long have you been teaching?
What courses do you teach?
[At this point, I tell the respondent that I will now explain each of the dimensions of multicultural education and answer any questions he or she may have. After I explain each of the dimensions of multicultural education, I field any questions the respondent has and ask that he or she explain how the dimensions of multicultural education are implemented.]
Do you have any questions about content integration or any of its levels?
How do you implement content integration?
Do you have any questions about the knowledge construction process?
In what ways do you implement the knowledge construction process, if at all?
Do you have any questions about equity pedagogy?
How would you say you implement equity pedagogy?
Do you have any questions about prejudice reduction?
How do you reduce prejudice in your students, if this is something that you do?
[At this point, I ask the respondent when it would be convenient for me to observe her or him teaching a class.]

Additional Resources

Aragon, S. R. (2000). Beyond access: Methods and models for increasing retention and learning among minority students. *New Directions for Community Colleges,* no. 112. San Francisco: Jossey-Bass/Wiley.

    Aragon has provided the reader with an abundance of practical resources for creating and executing cross-cultural courses in the college context. The author also discusses the intersection of learning styles and culture, work-based programs, and the particular needs and issues relating to minority instructors. Aragon examines and critiques assessment at various levels (admissions, placement, and classroom assessment) and the ways in which students of all ethnic groups can be engaged and included in both pedagogies and assessment practices. Finally, he provides a useful case study, detailing the efforts of one college campus to create more multicultural and inclusive classroom contexts.

Delpit, L. (1996). *Other people's children: Cultural conflict in the classroom.* New York: New Press.

Lisa Delpit, a McArthur Award winner and an African American, argues that many of the academic problems faced by students of color are the result of an imbalance of power between White teachers and the cultural values that they represent, on the one hand, and students and the values they prize, on the other. The *Harvard Educational Review* notes that this volume "provides an important, yet typically avoided, discussion of how power imbalances in the larger U.S. society reverberate in classrooms."

Henson, K. T. (2000). *Curriculum planning: Integrating multiculturalism, constructivism, and educational reform.* New York: McGraw-Hill.

This book focuses solely on the issues raised by the author of this chapter: multicultural curriculum planning for graduate courses and upper-division undergraduate courses. The author uses scenarios and case studies to give life to this discussion and also provides practical suggestions for working with culturally diverse students as well as with students with disabilities.

McTighe, J., & Wiggins, G. P. (2000). *Understanding by design.* Englewood Cliffs, NJ: Prentice-Hall.

What does it mean to understand? The authors suggest six facets in their model: explanation, interpretation, application, perspective, empathy, and self-knowledge. Using the term *backward design,* they propose using these facets in designing instruction that starts with the desired student outcomes and then turns to pedagogies. They propose framing content around essential questions and big ideas, and they suggest a formative assessment process for determining to what degree students understand an issue. In keeping with their theories, they present ways for engaging students in rethinking issues, thus resulting in greater depth of discussion and understanding. Though written for the K–12 classroom, this well-respected volume has much to say to the college instructor.

APPROACHES FOR DIVERSE CLASSROOMS

4

Culturally Relevant Strategies for the Classroom

Evangelina Bustamante Jones

Now as never before, U.S. college student populations better reflect the ethnic and linguistic diversity of the people of the United States. This positive change brings with it the need for instructors to teach differently from the ways in which we were taught. Because our diverse students bring their unique strengths and needs into our classrooms, we must support their learning by using approaches that affirm value systems perhaps different from our own and that more directly elicit students' experiences. Value systems and lived experiences, along with the interpretation of those systems and experiences, are directly linked to the culture or cultures in primary communities.

The appropriate use of culture in teaching and learning makes a positive difference in classroom environments and in the degree of student engagement with content. I am a Mexican American who still remembers what it was like to try to understand norms and values practiced at school that often conflicted with those in my home and community. Throughout my thirty years of teaching experience as a bicultural instructor with increasingly bicultural classrooms, I have learned to create culturally relevant learning settings and lesson designs, which I believe promote high academic achievement. I write this chapter hoping that some of the classroom strategies and practices I describe here will assist others in their efforts to explore the role of culture in learning.

I begin with descriptions of two theories that explore how culture affects the totality of the learning experience: Hollins's (1996) theory of culturally mediated instruction and Wlodkowski and Ginsberg's (1995) motivational framework for culturally responsive teaching. Hollins uses Vygotskian concepts to explain how culture shapes learning, while Wlodkowski and Ginsberg base their framework on intrinsic motivation as a means to engage diverse learners specifically in higher education settings (see also Wang & Folger, this volume). Following this overview, I employ Wlodkowski and Ginsberg's framework to organize examples of culturally relevant classroom strategies I have used in my courses, as a means to illustrate principles of culturally relevant instruction for all classrooms.

Conceptual Frameworks

Culturally Mediated Instruction: Understanding the Relationships between Culture and Learning

In *Culture in School Learning: Revealing the Deep Meaning* (1996), Etta R. Hollins places culture at the center of school learning. The basis of her theory is that "classroom instruction is influenced by the extent to which it incorporates critical aspects of the home-culture" (p. 137). The theory of culturally mediated instruction consists of linking culture with cognition, social contexts for learning, and curriculum content.

The foundational postulate of Hollins's theory is that the principal bridge between culture and instruction is the effect of cultural practices on cognitive development. Hollins uses the term *culturally mediated cognition,* which is based on Vygotsky's (1978) use of sociohistorical theory in psychology and human development. Vygotsky claimed that a person's schemata and mental processes are developed and organized through cultural and historical contexts. Schemata are theoretical knowledge structures organized to show the relationships among facts, information, and principles (McCown, Driscoll, & Roop, 1996). Among other things, the schemata created through an individual's cultural values affect his or her socialization; in turn, socialization practices create particular patterns in learning styles, incentive-motivational styles, human relation styles, and communication styles.

Hollins claims that culture and its relationship to learning contexts determines what people perceive as culturally appropriate social situations for learning, affecting the quality of relationships between teacher and students, as well as among students. When cultural appropriateness is consistent with the home culture, as is the case for many Euro-American middle-class students in American schools, it is more likely that a classroom will be congruent in behavioral expectations, relational structures between teacher and student, and peer dynamics. The harmonious match between home and school contexts creates positive culturally mediated instructional settings. Instructional practices in these cases are "an extension of cultural knowledge associated with customs, traditions, and values from the students' home-culture" (Hollins, 1996, p. 140).

Equally as important, however, is the social context for learning that is present in the classroom. Euro-American middle-class students are raised to appreciate individualism, a cherished value in this country; however, about 70 percent of the world's population, both in the United States and abroad, value collectivism within their communities (Bell, 1987, cited in Shade, Kelly, & Oberg, 1997). These communities include the Chinese, Japanese, Filipinos, Pacific Asians, Italians, Jews, Greeks, and Africans, as well as Cubans, Mexicans, Puerto Ricans, American Indians, African Americans, Asian Americans, and other Latinos in the United States. Values derived from collectivism, such as reciprocity, duty, tradition, dependence, harmony, and the priority of family integrity over personal gain, contrast with the values derived from individualism: seeking ownership, dominance, competitiveness, and aggression (Shade et al., 1997). Nonetheless, individualism is embedded in American school practices, and students whose cultures value collectivism over individualism find it difficult to break from their socialization patterns within the schools.

Culture and its relationship to curriculum, or "culturally valued knowledge," refers to the inclusion of knowledge that is valued in the student's home culture. As mentioned earlier, teachers can use historical and cultural events and role models from the home culture to teach or elaborate on concepts in the curriculum. But there are other approaches. Two of these approaches are represented by the Algebra Project, a math-science project that serves inner-city students in Cambridge, Massachusetts. Founded by mathematician and civil rights activist Bob Moses, its goal is to create structural equality for students of color by insuring that all students receive instruction in algebra regardless of skill levels or academic achievement. Instead of rote-based, traditional math instruction, for instance, the Algebra Project uses imaginative and creative activities that are strongly connected to African American cultural touchstones in order to generate complex mathematical thinking, such as a fourth/fifth-grade African drums curriculum unit that pairs a drummer and teacher to show ratios, proportions, fractions, and rates (see also Mukhopadhyay & Greer, this volume).

The Algebra Project program also generates critical consciousness in both students and parents, because teachers begin with the question, "What is algebra for?" posing it as a political question. Thus, the question delves into the issue of access to college prep courses and equity for all students, which are clearly values held by communities that have been politically and educationally marginalized (Moses & Cobb, 2001;

Moses, Kamii, Swap, & Howard, 1989). Now with eighteen sites, over one hundred schools, and forty thousand students, the Algebra Project "affirms local people's cultural values and capacity to deepen community life through shaping the public institution most likely to have a profound impact on their children" (Levine, 2001, p. 15).

In sum, Hollins's theory of culturally mediated instruction, augmented by the examples provided here, proposes that interactions with the people and immediate environment of our earliest years are shaped by the cultural and social contexts in which we live. We organize in particular ways what we perceive and learn through these conditions, thus shaping our theoretical knowledge structures or schemata. These schemata are, in effect, driven by the values in the culture that surrounds us; they are enacted in the ways we learn, in what motivates us and serves as incentives for us to persevere, in our norms and expectations for our relationships with others, and in our preferred ways of communicating. When we are students, these mental structures can shape our approaches to learning, as well as what we do or do not pay attention to; they can determine how we feel as we work in the classroom by ourselves, with other students, and with the teacher; and they can affect our perceptions about what is worth learning. In the next section, the relationship between culture and motivation is described through a framework that addresses postsecondary teaching and learning.

Culturally Responsive Teaching: Understanding the Social and Curricular Context

Raymond J. Wlodkowski and Margery B. Ginsberg (1995) propose that at the postsecondary level, there needs to be a framework based on "principles and structures that are meaningful across cultures, especially with students from families and communities who have not historically experienced success in higher education" (p. 9). Furthermore, they believe that the educational system of a society claiming to value cultural pluralism must "create learning experiences that allow the integrity of every learner to be sustained while each person attains relevant educational success and mobility" (p. 18). But in postsecondary education, such instruction is all too rare.

Wlodkowski and Ginsberg describe most college-level instruction as organized around extrinsic motivation, that is, teach-and-test practices, competitive assessment procedures, grades, and grade point averages. In contrast, they propose that intrinsic motivation should be the framework for creating culturally responsive learning environments in higher education. Intrinsic motivation underlies people's willingness to work on tasks because of internal reasons like enjoyment and pleasure, the satisfaction taken from learning something new, or curiosity and interest in the topic (McCown et al., 1996). The sense of autonomy, or self-regulation, also enhances intrinsic motivation (Deci & Ryan, 1985). Wlodowski and Ginsberg (1995) reason that although diverse learners are likely to have values and norms different from the instructor or other students, the connection between motivation and learning crosses all cultures. They warn that we must start thinking of motivation as powered not by manipulation and control but by communication and respect. For that to happen, we must be willing to understand perspectives different from our own and to "co-create with the learner a motivating educational experience" (Wlodowski & Ginsberg, 1995, p. 23). However, we cannot really begin to do so until we have examined our own cultural paradigms and how these have driven our assumptions, goals, and expectations.

Wlodowski and Ginsberg's framework focuses on the relationship between teachers and learners and is composed of four intersecting motivational goals or conditions (states of being). Each goal has two criteria and a key question for teachers and learners.

- Establishing Inclusion. The criteria for establishing inclusion are "respect" and "connectedness," which are prerequisites for feeling included in a group (p. 62). The key question for this goal is, "What do we need to do to feel respected by and connected to one another?" (p. 33).
- Developing Attitude. The criteria for developing attitude are relevance and self-determination. The key question is, "How can we use relevance and choice to create a favorable disposition toward learning?" (p. 33).
- Enhancing Meaning. The criteria for enhancing meaning are engagement and challenge. The key question is, "What are active ways to increase the complexity of what we are learning so that it matters to us and contributes to a pluralistic democracy?" (p. 33).
- Engendering Competence. The criteria for engendering competence are authenticity and effectiveness. Its key question is, "How can we create an understanding that we are becoming effective in learning we value?" (p. 33).

To broadly illustrate the four motivational goals, Wlodkowski and Ginsberg relate a rather lengthy example of a teaching/learning process conducted at the first session of an introductory course in research (pp. 30–31). We summarize that example here.

After the syllabus and its content are discussed, the teacher randomly assigns students to small groups and asks them to discuss previous experiences with research, as well as expectations and concerns about the course. After this activity, a volunteer from each group summarizes the experiences, hopes, and concerns of its members, thus helping students to establish rapport and trust among themselves. (Establishing Inclusion)

The teacher proposes her belief that most people actually exhibit many characteristics and behaviors of researchers in their day-to-day lives, and she asks the class what they would like to research at this present moment. Students choose to investigate the amount of sleep some of their fellow classmates had the previous night. (Developing Attitude)

Five students volunteer as subjects, and teams decide what set of observations and questions to ask, other than directly asking them how many hours of sleep they had. After the question session, teams rank the volunteers from most to least amount of sleep. The volunteers reveal to the class their amount of sleep time, and it turns out that none of the teams have correctly ranked more than two of the volunteers. Then the volunteers tell the teams questions they could have asked that would have elicited better information, such as "How much coffee did you drink before class?" (Enhancing Meaning)

In the final part of the activity, the students hold a discussion, and then each student writes about what she/he has learned from this process or about research. Finally, in randomly assigned groups, they share their insights, thus allowing them to see for themselves how their understanding of what research is has already grown. (Engendering Competence)

While the preceding example illustrates the framework's four motivational goals, Wlodkowski and Ginsberg provide three additional supports, or heuristics, that offer more specific guidance for reaching each goal (pp. 34–35).

- Norms communicate "the explicit assumptions, values, and purposes" that the learning group will live by.
- Procedures are "teaching and learning strategies" that can assist the teacher and learners to reach their "learning objectives."
- "Structures are formal patterns of organization, rules of operation, and other arrangements" that describe how the learning

group will work—often these are explicitly stated in course syllabi.

While these are general definitions, each motivational goal has a particular set of norms, procedures, and structures. For example, for the goal of Establishing Inclusion, one procedure could be collaborative learning, which would not necessarily be the procedure for Engendering Competence.

It is clear that the motivational framework is an ambitious, well-developed road map that can guide teachers toward designing more dynamic, more equitable, and more transformative classrooms.

There are significant connections between the components of Hollins's theory and Wlodowski and Ginsberg's motivational framework (see table 1). Hollins's theory explains the impact of a person's primary culture on learning, starting from birth. For individuals whose primary culture matches the culture of the dominant society, enculturation continues throughout life in a relatively harmonious way, but immigrants and children raised in other cultures can experience significant problems. Although most bicultural individuals become equally adept in both cultural systems (our college students are fine examples of this), many characteristics of their primary culture may continue to feel more "comfortable" than those of the dominant culture, especially when it comes to social contexts and relational structures.

Various researchers describe teaching and curriculum design that is sensitive to students' cultures with terms like *culturally harmonious, culturally synchronic, culturally appropriate,* and *culturally congruent.* It is important to note that the practice of culturally relevant instruction should go beyond personal student experiences and standard texts to deepen the students' understanding of what is being studied through

TABLE 1. Alignment of Wlodkowski and Ginsberg's Motivational Framework (1995) and Hollins's Theory of Culturally Mediated Instruction (1996)

Motivational Framework for Culturally Responsive Teaching	Theory of Culturally Mediated Instruction
Establishing Inclusion	Culturally appropriate social situations for learning
	Culturally mediated cognition
Developing Attitude	Culturally mediated cognition
	Culturally valued knowledge
Enhancing Meaning	Culturally valued knowledge in the curriculum
Engendering Competence	Culturally mediated cognition

cultural and historical examples from the students' own cultural and ethnic group (Jones, Pang, & Rodríguez, 2001). We can go farther still by also examining the effects of oppression and marginalization with our students within the context of what we teach, thus developing a critical consciousness that directly relates to what they are studying (Jones, 1998b; Shor, 1992). The inclusion of this last feature of culturally relevant instruction is especially crucial to the engagement of lived experiences at the college level. In the next section, the relationship between lived experiences and schooling is explored.

Culturally Relevant Teaching: An Application of Wlodowski and Ginsberg's Theories

I teach courses in literacy methods for multiple-subject classrooms (elementary grades) and single-subject classrooms (secondary grades), in a Bilingual, Cross-Cultural, Language and Academic Development (BCLAD) credential program. My students are, for the most part, Latinos who are themselves immigrants or whose parents were immigrants. There are also students of other ethnicities, primarily Euro-Americans, who have developed a high level of language proficiency in Spanish and deep knowledge of Latino cultural groups. Most of the Latinos in the program are from the first generation in their families to attend college, while most of the Euro-Americans come from families with longer traditions in higher education. My goals for our credential students are very clear: I want them to have learning experiences in my classes that develop high levels of competency in pedagogy so that they can raise academic achievement in all marginalized communities. In addition, I want our students to become reflective individuals who are critically conscious of equity and social justice issues as manifested in schools and thus will work for school transformation.

Because I believe that culturally relevant practices are crucial to reaching the goals I have for my students, I continually self-assess and reflect upon my work in the courses I teach, by asking myself the following questions.

- In my own teaching, am I using culturally relevant practices that model equity, promote high levels of participation, and develop and nurture positive ethnic and cultural identity?
- Which of these practices provide the best modeling so that my students can experience (and, hopefully, implement) them in their future classrooms?

At each semester's end, I take stock of my work in the classroom by analyzing multiple artifacts and data related to my courses relative to the qualities of culturally relevant practices described in the first part of this chapter. One set of artifacts considered is my output to students: my syllabi, my teaching notes and lesson plans, and the texts and readings I assign. Another set of artifacts is comprised of student feedback and assessments—student products such as *quickwrites* (on-the-spot responses to a question related to an assigned reading or brainstorming about a new topic), assigned reflective essays, student-designed lesson plans, midterm assessments, collaboratively produced thematic units, and the narrative sections of my teaching evaluations. This past year, I used Wlodkowski and Ginsberg's framework as an additional dimension by which to examine my teaching. Though I had, over many years, incorporated many of the norms, procedures, and structures proposed in the framework, I had not examined my work through the lens of motivation. This framework has added clarity to my self-assessment, as its holistic nature encompasses all of my previous assessment criteria.

Here, I use the framework's four motivational goals as a means to organize my teaching examples, although each example is illustrative of more than one goal. Additionally, I have included quotes from some student feedback artifacts (course evaluations, quickwrites, and reflective essays) to confirm the effectiveness of the classroom practices (see table 2 for an overview). I recognize that my examples are specific to teaching in credential courses, and I am not proposing that the strategies as described will apply directly to courses of all types. However, I believe that some general principles of culturally relevant pedagogy as defined earlier will emerge through the descriptions.

TABLE 2. Overview of Motivational Goals, Classroom Examples, and Evaluation Tools

Motivational Goals and Criteria	Classroom Example	Student Feedback Artifact
Establishing Inclusion: Respect and connectedness	Collaborative groups Carousel Trade books	Course evaluation Quickwrite
Developing Attitude: Relevance and self-determination	Weekly experiential learning activity	Course evaluation
Enhanced Meaning: Engagement and challenge	Simulation/performance assessment	Quickwrite
Engendering Competence: Authenticity and effectiveness	Layered reflective essays	Reflective essay

Goal One: Establishing Inclusion Criteria through Connectedness and Respect

As mentioned earlier, the key question for establishing inclusion is, "What do we need to do to feel respected by and connected to one another?" (Wlodkowski & Ginsberg, 1995, p. 36). I promote a sense of connectedness primarily through *confianza,* collaborative and coopera- tive groups, a specific collaborative structure called "the carousel," and the affirmation of ethnic and cultural identities.

Confianza

What is *confianza?* The English translation of *confianza* is "confidence," but this is insufficient in translation. In a Latino context, *confianza* denotes a sense of mutual or reciprocated trust about events or interac- tions that parties undertake together (Greenberg, 1989, cited in Moll & Greenberg, 1990; Vélez-Ibáñez, 1983, 1996; Walsh, 1991). The devel- opment of *confianza* takes place through a series of events that consti- tute social contexts for learning, most often in the homes of extended family members and fictive kin, that is, people who are not blood rel- atives but who play important roles in a family, such as godparents (Vélez-Ibáñez, 1996). Although *confianza* is not one of the norms pro- posed by Wlodkowski and Ginsberg, the term epitomizes Hollins's proposition that culture and its relationship to learning contexts deter- mines what people perceive as culturally appropriate social situations for learning (1996).

In my earlier research, I found that *confianza* was the genuine basis for the relationships between teachers and students (Jones, 1998b). Students felt that what teachers asked them to do in class was in their own best interest because of their previously established mutual trust. In thinking about the relationship between college instructors and their students, I believe that most instructors communicate a positive belief in students' abilities to become competent in developing and mastering their course knowledge. Such a demonstration of trust matters because at the begin- ning of a course, students often do not feel very confident about their present level of knowledge, and it can be difficult for them to take risks in participating or asking questions in class for fear that other students or the teacher will perceive them as unintelligent. Establishing a sense of safety and acceptance must precede such candor. By communicating that we hold a hopeful view of our students' capacity to become com- petent in our course of study—in other words, by our trusting them— students will rise to that expectation. In one of my course evaluations, a student wrote the following when asked to list the strengths of the instructor: "A real teacher knows how to build rapport with students." The statement tells me this student felt that creating rapport, which implies the existence of a common ground between teacher and student, was the most significant element of my teaching and was perhaps foundational to achieving the course goals and objectives.

Collaborative and Cooperative Groups

It is crucial that our classes are designed to promote different participation structures to accommodate everyone's comfort level. From the very first class session and at each session throughout the semester, students work in groups of varying compositions for at least part of each class session. Working in pairs and small groups allows even quiet students to voice their thoughts and contribute ideas. In large classes especially, a few students tend to dominate the discussion or answer questions posed by the instructor. I find that students whose second language was at one time their weaker language, even though they are presently fluent, tend to remain silent in spite of the fact that they have much to contribute.

Over the semester, I make sure to vary the ways groups are formed so that students eventually have the opportunity to work closely with all members of the class. One exception to this is the use of permanent groups based on their content areas, such as math, science, social science, English, Spanish, kinesiology, or art. These groups meet throughout the semester and have the opportunity to develop together a deepening understanding of teaching their specific subjects. As groups, they function much like miniature learning communities. I have found that students really value social structures where participation is built in. When asked to list the strengths of the course, one student wrote, "Students were engaged in every session."

This observation reinforced earlier student feedback garnered through an in-class quickwrite exercise. As mentioned earlier, quickwrites are short, focused responses to particular questions, and I use them throughout the semester to gauge students' growing awareness of effective teaching. When asked the question "What advice would you like to give college instructors that would make their classes a more successful experience for their students?" one student's response was, "For the professor to allow students the opportunity to engage with each other not only on outside time, but during class time."

The Carousel

In addition to the use of collaborative groups as participatory structures, I introduce students to specific collaborative structures they can try in their student teaching assignments. One of the most popular is the carousel (Schulz, 1998), judging from its mention in several course evaluations and self-reports by students. The carousel activates prior knowledge about a topic and can be conducted before starting a unit of study or for review after a unit has been completed. The resulting high level of interaction allows students to discuss and dialogue, build on or extend other students' points, and engage in problem solving. With my secondary teaching students, I begin the carousel by taping around the room a number of large pieces of chart papers on which I have written different open-ended questions. These questions may be based, for example, on the Aztec culture in general and the impact of the Spanish invasion and colonization in Mexico. Two examples of such questions are "What were some features of Aztec society?" and "List as many causes you can think of to explain the Aztecs' defeat at the hands of the Spaniards." In random groups of four or five, students go to one chart and brainstorm as one group member records their responses, using an assigned color marker. After a very few minutes, I ask them to move to the next chart, whereupon they begin the process again by reading the previous group's answers to the question, adding a check mark to answers they agree with, and writing additional responses below those of the first group. Because each group uses a different-colored marker, it is easy to see each group's contributions. As groups continue to rotate through all the charts, it gets progressively more difficult to come up with new answers, and students must dig much more deeply into their knowledge or rely more on critical thinking, often leading to more creative and divergent answers. For the final rotation, groups return to their original question, read and discuss the answers other groups added to theirs, and analyze the whole. At this point, they can compose a summary or place all of the responses into categories or classifications.

If this strategy is used before starting a unit, students can predict what the unit will be about or compose questions that will set purposes for reading. Used as a review, students can synthesize what they know and understand before working on a culminating essay, designing a project, or taking a test.

Affirmation of Ethnic and Cultural Identities

Until very recently, most school materials and library books did not reflect the diversity of cultures and ethnicities present in our schools. Over the years, I have collected many multicultural children's and adolescent fiction and nonfiction trade books that affirm identity and cultural values from various ethnic and cultural groups or relate in some way to issues of adolescence, social injustice, or stereotypes. I share these with my secondary credential students for two important reasons. Of course, as teachers of literacy in their respective content areas, they should know about such books so that they can use them as resources. But the other significant reason is that exposure to such books provides my students the first opportunity to see themselves or their family members reflected and celebrated in stories or informational texts, to experience seeing someone that "looks like them or feels what they feel." A couple of course evaluation remarks stated: "She picks appropriate materials and is inclusive of all students"; "We read and discussed various books with a variety of cultural themes, especially from Mexican and Latino cultures." In addition to evidencing their interest in books that affirm ethnic and cultural identity, I learned that students felt their previous content courses could have utilized resources that exposed them to the contributions and achievements of people of color in those subjects. In a quickwrite, one student said: "I would have liked to have learned about the significant contributions in science and math from diverse cultures and women. My current knowledge is heavily biased to contributions made by American and Western European males." (For more on math and science education, see Yerrick and Mukhopadhyay & Greer, this volume.)

The use of these texts fits well within my course, but similar sharing can be implemented in a more global way in other disciplines. Students appreciate it when their instructors share their personal knowledge and passion for their subjects with them through brief book talks. Instructors can do this with an occasional display of books in their field that made an impact on them or of books, posters, or memorabilia that represent a meaningful event in their development as mathematicians, biologists, or historians. Such a display reminds students that they are also in the process of developing a part of their identity through study.

Goal Two: Developing Student Attitude through Relevance and Self-Determination; Experiential Learning

The key question for developing attitude is, "How can we use relevance and choice to create a favorable disposition toward learning?" (Wlodkowski & Ginsberg, 1995, p. 37). Norms related to this goal further articulate the question: "Teaching and learning activities are contextualized in the learners' experience or previous knowledge and are accessible through their current thinking and ways of knowing" (Wlodkowski & Ginsberg, 1995, p. 37). The entire academic process of learning, from content selection to accomplishment and assessment of competencies, "encourages learners to make real choices based on their experiences, values, needs, and strengths" (Wlodkowski & Ginsberg, 1995, p. 37).

I have established a routine that works particularly well to reinforce theory-based pedagogical concepts in weekly reading assignments. It is effective for a number of reasons, but mostly this one: if my goal is to get students to actually use what they are reading about, they need to have a firsthand experience with the ideas in the text, have time to think of how to apply these to their particular needs, and have time to refine or revise their understanding of the ideas. Interestingly enough, I found an almost identical routine for experiential learning, the Kolb model, in Wlodkowski and Ginsberg's (1995) book, even though I developed my routine through trial and error. Briefly, the Kolb model offers active learning as well as observing, theorizing, testing, and reflecting. Although I use my routine as a reinforcement for reading assignments, Wlodkowski and Ginsberg point out that instructors can use experiential learning when students are not already interested in or lack experience in a topic, in order to make such a topic relevant by providing an immediate experience. To illustrate the active learning cycle, I will summarize the steps in my weekly classroom routine and then introduce the related Kolb model.

Step 1. Students come to class having read a chapter in the course text, such as "Vocabulary and Concepts." After offering a brief overview of the chapter and eliciting questions or comments about the reading, I ask students to join their content-area groups.

Step 2. I model a few of the strategies for teaching suggested in the book as well as additional ones from my own strategy collection, using the overhead projector or posting samples on walls, then ask students to discuss in their groups which strategies (a minimum of four) they wish to select as most appropriate for the content they teach. Given about 45–50 minutes to complete their task, each group divides into pairs if needed in order to construct, draw, or design an approximation (model) of the teaching aids with materials I bring to class (markers, newsprint, glue, tape, scissors). During this time, I talk to each group in order to answer their questions, to clarify the purpose of and need for the strategies, or to help them refine their ideas.

Step 3. Students present their strategy models to the class. The instructor and/or fellow students comment, ask for elaboration of ideas if needed, or share new ideas triggered by the presentations; the audience applauds.

Step 4. The following week, students submit individually created lesson plans that use any of the strategies modeled in class that can be used in their teaching assignments. The students also read the next assigned chapter to be ready for the following week's routine.

The Kolb model, which is closely related to my steps, provides various opportunities to engage with a given concept or skill through the alternating of hands-on and thinking phases. It consists of two intersecting continua: the perpendicular continuum ranges from "Concrete Experience" at one end to "Formation of Abstract Concepts and Generalizations" at the other, while the horizontal continuum ranges from "Reflective Observation" to "Active Testing" (Wlodkowski & Ginsberg, 1995, p. 149). An instructor can organize a set of experiential learning activities by exploiting these continua (see fig. 1). Starting clockwise, with concrete experience at the top, students can engage in a laboratory session; read a primary source text, for example, a diary entry from a historical figure; or participate in a simulation or game. Then, in the reflective observation stage, activities can include discussions, brainstorming, or reflective papers. Next, students develop abstract conceptualizations by hearing a lecture, building models, or creating hypotheses. The fourth phase is active experimentation, in which students can construct artistic creations, conduct a laboratory experiment (to test a hypothesis), or design a project (cited in Wlodkowski & Ginsberg, 1995, p. 154).

As I have mentioned, the steps in my routine line up with the Kolb model quite well. Starting with a concrete experience (reading the text and seeing models of the teaching aids), students engage in reflective observation through brainstorming or discussions (in my class, brainstorming, clarifying, and selecting the specific strategies most relevant to their subject). Then, arriving at the stage of abstract conceptualizations, they create hypotheses or models (pairing up, students construct selected teaching aids, customizing them for topics customarily taught in their content areas). Finally, they proceed to active experimentation by creating projects and conducting fieldwork: students individually design a lesson plan that uses one of the ideas they tried or saw presented and then implement these ideas in student teaching classrooms.

The Kolb model is an extremely useful planning tool. While I use these steps in a weekly routine, it might be more realistic for me to use

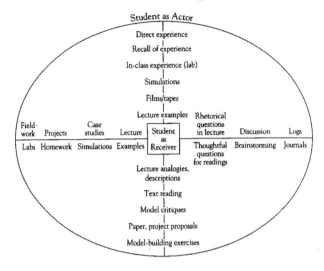

Fig. 1. Degree of direct student involvement in various teaching methods

the Kolb model only with topics or concepts that students have the least experience with or that seem to be the most challenging to teach in a given semester. Several comments in the course evaluations attest to the effectiveness of these active learning approaches. In response to the evaluation prompt "Describe the positive outcomes you have experienced as a result of taking this course, such as increased knowledge, greater vision, personal growth, broader perspectives, etc.," one student answered, "My strength has always been a hands-on approach and the fact that I could do that with all concepts [in the reading assignments] just made them more meaningful." My goal of modeling strategies that students would readily adopt as their own seems to have been met with at least one student. Asked to list the strengths of the course, one reply was, "Many useful strategies that can be applied in our teaching."

Goal Three: Enhancing Meaning through Engagement and Challenge; Simulation of a Grade-Level Planning Process

Wlodkowski and Ginsberg (1995, p. 164) believe that learners are able to enhance meaning in what they study when they have opportunities to "expand, refine, or increase the complexity of what is learned in a way that matters [to them], includes their values and purposes, and contributes to a critical consciousness." The key question for this goal is, "What are active ways to increase the complexity of what we are learning so that it matters to us and contributes to a pluralistic democracy?" (Wlodkowski & Ginsberg, 1995, p. 39).

Probably because I started out as a writing teacher who believes in the importance of a process approach to writing development, I customarily plan an assortment of academic tasks over the semester that, when linked together, allow students to weave these products toward a larger, more complex project. One example, a midterm simulation activity, helps students understand how everything they have read and worked on becomes relevant for the next stage. In the process, they gain deeper understanding of the theoretical- and practice-based contents of the readings and class presentations.

In the form of a letter to the faculty of a new school, I explain the task, which is to design as a team an interdisciplinary curriculum unit for a group of 120 students they will teach throughout the day in a "school within a school" setting. This "authentic" document helps students to visualize themselves as team players in a faculty organized to plan instruction directly linked to the needs of their students. The step-by-step tasks involve both consensus-oriented and individual work.

Step 1. Students work from a scenario that places them in positive interdependent roles—they cannot succeed without the efforts of all group members. Given clear step-by-step goals to reach in the allotted time, they must bring with them their working knowledge of the course text's features as well as their prior knowledge of the content standards in their particular disciplines—in other words, they must have excellent command of the class resources or they will not finish.

Step 2. Students are asked to refer to previously gathered data about which learning strategies and study skills second language learners use (and do not use) in their classes; then, by discussing and prioritizing, they select learning and study skills or strategies that must also be included in their integrated unit to assure mastery of content.

Step 3. Using a guide for designing an integrated unit, each "faculty team" collaboratively creates a graphic organizer or web that shows how each content area's specific topics and content standards are related to the unit's theme.

Step 4. Individual students turn in their own preliminary plan that includes state content standards, content objectives, and learning strategies that will support their attainment.

This simulation, though highly stressful because of its complexity and time constraints, gives students an experience in which they must bring everything they have learned in my class together toward a synthesized product. In a quickwrite at semester's end, a student commented on this introduction to thematic planning: "I hadn't realized how much I really knew and had learned in this class until we had to come up with this unit. After my group was finished, we were amazed at how our work for the final project was already organized; all we had to do was follow our plan."

Goal Four: Engendering Competence through Authenticity and Effectiveness; Connecting Assessment to the Learners' Worlds, Frames of Reference, and Values

The key question for this goal, voiced from the perspective of the student, is, "How can we create an understanding that we are becoming effective in learning we value?" (Wlodkowski & Ginsberg, p. 40). Clearly, assessment is central to everything instructors do throughout a course. Our course objectives define the skills, content knowledge, and academic processes or discourse we identify as necessary evidence that students have attained a level of competence appropriate for the course. Wlodkowski and Ginsberg (1995) believe that instructors need to examine their philosophies on assessment to see how well our current practices match with the ways we measure, or assess, our students' level of competence.

My hope is that critical reflection based on lived experiences will enable our preservice teachers to challenge and withstand the power of routinized, institutionalized, and unquestioned practices that relegate students of color to limiting environments (Jones, 1998a). It is through dialogue and a problem-posing process that critical reflection develops, and it is only through that same process that it can be "assessed."

As faculty and students examine their lived experiences in the context of the subject under study, they engage in problematizing what they are studying. This consists of looking underneath the surface in order to understand how a body of knowledge originated, how it is structured, who participated in its structuring, and the consequences of this knowledge (Shor, 1992). Problematizing is approached as problem posing, or the asking of questions that strive to focus critical analysis upon previously unquestioned events. In my final example, I describe a process that I am privileged to introduce and nurture in another group of students, multiple-subject (elementary) student teachers, over the course of one academic year. The end product of this critical analysis is a philosophy-of-literacy essay placed in a portfolio that contains comprehensive, well-organized representations of what has been learned and achieved during the program. This portfolio is an important part of the year-end assessment of teacher candidates (See Zuniga, this volume, for a discussion of portfolios.)

I will summarize the process I use to promote the richness of dialogue and the development of critical reflection based on students' lived experiences as second language learners and as student teachers in elementary bilingual classrooms. During the first semester, students write a series of "layered" reflections (seven one- to two-page essays) about their literacy experiences. These form the foundation for a preliminary position paper on literacy written at the end of the first semester. In the second semester, they rethink and revise this essay to more closely reflect their increased depth of knowledge. Thus, the final paper represents a yearlong exploration of lived experiences, direct observation, firsthand teaching experiences, and theoretical frameworks.

The focus of each reflection shifts so that students will gradually widen their scope as they view all of the literacy events in their lives. Briefly, here is the sequence of the first four of the seven essays:

1. earliest recollections of being read to or of being told stories by their parents, grandparents, other family members, or caregivers (in class, we discuss the connection between hearing stories told by people who loved them and the resulting motivation they felt to retell or read stories);
2. roles played by family members in literacy events and ways in which literacy was used in the home;
3. school literacy reflections dealing with their first day of school and/or first experiences in an English language classroom; experiences related to the differences they encountered at school in reference to the language status of Spanish compared to English; roles they played as language brokers for non-English speakers;
4. analysis of the ways their teachers taught (good and bad examples); reflection of the quality of their teacher-student relationships and those of their classmates with regard to their status and treatment.

I want to emphasize here that, for many students, the school literacy reflections are difficult to write. Over a period of several weeks, however, most students shift their focus from the pain they felt to the reasons they think these events were so difficult for them. In essence, they are able to shift to the problematizing of their experiences and thereby start the process of becoming critically conscious, an important first step.

Each time I assign a reflection paper, there is dialogue within the classroom, and additional memories are jogged through peer response *read-arounds* (in small groups, students read their essays and receive feedback, questions, or suggestions). Students begin to ask each other and themselves ever deeper questions, and they gradually take the lead (as the teacher recedes) during whole-group and small-group discussions as they engage the problem-posing process. By the end of the academic year, most of the final essays display a thoroughness and depth of understanding about literacy development that is grounded in both theory and practice. However, one particular paper has stood out for me. Like many others, it described a culturally relevant classroom where children's ideas would be listened to and validated, biliteracy would be valued, and parents would be welcomed. In recalling this student's reflections throughout the year, I knew she had experienced quite the opposite as a second language learner. She concluded her essay by saying, "I want to be the teacher of literacy that I didn't have, and needed, when I was a child."

In one poignant sentence, this young Chicana demonstrated her ability to examine her own lived experience as a bicultural student in order to inform her practice as a biculturally conscious literacy teacher. With that sentence, I knew she had learned to critically examine her lived experiences and to use them to transform the learning experiences of the fortunate children in her classroom (Jones, 1998a).

Conclusion and Recommendations

At the beginning of this chapter, I stated that we instructors must recognize that the strengths, needs, and cultural values of our diverse student population may be quite different from our own or those of previous generations of university students. We must be open to new ways of developing learning events and generating competency in the subjects we teach; however, this is a daunting task that many of us resist because of its immensity. Wlodkowski and Ginsberg (1995, p. 287) propose the following guidelines:

- Proceed carefully and gradually
- Create a safe climate in which to learn
- Learn with others
- Identify new roles
- Create action plans

- Acknowledge doubt and anxiety as signs of change and potential professional and personal development
- Recognize the power of self-generated knowledge
- Share your work with others

Paulo Freire (1970) wrote about the courage it takes to be a transformative teacher. We need courage because we must constantly create new ways of doing, and thinking, and not rely so much on previous practice. As Antonio Machado said, "Se hace camino al andar" [We make the road by walking] (1982, quoted in Ada, 1995).

Additional Resources

Garcia, E. E. (2001). *Hispanic education in the United States: Raíces y alas*. Lanham: MD: Rowman and Littlefield.

This book is from the series Critical Issues in Contemporary American Education. Garcia, formerly dean of the School of Education in the University of California, Berkeley, and current dean of the College of Education at Arizona State University, uses data from many studies, including his own, that focus on different experiences of Hispanic students and their engagement with education. Garcia describes principles and practices shown to be successful at various levels of the education system.

Ladson-Billings, G. (1994). Culturally relevant teaching: The key to making multicultural education work. In C. A. Grant (Ed.), *Research and multicultural education: From the margins to the mainstream* (pp. 106–121). London: Falmer.

Culturally responsive teaching and learning, a common terminology (Wlodkowski & Ginsberg, 1995), more explicitly address instructional methods, interactional practices, and social contexts for learning compatible with the students' cultures and use students' lived experiences as central links to the curriculum and classroom instruction (Hollins, 1996) on the development of positive self-empowering skills.

Sheets, R. H. (1999). Student self-empowerment: A dimension of multicultural education. *Multicultural Education, 6*(4), 2–8.

This article examines the effect of facilitation and affirmation of ethnic identity development, access to the significant contribution of friendship to coping behaviors, and culturally mediated instruction. Students also play an active and decisive role in the learning process. There are at least three student-oriented dimensions of multicultural education—ethnic identity development, interpersonal relationships, and self-empowerment—that must operate in tandem with Banks's five dimensions for multicultural education to affect students' social and cognitive development.

Forest, J. F. F. (Ed.). (1998). *University teaching: International perspectives*. New York: Coarland. *University Teaching* is a collection of eighteen independent essays and case studies that explore several dimensions of university teaching, including the impact of cultural and social environments. The book, edited by James Forest, is divided into four topic-specific sections: (1) issues of instruction, (2) perspectives on student learning and assessment, (3) training and development of university teachers, and (4) issues of policy, structure, and organization. Chapters are authored by an international group of faculty and administrators with significant experience in the areas of teaching, learning, and assessment at the postsecondary level. Although it includes far too much information to highlight in a brief review, this book is a good resource for readers interested in examining how issues of university teaching transcend national boundaries.

University Teaching makes an important contribution to the comparative study of higher education because the extant literature has tended to focus on academic systems and policy. Academic administrators and policymakers will appreciate the pragmatic suggestions for improving institutional teaching policies and practices, and researchers will find beneficial the extensive and thorough reviews of relevant theory and research. Because each chapter makes an individual contribution to the literature, the book can be used in whole or in part. It requires the reader to tie together emergent themes, key findings, and conclusions rather than to rely on introductory and summary chapters. Although the book could be more consistent in the reporting of research results, I found it particularly informative and useful in documenting how specific programs and practices are being used to improve teaching in different countries.

5

Using Portfolios in Classes with Diversity Content: Enabling Deep Learning, Student Awareness, and Effective Assessment

Maria Zuniga

The publication of the new census data in March 2001 startled demographers and those who had made projections about the U.S. population. The Latino population had grown so dramatically that it had become as large as the African American population (Cohn & Fears, 2001). For the first time in the nation's history, almost half of the country's one hundred major cities had larger populations of people of color than of Whites. These statistics highlight the major population shifts in the United States that are occurring more quickly than anticipated.

On many university campuses, the diversity of students from populations of color has increased as well. Thus, as faculty, we must be aware of, and concerned with, both classroom and community diversity. In the discipline of social work from which I come, the challenges of diversity have been a major impetus in curriculum development and mandated efforts to train students both at the undergraduate and graduate levels to become prepared to serve diverse clients, families, and community populations. For the past twenty years, standards for accreditation from the Council of Social Work Education (CSWE) have included mandates for diversity content in curricula. This has enabled some faculty in schools of social work to pioneer efforts for both teaching an increasingly diverse student population and training all students to be prepared to serve a diverse clientele (Van Voorhis, 1998).

Like the discipline of social work, other service disciplines—teacher education, counseling education, psychology, nursing, and communicative disorders, to name a few—have been concerned with training students to effectively serve client populations that are diverse in terms of ethnicity, race, immigration status, and class. Even business administration curricula reflect the concern for commercial ventures with culturally diverse clients (DeAngelis, 2001). In disciplines that are not necessarily service oriented, the general goal of incorporating diversity content into course work is to educate and prepare students to be productive workers and citizens in a society characterized by diverse populations.

There have been great strides made in offering content on the culture and lifestyles of underrepresented groups, as well as content that indicates how the history of oppression in U.S. society has affected people of color (Lum, 1999). The paradox is that while there is a growing interest in and knowledge about multiculturalism, at the same time there is a backlash against it (DeAngelis, 2001). It is not unusual for people to feel the need to be politically correct yet have sentiments that are laced with subtle racist attitudes and feelings.

De Angelis (2001) cites some of the work of John Dovidio, who comments on this phenomenon. A social psychology researcher, Dovidio found what he calls "a type of modern racism," in which a person may, on the surface, express a belief in racial equality. However, this masks a latent, though unconscious, prejudicial feeling that often gets played out in ambiguous situations such as job interviews where a Black person is as qualified as a White person but the latter is selected for the job. Thus, it can be argued that many people have addressed racism only on a surface level. They may cooperate with legal prohibitions against discrimination but have not identified and reflected on their own subliminal attitudes (DeAngelis, 2001).

What is hopeful about the current situation on university campuses is that there is more willingness to address diversity issues in courses, which therefore addresses these unconscious feelings. However, the complexity of addressing such content as prejudice, racism, and oppression related to historically underrepresented populations remains a major challenge for educators. How can we hope to teach students how to recognize, admit to, and then change their prejudices? Moreover, how can we, as faculty, enable students to recognize how discrimination harms both themselves and those victimized? This is a tall order for any instructor, regardless of her or his background and discipline.

As a Latina instructor who has presented diversity content in courses for many years, I have found that the use of portfolios has facilitated the teaching, learning, and assessment of this content. In this chapter, I discuss the use of portfolios as an adapted method that facilitates teaching diversity content to undergraduate students as well as to graduate students in human behavior courses, which are similar in content to courses in sociology, psychology, counseling education, family studies, child development, and some ethnic studies courses.

Specifically, this chapter addresses some relevant questions, drawing upon examples from the literature, my courses, and courses designed by others. I approach this discussion by addressing questions under three major categories: background, portfolios and diversity content, and portfolios in classes with different levels of content integration. I complete the chapter with general suggestions for teachers. Here are the questions addressed in the chapter.

Background: Definitions, History, and Critique

- What are portfolios?
- How have portfolios been used in university courses?
- What are the advantages and disadvantages of portfolio curricula and assessment?

Portfolios and Diversity Content

- What challenges face the instructor attempting to combine portfolios and diversity content?
- How can these challenges be met?
- Why are portfolios the ideal approach for some diversity courses?

Portfolios in Classes with Different Levels of Diversity Content Integration

- How can portfolios be employed in classes in which diversity is the central focus?
- If the central focus of the class is different and diversity content is integrated, how can portfolios be introduced?

Background: Definitions, History, and Critique

Defining and Explaining Portfolios

What is a classroom portfolio? The following definition of a portfolio was formulated by a group of educators from seven states who were working together with the Northwest Evaluation Association.

A portfolio is a purposeful collection of student work that exhibits the student's efforts, progress, and achievements in one or more areas. The collection must include student participation in selecting the contents, the criteria for selection, the criteria for judging merit, and evidence of student self-reflection. (Paulson, Paulson, & Meyer, 1991, p. 60)

As these writers and others have noted, a portfolio is a powerful tool that enables students to take charge of their own learning. If designed appropriately, this tool can offer to students and their instructor a way to integrate sensitive content, as well as providing "an intersection of instruction and assessment" (Paulson et al., 1991, p. 61). To insure that portfolios can, in fact, produce these results, instructors are advised to follow these guidelines (adapted from Paulson et al., 1991):

- A portfolio assignment must integrate the purpose for the portfolio, its goals, its content or displays, and its standards or means of assessment.
- Models of student portfolios should be provided by the instructor, in addition to illustrations of how others have composed and assessed their portfolio work.
- A portfolio must be an enterprise undertaken by the student, not something done to the student. It should provide an avenue for students to learn to value their own work and thus to learn about and value themselves. Students must have the freedom to select what they will include in their portfolio.
- A portfolio should provide the learner with opportunities for developing metacognition, thinking about thinking and learning about learning. The product should contain information that shows that a student has undertaken self-reflection.
- A portfolio is different and separate from the students' tests and other assessments—though it can be used as an assessment tool.
- A portfolio may serve different purposes at different times of the year, with inputs at the beginning of the year serving to guide learning and with inputs at the end of the year serving to guide assessment.
- A portfolio can have various purposes, but it must not conflict with students' goals or with the goals of their teachers. Importantly, the portfolio should provide information that depicts growth, such as evidence that demonstrates skills that have improved over the time period or attitudes that have changed.

As can be seen from this list, one of the many positive aspects of portfolios is that they enable instructors to see and assess student work not just from results of a test but in a broader spectrum—one in which students are taking risks, developing creative solutions, and learning to self-evaluate and make judgments about their own work or performance (Paulson et al., 1991). A critical trait is that portfolios should be based on competency or mastery. This assumes that the ideal end result is that all students are able to succeed in the class, since they are given enough time, help, and support to complete, and reflect on, what instructors ask of them (Elbow & Belanoff, 1986). Portfolios ensure a more equitable teaching process and assessment, especially for a range of diverse students enrolled in a class.

Portfolio Use in Higher Education

Traditionally, artists, writers, and architects have utilized portfolios, since they are all involved in selecting their own work for presentation. An artist's portfolio captures the selection of work she or he feels represents knowledge and skills for a particular art medium, like use of watercolor or oil. It offers the audience an overview of the person's abilities in various formats. This artist's collection can be used to seek employment or to obtain a commission.

However, the use of portfolios now extends way beyond the artist's studio. Public school districts have incorporated portfolios in math and science projects. Applicants to the University of Wisconsin use portfolios of their collected high school work as part of their application documents. Seniors in Vermont high schools are using portfolios as part of their graduation requirements. A joint research program between the Pittsburgh school district, the Educational Testing Office, and Project Zero at Harvard, called the Propel Project, involves the use of portfolios for assessment in schools (Williams, 1990).

When did portfolios become curricular and assessment tools in higher education? It began with the emphasis on the assessment of student writing in many English departments and then moved to other areas of the university in the 1980s. The portfolio movement was, and continues to be, a major effort that challenged faculty to clarify their goals for their courses and realize these goals in a particular, and often varied, collection of assignments. The use of portfolios changed the traditional process for grading, in which students are ranked or differentiated into as many different "grades" as possible, with the intention of simulating a bell-shaped curve (Elbow & Belanoff, 1986). Portfolios also changed the traditional role of the instructor, from one who grades papers and tests to a person who is the class facilitator and coach. The instructor becomes the person who helps the students overcome obstacles and encourages the learning process. Portfolios encourage teachers to concentrate their energies on useful comments on work rather than just on the grade and on traditional comments that typically do not contribute to further learning (Curran, 1989). Despite their somewhat unusual nature, portfolios have been used on many campuses by a range of faculty in such departments as recreation, chemistry, policy studies, classics, art, teacher education, and social work (Williams, 1990).

Here are some examples.

1. At the State University of New York at Stony Brook, portfolios have replaced the writing proficiency examination. The old exam, requiring only one timed writing in draft form, was viewed as too limiting for evaluating a student's writing, for it did not provide a valid picture of a student's proficiency, particularly if she or he was not a native speaker of English. Rather, having two or three student writing portfolio samples in two or three genres, written at more than one sitting, was viewed as offering a more reliable and valid evaluation (Elbow & Belanoff, 1986).

2. In the discipline of social work, the portfolio enables students to evaluate their class work in relation to their agency internship and to practice applying what they have learned with clients, groups, and communities. At Colorado State University, senior social work students use portfolios to prepare for the real world; this tool prepares them to evaluate their readiness for client practice in particular agencies with identified populations (Simon & Schatz, 1998).

3. Nona Lyons (1998) illustrates how portfolio endeavors have been used in teacher education. She notes that the various types of portfolio experimentation that have developed in teaching and teacher education have resulted in "the dynamic process of teachers documenting the evidence of their work and growth, gathered and authored by them through careful reflection, shared with colleagues and students, and presented for public discussion and debate about their conceptions of good teaching" (p. vii).

Advantages and Disadvantages

What are the advantages and disadvantages of portfolios? A major advantage is that students are free to select for their portfolio entries what they feel represents their best individual work, as well as their goals, efforts, and struggles. This freedom also enables them to be creative in how they want to present their work. The disadvantage is that the instructor is challenged with a large variety of work to evaluate and on which to offer feedback, support, and guidance. For large classes, such as undergraduate general education courses with enrollments of fifty to sixty students, organizing and evaluating student portfolios can be overwhelming.

However, some of this effort can be seen as an advantage, for the instructor is not limited to correcting fifty to sixty papers that are all very similar in their focus. The tediousness in this kind of grading task is exchanged for other, more interesting time investments. Not surprisingly, the instructor may find herself or himself looking forward to how students have organized their portfolios and being impressed with the range of novel and fascinating entries. It is important to note that through portfolios, students who may be more reserved in class for cultural, linguistic, or other reasons may offer insights into their strengths and struggles that would otherwise be unreported.

Portfolios and Diversity Content

Challenges of Teaching Diversity Content

First of all, it is necessary to define "diversity content." For purposes of this chapter, diversity content refers to the historical as well as contemporary, political, economic, and cultural knowledge about underrepresented populations in the United States who are often classified as people of color. Classroom content can contain information about diverse people's experiences with oppression and its impact on them as individuals, families, and communities. An important aspect of diversity content refers to how prejudice, discrimination, and oppression adversely affect both the individual who is oppressive and those being oppressed.

I have learned from twenty-six years of teaching content on diversity, racism, and oppression that I am dealing with very sensitive material. Students find it complex, difficult, and painful to address. Euro-American students often react by feeling guilty about historical wrongs and then frustrated about what they cannot do about the past. Students of color may feel angry or frustrated when they perceive majority students as insensitive to the pain they have suffered due to discrimination. In addition, Euro-American students tend to feel angry when they attempt to reach out to students of color and are rebuffed or experience reverse discrimination. Students of color may be hesitant to admit their own racism or prejudices toward other groups of color.

Thus, this content is extremely difficult to teach successfully. It becomes a major challenge for faculty to devise methods to teach sensitive course content and design student requirements that facilitate successful, but difficult, learning experiences. In light of this challenge, and given my experience with experimenting with methods and techniques for effective teaching and learning of diversity content, I have found that the use of portfolios as student requirements addresses a multitude of learning and affective needs and makes the understanding of diversity among my students richer and deeper than it might be otherwise.

Meeting Challenges through the Use of Portfolios

If designed appropriately, portfolios can result in the intersection of instruction and assessment (Paulson et al., 1991), and more important, they can show a process of discovery and insight. Students can present their experiences with diversity related to various times in their lives and in different contexts through a collection of documents used as entries. Students are given the freedom to choose how they will present this material, in what format, and what will be actually shared. Thus, the portfolio serves as a major breakthrough in their understanding of others. The students are not being acted on as they work through sensitive material but are choosing to act themselves by including entries in their portfolios. They offer their "creative" endeavor knowing that they will need to reflect on it. The instructor has access to their thinking and working processes, providing "instruction" and evaluation, and thus the "intersection of instruction and assessment."

Another critical facet of portfolio work is that it promotes metacognition, or thinking about thinking (Johns, 1997)—in this case, as it relates to racism, prejudice, and cultural and racial differences. This thinking about thinking is the heart of the portfolio process, since it allows students the freedom to choose what they will analyze and share with their instructor—and it encourages them to reflect on their choices. This freedom to decide what to think about again offers the license students typically take to analyze sensitive areas of prejudice and discrimination, whether they are Euro-American students or students of color.

This process of self-reflection promoted by the portfolio can be the "nuts and bolts" of change that is demanded by themes presented in a class addressing sensitive diversity issues. The students' freedom to decide how deep and how personal they want to reflect enables them to pick and choose what "texts" they want to include; again, they act on themselves rather than being acted on (Paulson et al., 1991). Throughout the process, the instructor acknowledges its difficulty and highlights the commonality of the dilemmas of prejudice, especially by the media that feeds stereotypes about populations of color. Providing feedback, support, and facilitation, the instructor enables students to value their efforts and struggles, to value this work they are undertaking, and then to learn to value themselves for their courage, honesty, and openness, this valuing being the expected outcomes of portfolio endeavors (Paulson et al., 1991).

For diversity content that is so sensitive, this classroom tool for self-evaluation is especially critical for motivating students to pursue their efforts, even without the course. The instructor must indicate both in class and in personal feedback that students are learning about content most people do not want to discuss. In my class, I let students know that what they are doing is difficult and can even be painful but that they are making the commitment to reflect on, and undertake, positive change. The portfolio work enables students to evaluate where they need to grow and, particularly at the end of the course, the extent to which they have learned and changed. This reflective self-evaluation enables them to make judgments about their own work and their progress toward a better understanding.

Throughout the course, students should be judging themselves before they receive feedback from the instructor, who is acting as coach and facilitator. Again, this is a crucial point for teaching diversity content, since the students choose how much and what kind of work they will undertake and, in the final analysis, are the ones to judge and/or evaluate their efforts.

Thus, the portfolio is a purposeful collection of work that exhibits efforts, progress, and achievements in one or more areas (Paulson et al., 1991). In this case, the area of learning is diversity content that is designed to prepare students to live and work in a diverse social arena, in their work or in the community. As I have noted, knowledge of self and others is demanded if students are to serve diverse clientele in an effective professional manner. In all the examples already noted, I have found that portfolios provide a viable fit as a medium for teaching diversity content in an effective and meaningful manner.

Portfolios, Diversity, and Professional Classes

After having been introduced to portfolios as a tool, I became interested in adapting the portfolio concept as a way to elaborate on and strengthen the ability of students to "compose a powerful personal reflective learning experience" (Paulson et al., 1991, p. 5). Portfolios were adapted for my social work classes in a way that permitted the following:

- a powerful, personal reflective experience that was process based;
- a self-assessment of the impact of a student's family on values, culture, and traditions;
- a self-assessment of experiences with oppression;
- a tool with which students select the format (e.g., visual, auditory) they prefer to work in, providing them with the choice of a learning style that fits them;
- a way for students to reflect on what they had learned and how they had changed and to debrief that with the class after each assignment and at the end of the semester; and
- a tool that would allow them to use their creativity so they could experience the freedom/challenge of "finding their own voice" to express themselves.

Pedagogical Implications for Classes with Differing Levels of Diversity Content Integration

In this section, I discuss the details of using portfolios as a teaching and assessment tool in two types of classroom, one in which diversity is the central focus and one in which diversity is not central but integrated (see Branch and Jones, this volume, for more complete presentations of diversity integration). I begin with the class in which diversity is central.

Classes in Which Diversity Is the Central Focus

Some disciplines, like counseling, education, psychology, or social work, may develop a course at the undergraduate or graduate level that has as its entire focus themes of cultural and racial differences, the history and reality of oppression, and examination of students' prejudices and racism (see Hohm and Venable, this volume). Typically, the goal in this kind of course is to enable students to scrutinize and change their prejudice and racism so they will not harm clients they will be serving. In concert with this is the goal that they will attain the cultural competence to viably serve those clients who are racially, ethnically, or culturally different. (For valuable insights on cultural competence, see Lum, 1999; Fong & Furuto, 2001; Sue & Sue, 1990.)

A central-focus course generally provides content and activities that encourage student self-assessment and change throughout the term. This course is central, but it is only part of students' preparation for gauging personal change in attitudes and behavior, because they fulfill the requirements for their major or professional degree over several semesters and in other course work with diversity content.

In central-focus classes, diverse speakers may be interspersed with faculty lectures throughout course sessions to reflect the unique history and experiences of different populations of color. The design may include lectures and films that depict realities of discrimination experienced by diverse populations, supported by texts devoted entirely to this content in historical, contemporary, and practice dimensions. Course requirements may demand major papers through which students learn about one culture or population, group presentations on diverse families, or "plunge" experiences in which students might, for example, visit a church service in a setting culturally or racially different from their own and write about this experience (M. Senour, personal communication regarding assignments used for the degree in counselor education, April 1999; see also Young, this volume).

How do these various activities play out in an actual central-focus course? Here, I offer as an example a course taught in the School of Social Work in another California State University by a professor who asked permission to borrow my portfolio assignments. The entire course was focused on issues of discrimination and oppression of populations of color, with a further focus on Latino people. The objectives for students, found in the class syllabus, were the following:

- To develop insight on the impact of your family on your value system
- To examine the origins of your family history in the United States
- To delineate the influence on you of the cultural group with which you identify
- To examine your experiences with Latinos or if you are a Latino to examine what it feels like to belong to this ethnic group
- To develop knowledge and insight on diverse populations, especially as reflected by the student population in this class
- To develop knowledge and insight on one diverse community

The course had an enrollment of eighteen students: five Latinos, one Latina who was also Anglo, two Filipino students, one Cambodian, one Hawaiian, one African American, and seven Euro-American students. All students were undergraduate social work majors.

The course used four portfolio assignments to cover 40 percent of the course requirements. In addition, students were also required to read one novel on a diverse group and to write a report on their reading. Finally, each student was asked to write a paper on how to develop ethnic-sensitive services for Latinos in the field of service for which the student was being trained, such as services for youth, services for the mentally ill, or services for the elderly.

Here, I will discuss only the portfolio assignments, since that is the topic of this chapter. The first two assignments focused on the development of self-knowledge, the third assignment emphasized the development of cultural knowledge, and the fourth assignment focused on the development of both self-knowledge and cultural knowledge. These assignments included the following:

- A creative work that signifies the "imprint" your family has made on you. Couple this with a brief narrative explaining this imprint, and utilizing course content to highlight your insights (self-knowledge).
- A depiction of one or more aspects of the cultural group you identify with that illustrates important cultural influences that comprise who you are. Creatively depict these cultural imprints via a collage, graphic representation, poem, song, or other creative medium to highlight the importance of this culture on your development and meaning making. Provide a brief narrative explaining this influence (self-knowledge).
- Select a Latino cultural guide who can help you learn about some aspect of the Latino Community. Participate with this individual in different activities you choose within the Latino community that you feel will feed your cultural knowledge. Keep a portfolio log of these experiences which you will analyze in a brief narrative that summarizes your community cultural knowledge development (cultural knowledge).
- Keep a portfolio journal from week two to week thirteen (hand in at week fourteen). Reflect on your reactions to the class, readings, and other assignments. A handout will be provided by the instructor which will offer a variety of questions you can use for this class reflection, including asking yourself a) to examine what you liked/disliked about each class; b) what were class experiences that you found meaningful and why; and c) what were experiences that were challenging, why, and what you learned

from them? (We will debrief in class regarding your insights over
the semester.)

The first two portfolio assignments were process based (Williams,
1990) and fit nicely into the overall course content. The third portfolio assignment served as a journal, which allowed students to take a
more active role in their learning (Williams, 1990) by choosing what
Latino guide they would accompany and then by scrutinizing their
reactions to and experiences in this endeavor. The fourth portfolio
assignment was a critique type of entry, based on a series of questions
and instructions distributed early in the term. The following is a typical example.

- Spend five minutes before the end of each class (which will be
  allotted by the instructor) to jot down ten words that each characterize different experiences you had in class that day. After class
  write a one–two page assessment utilizing these terms to reflect
  on what you felt in class, what you learned, what surprised you,
  what was difficult for you. At the end of your analysis, note an
  area where you feel you would like to pursue more knowledge
  or insight for your further development.

When each of the four portfolio assignments were turned in, part of
the class time was spent "debriefing" students, who were asked such
questions as

- What was difficult about doing this portfolio?
- What surprised you about what you learned?
- In what way did your experience doing this portfolio relate to
  any of the course content? Explain.
- What did you learn about yourself/your family?
- How can you use this experience for further growth?

Asking students to think about their learning (metacognition) and to
reflect upon their experiences was essential to the success of the portfolio. The students also debriefed: the preceding questions served as a
generic guide to their evaluation of their work in class. Questions that
are more specific to assignments were also used, since the substance of
the class was being addressed in various ways via each portfolio entry.

Students responded in this course by using a variety of "texts" for
their first two portfolio entries: poems, collages, boxed art, paintings, a
genogram of family pictures, and/or a newspaper. Toward the end of

the course, when all the entries had been completed, part of a class session was spent on evaluating the portfolio experience in its entirety. When asked if this part of the assignments should be kept for the course, all students agreed that it should. What was powerful for this class was that the portfolio on family provided several Euro-American students with the opportunity to contact their families to seek out family history they had not thought to ask about before. Table 1 lists comments from several students in the class.

Classes That "Integrate" Diversity Content

Classes that integrate diversity content are probably more common than those that focus solely on this content. Therefore, I will discuss two levels of class integration: one on the undergraduate, general education level and one on the graduate, professional level.

General education (or breadth) classes often integrate issues of population diversity, racism, and prejudice with other, major content areas. For example, the major class goal may be to expose students to the challenge of being a competent citizen in a diverse society. The objectives are aligned with efforts to socialize students to the realities of diversity, perhaps without making immediate substantive changes in their attitudes. Despite other goals, faculty can motivate students to recognize their need to expand their thinking and behaviors about diversity, offering an initiation process that enables them to recognize the importance of life-long self-evaluation in order to effectively live in a diverse society. Although the outcome of this course type might be less intense than in the central-focus type, the goal of beginning a process of openness to diversity would be present.

TABLE 1.   Student Comments on Portfolio Assignments

- I learned that when my grandfather immigrated he said he was Irish although he was a Jew from Russia and for three generations we did not know we were Jewish. (genogram)
- I learned about my grandfather's immigration to the U.S. and that he entered from Europe illegally; given the reaction today about illegal immigrants, it provided me with an important insight. (genogram)
- As a middle aged Chicano, I learned how much I have grown to respect my parents' sacrifices and their strengths. (poem)
- As a Cambodian I see how easy it is to lose your culture if you are not careful; I can see how acculturation has already changed me in my values and behaviors compared to my parents. I want to make my choices now more consciously. (collage and poem)
- I have a better understanding of who it is that I am and what it was that caused me to be this way.
- It is challenging; it makes you stop and take time to realize who you really are.

Generally, diversity themes are woven into assignments so students will consider them as they write papers or make class presentations. A course on social problems might address the importance of economic factors among diverse populations. Implications for how populations are affected by a recession might include data on employment rates, with an emphasis on examining the employment rates of persons of color.

Undergraduate, general education classes that integrate diversity content, rather than having it as a focus, can be more challenging to teach, since the instructor must balance methods for teaching and student requirements that ensure that the major course content is thoroughly covered. Either the main texts have to reflect the diversity weaving, or faculty must find supplementary texts or course readings that provide the necessary information.

Another example of integration of diversity content can be found in graduate course work for disciplines like psychology, counselor education, communicative disorders, or social work, courses that prepare students for professional service. Often, the course incorporates content on diversity that complements the major content being taught, like stage theory on human development. The integration may reflect slivers of diverse content, for example, human development stage theory (Newman & Newman, 1999) that elicits the special issues for adolescents of color who are challenged to form a positive identity in light of societal racism and discrimination (Phinney & Rotherham, 1987). In this case, the course requires students to take command of the general content while also considering the special themes in development or in human behavior that characterize the experiences of clients of color. Although a goal may be to enable students to be less prejudiced or racist, this is not the principal goal of the course.

Again, faculty are challenged to design the course so that the integrated content on diversity is meaningful for student learning. The instructor must balance how much time and content will be devoted to diversity themes and what kinds of student assignments and assessment will be made to cover the general content as well as the diversity content.

I will now turn to one of my own courses as an example. I teach a graduate three-unit course on human stage development for first-year graduate social work students, using three-entry portfolio assignments as one learning and assessment component. This course would be comparable to some of the human behavior courses in psychology, family studies, and child development. In the class on which I base student examples cited here, there were twenty-eight students—two African

American, eight Latino, five Asian, one Iranian, and twelve Euro-American.

The basic goal for this course is for students to learn theories of stage development, including those of Erikson, Piaget, and Vygotsky, which are highlighted in the course text on development by Newman and Newman (1999). By the end of the course, students should be able to utilize the theories to assess a family with members at different levels of development, knowing if and how each member is on or off task in terms of the developmental expectations for each respective stage, so they can formalize a sound developmental assessment for a social service agency or health agency. The course's objectives follow.

- Students will comprehend how environmental, physiological, biological, cultural, and social factors facilitate or interfere with optimal development throughout the life span, with particular cognizance of how those from non-Western cultural groupings have similar and possibly different developmental milestones as they pass through the development schema.
- Students will develop perspectives on the unique challenges minority and biracial children/teens encounter regarding identity development. Similarly, these issues will be examined in relation to gay adolescents.
- Students will describe and analyze the concepts, framework, and main hypothesis of each theory of behavior presented.
- Students will be able to evaluate their growth in comprehending development, with special insights on diversity themes. They will examine their own development as a means for understanding their professional growth.
- Students will develop the ability to select those theories that contribute to the comprehension of how poverty and oppression challenge growth and development; also, they will be able to discern how oppression can affect people so that strengths and resiliency are outcomes for individuals and family systems.

Readings on diversity are integrated into the course in such areas as identity development for children, using such supplementary readings as Phinney and Rotherham's (1987) work on minority children.

Students develop three portfolio assignments that are interspersed over the first eight weeks of the semester. Each portfolio is worth 15 percent for a total of 45 percent of all requirements. Students are assessed on their portfolio on the basis of the following:

- the extent to which the portfolio endeavor represents work that is thoughtfully and creatively put together, signifying they have spent time on self-reflection;
- the extent to which the portfolio incorporates and applies the related theory for that part of the assignment; and
- the extent to which the one- to two-page narrative summarizes the significance of the portfolio's relationship to the theory and, importantly, signifies personal development of knowledge and personal insight.

After students receive their first returned portfolio entry for the semester, I detail what they did or did not do to address the stated criteria, enabling them to undertake their second and third portfolio entries with more understanding of what is expected. Here, for example, is some feedback that I provided for one student.

> What a great portfolio. The anguish and pain was great as noted in your diary entries [she had based portfolio work on a diary she kept in grammar school] now that you have more perspective. You really pulled together the various issues; how your environment impacted you, and how your cognitive processes were functioning. You demonstrate the importance of identify formulations and how our differences can really be painful when we are so young and still in the process of learning who we are. You integrate Piaget very appropriately. The selection of issues was vividly portrayed in your collage. Thank you for your creativity; you applied the theory content in full force. Can you examine how this insight will help you work more effectively with clients? Explain.

Another example of my coaching involves a Euro-American student who used a storybook to depict her latency-age years developing a friendship with a child from another culture. The book depicts the hesitation that was initially experienced and then drawings/collage pages of different cultural experiences with the minority family's cooking, lifestyle, and rituals. My feedback follows.

> What a delightful way to tell your story. You apply the theory quite appropriately. The theme of working with your hands [hands on operations], being exposed to a different culture and style of operating, and their relation to logic and Piaget's concept of

accommodation were very applicable. What a lovely way to learn about difference and sameness. Can you remember if any of your experiences were uncomfortable, especially when you first engaged this friend and her family, and why? Full credit—thoughtful and creative.

What do my students' portfolio assignments look like? Specifically, the three entries for the portfolio are as follows:

- Use "the radius of significant relationships" (Newman & Newman, 1999) to examine how your family impressed you with your ethnicity, race and or culture as you were developing during childhood. Feel free to incorporate such theory inserts as Vygotsky's (Newman & Newman, 1999) cultural framework.
- Examine one or more experiences that you had with prejudice or discrimination being aimed at you. Note what state of development you were in and how you cognitively comprehended what occurred using the text's appropriate theorists. Attempt to express in a creative manner, how you felt, reacted, and now view this (these) experience(s).
- Use Piaget's theory on cognitive development to highlight what stage of cognitive development you were in when you first became aware of different sexual orientations. Use your 1–2 page narrative to elaborate on how your portfolio project elucidates the cognitive processes for the stage you are addressing.

Almost all my students choose to develop their portfolios by using a creative art form—such as a poem, a collage, a genogram of family pictures, a "nature" mobile, a sculpture, or an oil painting—to symbolize their experiences. What is striking is that this freedom they have to develop each entry is seen by them as the most difficult part of the assignment—yet the most rewarding. They struggle to find a medium and a product that symbolizes what they want to express—and that relates to both the theoretical and the personal requirements of the assignment.

Another difficulty they face is the two-page limit I impose for reflecting on what they have produced and its connection both to the theory and to their learning experience. Here, I wanted to make the assignment brief, since students invariably invest more time than they would normally and the paper often becomes too long. The page limitation also works by helping them learn to be succinct and focused in their analysis, which contributes to specificity related to theory, clearer writing, and personal meaning.

Invariably, many Euro-American students who complete this assignment are surprised by their discovery of roots, history, and culture that they had not previously known about. In order to get more information, some students contact extended relatives or parents to "investigate" their ethnicity, history, and familial idiosyncrasies. For students who are from a more traditional ethnic, racial, or cultural group, this entry offers them the opportunity to celebrate a part of their reality they had not stopped to think about in any analytical fashion. Often, for these latter students, theorists like Vygotsky (Badrona & Leong, 1996) take on added significance. Some are motivated to undertake more library research on the impact of culture on their lives.

A debriefing session is held in class after the students turn in each portfolio entry, to enable them to talk about the difficulty of the assignment and what they learned. This session often leads to more insight as they compare and contrast their experiences. Each successive portfolio assignment readies students for open dialogue and class interaction that becomes easier every time. What is remarkable is that the portfolio work prepares them to be open to discuss a topic that can be both sensitive and quite controversial. Students also become excited about the meaning of the entries. They share their experience with classmates by depicting the meaning or symbolism of the portfolio, if they so choose.

At the end of the course, students are asked to assess their likes and dislikes about the course in general and about the portfolio entries in particular. They are asked to make recommendations about how to change the assignments to make them more meaningful and effective. Invariably, students suggest that the portfolios remain, and they do not recommend major changes, although some would like to add pages to the narrative portion of each portfolio, moving from a limit of two to a limit of four. Their comments show important themes that characterize the portfolio work for these graduate students.

- Theory became more real to them as they applied it to their own experiences.
- Self-exploration (reflection) was seen as invaluable, albeit painful at times; they felt it readied them for their work with others.
- They experienced learning in a new manner that surprised them and enabled them to see issues in more depth and with more substance.

General Recommendations for Teaching

In order to accommodate the use of portfolios as a way to teach diversity, the following approaches are recommended.

- Specify in the first class and on the syllabus what is expected for the portfolio work in general and what is expected for each portfolio entry in particular.
- Give explicit examples of successful student entries written in past classes. Model!
- Make reflection and oral debriefing an important element in the course.
- Underscore the importance of using boundaries so that very personal content is not shared in class.
- Return the first portfolio assignment within a week, with comments, to moderate the students' concerns about "getting the idea" of the assignment.
- Discuss the differences, if any, among the entry types required.
- If you use "creative" portfolios, delineate size limitations and caution students to only use copies of important photos and other artifacts.
- If you use "creative" portfolios, instruct students not to utilize for their collages costly resources or personal mementos or elements that could easily break off or get lost.
- Build into your course, especially during debriefing sessions, a focus on process rather than on merely the final product.
- Model for students respect for their individual ways of interpreting, especially concerning creative and cultural portfolios.
- Remember to acknowledge—both in class and in your feedback to each student—the importance of addressing diversity and the respect you have for students who take this learning seriously.
- Use the students' experiences throughout the course to decide if the portfolio assignment fulfills the goals you have set.
- Use student evaluation to "tailor" or refine each assignment.

Conclusion

There is extensive literature that supports developing multicultural competencies in students. Examination of works in psychology and social work will facilitate insights on how diversity content is taught in an effective fashion (see other chapters in this volume; Lum, 1999;

Fong & Furuto, 2001; Van Voorhis, 1998; Garcia & Zea, 1997). In addition, there is a variety of work that uses social construction and social interaction theory to highlight the unique experiences of diverse subgroups (O'Brien & Kollock, 2001), providing instructors with more theory and process.

Highlighting the importance of diversity competence is important for both the general education (undergraduate) courses and the graduate courses discussed in this chapter, whether diversity is the major focus or integrated into other content. Expectations for the depth and level of integration of course theory in the portfolios will be different for undergraduates compared to graduates and for different types of courses. In my graduate class, I emphasize the importance of theory integration as a focal aspect of the entries. For undergraduates, the instructor's expectations for the depth and breadth of course theory integration is not as extensive as for graduates. However, for both groups, critical thinking and reflective skills are substantive aspects of their self-assessment in their portfolio endeavors. The goal of developing "formative assessments" for each student is a major outcome.

Because portfolio work is a unique way of facilitating student learning, the instructor must expect to also develop a new way of teaching. The instructor must provide time for a reflection and a learning process both in individual instruction (feedback) and in the class sessions. Sensitive issues will be raised, and the instructor needs to prepare to deal with them. Assessment of the portfolio may require that the instructor raise questions and challenge students to pursue further work on an issue or theme. Feedback that is sensitive and supportive, yet challenging, enables the students to pursue content they might not otherwise examine.

In addition, the instructor must model his or her belief about and commitment to multiculturalism, noting how knowledge, attitudes, and enjoyment of difference are invaluable life resources. Moreover, the instructor must delineate that learning to respect difference is a life-long project. This commitment is difficult; it can be challenging and is sometimes painful. Nonetheless, these are normative processes that each of us must engage in if we make a commitment to multiculturalism, whatever our chosen discipline or profession.

Guidelines on boundaries are important so students will realize that the instructor is not a therapist. They can refer to sensitive issues in a general way to make a point, but they need not divulge personal themes that only should be shared with a professional. This caution should be noted in the assignment section and also elaborated on in class. Since our work is heavily imbued around relationship competencies and suits the training of students who will work with clients, it may be more challenging for instructors in disciplines where this outcome is not part of their discipline repertoire.

My own experiences, those of my colleagues, and those mentioned in the literature demonstrate that portfolios are excellent tools for integrating diversity into the classroom, encouraging self-evaluation and reflection, and empowering students. However, they do require changes in some of our teaching approaches and assessment practices, but these changes will undoubtedly benefit the students we are serving and promote deep understanding of diversity.

Additional Resources

Curran, P. (1989, March). The portfolio approach to assessing student writing: An interim report. *Composition Chronicle, 2*(2), 6–8.

    Although this article is focused on writing competencies, it examines the roles the educator must take on when portfolios are used. It underscores how teaching should provide support for the student as she or he progresses in the learning spiral. It dramatically notes the importance of facilitation that characterizes the teaching role when portfolios are utilized.

Elbow, P., & Belanoff, P. (1986, October). Portfolios as a substitute for proficiency examinations. *College Composition and Communication, 37,* 336–339.

    This article examines how portfolios offer alternatives for the evaluation of student competencies. The discussion elucidates how teaching should be viewed in a more creative and supportive role when using portfolios with students. It is a good article for understanding less traditional formats for evaluating students' progress and competencies.

Lyons, N. (Ed). (1998). *With portfolio in hand: Validating the new teacher professionalism.* New York: Teachers College Press.

    This book offers several chapters that examine how portfolios are effective in teacher training. Use of portfolios enables teachers to glean more precise insights on the roles of the teacher. Portfolio use facilitates the teacher trainee's development of conceptions of good teaching.

Paulson, F. L., Paulson, P. R., & Meyer, C. A. (1991). What makes a portfolio a portfolio? *Educational Leadership, 48* (5), 60–63.

    This article highlights the intersection of instruction and assessment that should occur in the use of portfolios. A group of educators from seven states, the Northwest Evaluation Association, provide excellent definitions and types of portfolios. Although their work is focused on use of portfolios in teaching children, their concepts on self-reflection and the student acting on self through the use of portfolio is readily applicable to any age-group.

Simon, S., & Schatz, M. (1998). The portfolio approach for BSW generalist social work students. *The New Social Worker, 5,* 12–14. This article is specific to the training of undergraduate seniors who are social work majors. It demonstrates how the use of portfolios offers students and instructors more process-oriented tools for evaluating their readiness for working with clients in the human services.

6
Collaborative Learning in the Diverse Classroom

Carol F. Venable

Conceptual Frameworks: A Review of the Literature

Wide diversity among students has become the norm in undergraduate education. Only about one-sixth of undergraduate students meet the traditional characterization of being full-time students between ages 18 and 22 living on campus (Kuhn, Baird, & Leslie, 1992). Students now include those who are economically disadvantaged, academically underprepared, challenged by disabilities, older, from other countries, or from diverse ethnic or cultural backgrounds (Hughes, Frances, & Lombardo, 1991; "The Landscape," 1993; Wagener, 1989).

In addition to diversity of demographics, diversity of learning styles emerges as a significant factor in today's higher education classroom. Claxton and Murrel (1987) review models and empirical findings that reflect more than fifteen different learning styles. They define learning styles to be ways of "perceiving, interacting with, and responding to the learning environment" (p. 71) that reflect differences in various personal characteristics (i.e., personality, information-processing ability, organization and depth of existing knowledge, social interaction style, and motivation).

Recognizing that no two students are exactly alike and that not one set of homogeneous learning characteristics uniquely identifies each student in a demographic category leads to the following question: How should instructors design classroom experiences? Wlodkowski and Ginsberg (1995) suggest using a culturally responsive teaching framework with four intersecting motivational goals: establishing inclusion, developing attitude, enhancing meaning, and engendering

96

competence (also see Yerrick, this volume). They suggest that pedagogies that fit this framework include collaborative and experiential learning. These pedagogies, which incorporate student interaction in the classroom, can be designed to include students' personal experiences and bring out diversity issues. Diversity in the classroom allows for not only content learning but also the development of other desirable learning outcomes (Astin 1993a, 1993b; Gurin 1997; Chang 1999). Jones and Clemson (1996, p. 150) argue that with an increasingly diverse student population, there is a need to ensure "that all teachers, regardless of their ethnicity, are prepared to teach effectively in multicultural classrooms and therefore are culturally responsive and sensitive to the ethnic backgrounds of their students."

This chapter first discusses diversity-related learning outcomes and the use of collaborative learning strategies. It then provides a description and assessment of an experiential, collaborative assignment that was designed to incorporate the personal experiences of students in the classroom. Learning outcomes that resulted from the project are identified using content analysis. An examination of the diversity factors that were observed, mentioned, and considered and that influenced the design of the projects is discussed.

Diversity Outcomes and Pedagogy

Evidence of the positive effects of diversity experiences on student learning outcomes continues to grow and expand. Positive effects on satisfaction measures, self-concept, values development, and academic and intellectual skills are reported. Astin's (1993a, 1993b) initial studies show that socializing and discussing racial or ethnic issues with individuals from another racial group have specific positive effects on retention, overall college satisfaction, intellectual self-concept, and social self-concept. Chang (1999) replicates these findings and notes, "when campuses genuinely value diversity and take it seriously, at all levels and in all parts of the campus, the quality of the environment is improved and benefits accrue not only for underrepresented students but for all students" (p. 392). Further, institutional and faculty diversity emphasis and individual student diversity experiences have positive effects on two value outcomes: cultural awareness and commitment to promoting racial understanding (Astin 1999).

Evidence to support growth in academic skills and intellectual development also exists. Gurin (1999) provides empirical evidence that "students who had experienced the most diversity in classroom settings and in informal interactions with peers showed the greatest engagement in active thinking processes, growth in intellectual engagement and motivation, and growth in intellectual and academic skills." In addition, empirical evidence suggests that Latinos and African Americans may achieve more when working in collaboration with others (Slavin, 1990; Cohen 1994a), especially when working on real situations and whole concepts rather than abstractions. An example of such collaboration is the successful experience-based science program with heterogeneous groups of Latinos and Anglos where the groups rotate among classroom "centers" to work on complex science problems (Cohen, 1994a; Cohen, Kepner, & Swanson, 1995).

These results suggest that the use of collaborative learning within a diverse classroom creates an environment that enhances multiple learning outcomes by providing more opportunities for discussion and interaction between individuals of diverse backgrounds.

Experiential and Collaborative Learning Pedagogies

Experience, both past and current, forms the basis for learning. Kolb's experiential learning model (Kolb, 1981; Smith & Kolb, 1986) depicts the dynamics of learning as progressing through various stages from concrete experience, to observations and reflections, to the formation of abstract concepts and ideas, to the testing of implications and concepts in new situations. Each element of the model provides a framework for organizing courses and lessons. Each element also represents a particular learning style. Since students and teachers may be predisposed to the use of a particular learning style, movement through each element provides a way for teachers to reach all of the students. Movement through the model also provides students with exposure to non-preferred learning styles that they may need to use in later school or career settings. Thus, activities at each stage should be incorporated in classroom planning.

Svinicki and Dixon (1987) identify activities related to each stage of Kolb's experiential learning model (see fig. 1 and Jones, this volume). For example, concrete experiences may include interviews, reading of primary texts, problem sets, laboratory work or fieldwork, role playing/simulations, games, and films; reflective observation may incorporate journals, discussion groups, brainstorming, thought questions, and reflection papers; abstract conceptualization may use lectures, papers, model development, analogies/metaphors, and hypothesis creation; and active experimentation may incorporate artistic creations, role playing/simulations, laboratory work or fieldwork, and projects.

Many of the aforementioned classroom activities can be designed as

CONCRETE EXPERIENCE Text Reading/ Problem Sets Interviews Laboratory Work or Fieldwork Role Playing/Simulations	REFLECTIVE OBSERVATION Journals Reflection Papers Brainstorming Discussion Groups
ACTIVE EXPERIMENTATION Projects Laboratory Work or Fieldwork Artistic Creations Role Playing/Simulations	ABSTRACT CONCEPTUALIZATION Lectures Papers Hypothesis Creation Model Development

Fig. 1. Examples of activities for the dimensions in Kolb's experiential learning model. (Adapted from Svinicki & Dixon, 1987, p. 142.)

collaborative assignments. Thus, a well-chosen set of collaborative assignments could expose students to activities that represent various learning styles, while also providing the setting for the positive learning outcomes (discussed in the prior section) that are associated with interactions between diverse groups of individuals.

Collaborative Learning: Cooperative and Participative Strategies

Collaborative learning is an umbrella term for various types of cooperative and participative strategies that involve team-based active learning (Smith & MacGregor, 1992). Collaborative learning provides a framework that fosters greater use of higher-level reasoning strategies and critical-thinking skills (Johnson, Johnson, & Smith, 1998), as well as the development of communication and interpersonal skills.

Rather than focusing only on output, collaborative learning projects are designed to emphasize process—or, rather, the "processes" that can be used. Individual processes differ because they are based on prior experience, skill sets, knowledge base, and cognitive capabilities. Collaborative learning can bring to the surface these individual differences, since group projects allow individual process differences to reveal themselves. Students often believe that that there is one way to solve a problem and that everyone does it in the same manner. Collaborative learning helps individuals to expand their knowledge of process because it allows them to observe and learn other approaches to problem solving, as well as differences in values and experiences.

Cooperative learning generally is described as a subset of collaborative learning that takes a more structured approach. Both share a philosophical framework and sense of community. Although the field of collaborative and cooperative learning contains a number of distinct approaches that differ on various attributes, common to all approaches are the following five attributes: (1) common tasks or learning activities suitable for group work, (2) small-group learning, (3) cooperative behaviors, (4) interdependence, and (5) individual accountability and responsibility (Davidson, 1994).

The requirement for tasks to be suitable for group work does not imply that projects or assignments must be highly structured or readily dividable into separate sections. Abstract problems need solution strategies that may require innovative and creative approaches. To solve abstract problems, group members must exchange ideas and information rather than parcel out the tasks of a project. In a comprehensive review of the cooperative learning literature, Cohen (1994b) proposes that under the conditions of a group task with an ill-structured problem, interaction is vital to productivity, because unless the group members exchange ideas and information, they are unlikely to come up with creative solutions to their assignment or to discover the underlying principles. Thus, the types of tasks suitable for group work are not limited to those that have well-defined solutions; they also include those that may require innovative, interactive, and inventive solution strategies.

Three Types of Cooperative Learning Groups

Johnson et al. (1998) identify three basic types of cooperative learning groups that are often used in higher education. These are formal cooperative learning groups, informal cooperative learning groups, and cooperative base groups. Instructors can use one particular type of group or a combination of the three types of groups in any classroom. The groups vary on several dimensions: group duration, purpose, and interaction activities.

- Formal cooperative learning groups. These groups provide a structure to accomplish specified learning objectives. Instructors design an assignment or task and organize the specific student interactions that are to take place. Any type of academic assignment can be structured for a formal cooperative learning group. Generally these groups stay together for a class session or for several weeks. Specific classroom interactions may range from a few minutes to the entire class period. Groups stay formed until the completion of the task, unit, chapter, or assignment. Rotation of students among groups during the course of a semester may occur.

- Informal cooperative learning groups. These groups are ad hoc groups that may last from a few minutes to an entire class period. These groups can be used to focus the attention of students during lectures, films, or experiments. By briefly discussing some aspect of the presentation, students in these groups become clearly focused on the instructor's learning objective and are cognitively engaged in the classroom session. There are a number of informal cooperative structures. Millis and Cottell (1998) note that the think-pair-share approach is one commonly used technique that individuals may not associate with cooperative learning. They note that its simplicity and versatility make it a low-risk activity for instructors new to the idea of cooperative learning (p. 72). In a think-pair-share activity, the instructor asks a question that does not have a definitive answer, and students are given thirty to sixty seconds to think of a response. The think time provides students time to retrieve their memories relevant to the question. Research shows that this time is critical to student learning. After the allotted time, students are paired to discuss their responses. In the final step, several students share their responses with the class as a whole, allowing the instructor to actively assess the learning process. Variations of the think-pair-share format can be used for more complex and extended student exchanges, as will be shown later in this chapter.

- Cooperative base groups. These groups are long-term groups, usually lasting for the entire semester when used within the context of a course. They are heterogeneous groups where the purpose is for members to provide support, help, and assistance in a long-term committed relationship. Groups meet at the beginning and end of each day or week. In addition to providing support, these groups manage class routines and administrative requirements such as attendance and homework. They may also review and edit papers and other assignments. At the college level, cooperative base groups can be used to support inclusion and student development. When used for this purpose, these groups are formed at the beginning of the college experience.

They last for at least a year and may stay together during the entire four years of school. Some universities may even assign members of base groups to the same classes, when possible, and provide special times and spaces for groups to meet.

Decision Making in Group Formation

After an instructor has determined course objectives, desired learning outcomes, and assignment/task parameters, a number of decisions still remain to be made when forming classroom groups. These decisions concern the group's duration, the size of the group, and the method of forming the group.

- Group duration. What should be the duration of a group (permanent or temporary)? The type of group (formal, informal, or base group) is the main influence on group duration, but some variability may occur due to the type of task assigned to the group. For example, a formal group assigned to a unit in a text may stay together for several months, whereas a group assigned a particular chapter may change after one or two weeks.
- Group size. What is the appropriate size for a group (dyad, triad, octet, etc.)? Again, the type of group and its purpose influences its size. Generally, informal cooperative groups are smaller and often are done in dyads during lectures or films. Johnson et al. (1998) note that groups usually range in size from two to four students, but size often depends on the time available, student experience with group work, the students' ages, and the amount of available resources or equipment for group work. The use of smaller groups makes it more difficult for students to hide and not contribute. Limited time and lack of group experience dictate the use of smaller groups.
- Group formation. How do you form the group (randomly, through instructor assignment, through self-selection, or with some combination of these methods)? A group's formation can have a very strong effect on its success. Johnson et al. (1998) note the benefits of heterogeneous groups where students have varying backgrounds, abilities, experiences, and interests, but they recognize that homogeneous groups may be appropriate in some circumstances. Random assignment often results in heterogeneity, but not always. Self-selected teams are rarely heterogeneous. Research shows that self-selected teams are likely to be unsuccessful (Fiechtner & Davis, 1985). Millis and Cottell (1998) note that most instructors prefer instructor-selected teams and that

"instructors should distribute students from team to team based on their academic preparation and ability, their gender, their ethnic background, and any other characteristics that might prove useful." They explain, "The idea is to create teams that will build on students' varied strengths" (p. 51). It also is possible to combine student-selected and instructor-selected choices and still maintain heterogeneity, by allowing students to name students that they would like to work with and guaranteeing that one of the named students will be in their group.

Resources for Designing Cooperative Groups

Basic resources that can provide more discussion of these questions and that examine the various modes of collaborative learning include, among others cited in this chapter, Johnson et al., 1998; Millis and Cottell, 1998; Cohen, 1994a; Bruffee, 1993; Michaelsen, 1992; and Johnson and Johnson, 1989. The following section provides an example of an exercise developed to incorporate collaborative learning and specifically to use the personal experiences of students from diverse backgrounds.

Pedagogical Applications

Setting/Background

Using the tenets of both experiential and collaborative learning, an exercise was designed for upper-division accounting students to learn about the topic "control systems and design options in the human resources and payroll system." The assignment was intended to introduce students to how their own experiences may bias technical decisions and to how various community factors may affect system designs. While the context of this assignment is accounting, the application and structure of the assignment can be applied across disciplines.

Objectives

The objectives of the assignment were based on the framework of the Teaching Goals Inventory (TGI) of Angelo and Cross (1993). They included seventeen of the fifty-one TGI items, representing six cluster areas.

- Higher Order Thinking Skills
    Develop the ability to apply principles already learned to new situations

> Develop problem-solving skills
> Develop ability to think holistically
- Basic Academic Success Skills
  > Improve speaking skills
  > Improve listening skills
- Discipline Specific Knowledge
  > Learn concepts and theories
  > Understand perspectives and values of the discipline
  > Learn to evaluate methods
- Academic Values
  > Develop an openness to new ideas
  > Develop an informed concern about contemporary social issues
  > Develop an informed appreciation of other cultures
- Work and Career Preparation
  > Develop ability to work productively with others
  > Develop leadership skills
  > Improve ability to organize and use time effectively
- Personal Development
  > Develop a commitment to one's own values
  > Develop respect for others
  > Develop capacity to think for one's self and make wise decisions

To ensure that the students would be able to bring their personal experiences to the assignment to design a payroll system, the context of the system was in a high school where students would be paid a salary. A description of the exercise and process is shown in table 1. In addition to the attainment of specific discipline knowledge, an objective of the exercise was to incorporate discipline values, which recognize that personal experiences may bias one's understanding of the needs and situations facing other individuals and groups when doing consulting work and designing systems.

The Prompt

The setting for this assignment is an upper-division course for accounting majors. The class includes students from various ethnic and cultural backgrounds, which are representative of the population at this large, urban, public university in southern California. A wide range of socioeconomic groups is represented in the class, and students report a wide range of related work experience that adds to the diversity. Some individuals have no experience, while others have experience in business that was, in fact, the impetus for them to enter school and major in accounting. Ages of the students vary from the early twenties to the fifties, with gender approximately equally divided.

Assignment Framework

This assignment is a variation of the think-pair-share format used for informal cooperative learning groups. It is designed for five-person groups who are experienced with group work. It uses an individual prehomework think assignment and has a full classroom period for the pair-and-share session. The assignment is structured to limit the group responses to specific questions in order to control the time allocated to the assignment, to focus the students on the relevant issues, and to allow for a comparison between groups.

Students are first given the assignment as individual prehomework, to provide time to those who need to formulate their ideas before they are comfortable participating in group discussions. Alternatively, this assignment has been used with comparable results for an in-class session

TABLE 1. Details of the Assignment

First, individuals are given a written homework assignment. In the classroom, participants are divided into five-person teams with twenty minutes to develop a team solution. Individuals are assigned to lead the discussion, record proposed solutions, record a bulleted design on the blackboard, present the results, and present alternatives that were considered. To structure the answers and provide a basis to compare the responses, students are given specific control objectives to apply to the design and a set of five specific questions to answer.

The Scenario:

The local community feels that secondary school education is a necessity in our society and that lack of education leads to a number of social problems. As a result, the local school board has been concerned about the rising dropout rate and has decided to take action. To reverse the trend, the board has voted to provide funds to treat education as a job. As of now, high school students will be paid. It is your job to devise a system to compensate the students.

Payroll Control Objectives to Apply to the Solution:

- All personnel and payroll transactions must be properly authorized.
- All employees must be assigned productive work, and they must do it effectively and efficiently.
- All transactions must be accurately recorded and processed.
- Accurate records must be maintained.
- All disbursements must be proper.

Questions to Be Answered:

- How should the students be compensated?
- How are the payouts authorized?
- How are the payments processed?
- How are the payments made?
- When are the payments made?

(without the individual prehomework) and with formal cooperative learning groups as out-of-class group homework. However, without the individual prehomework, the use of a four-person group is better for an in-class session due to the complexity of the assignment. A decrease in the number of group members reduces the number of necessary group interactions, countering the lack of preparation time. Thus, instructor objectives, student experience with group work, available time, and the nature of the assignment determine adjustments for group size and task structure.

The time line for the assignment follows.

- Day 1: Lecture on assigned readings and distribute the individual homework think assignment.
- Day 2, part 1: Form random five-person pair groups. Each group member is assigned to one of the following roles: the discussion leader, who guides the group process; the recorder, who takes notes on all the proposed elements; the reporter, who records the design on the blackboard; Speaker 1, who presents the design and rationale; and Speaker 2, who presents alternatives that were not included in the group's design.
- Day 2, part 2: Hold the share session (presentations) on the design components and the pros and cons of the proposed alternatives. Presentation order is determined randomly, since later groups will only present elements of their design that differ from the ones that already have been presented.
- Day 3: Assess the outcomes from the assignment, using anonymous student response sheets.

Student Assessments and Classroom Discussion

This section first reports the results of student assessments and then examines the diversity in the final projects and the cultural factors contributing to these differences. Sixty-two students in two sections participated in the assignment during the examined semester.

General Assessment Results

To assess the assignment, students were provided with a questionnaire at the class meeting following the exercise, asking them to list what they or their classmates had learned from the exercise and discussion. In addition, the questionnaire asked whether the exercise should be used again (and why) and whether after listening to the other groups and discussions, they would consider changing their system.

A faculty member who was not involved with the exercise but who had expertise in qualitative data analysis (see explanation of qualitative data analysis in Miles & Huberman, 1994) conducted an independent analysis of the responses on the questionnaire. Table 2 provides the analysis, which categorized the responses to the question that asked students to list what was learned from this assignment. Three clusters of responses emerged from the analysis; items with four or more responses are tabulated against these classifications.

- Content—Discipline Knowledge and Personal Awareness. The first cluster contains responses dealing with content. Students found that multiple solutions could exist and that there were many different opinions. Of particular importance, it was noted that values influenced the decisions and that various parties can be affected by systems.
- Task—Group Problem-Solving Issues. The second cluster has items concerning the task. Students found that teams generated more and better solutions but that reaching agreement could be a difficult task requiring accommodation.
- Process—Interpersonal Skills Issues. The third cluster contains responses dealing with the process. Several individuals noted that they found out the importance that effective communication skills could play in determining outcomes and influencing decisions.

In response to the question of whether the exercise should be used again, a majority of students (82 percent) were in agreement (see fig. 2).

TABLE 2. Content Analysis of Student Responses to the Question, "What Did You Learn from the Assignment?" ($N = 62$)

Content Related—Discipline Knowledge and Personal Awareness
- Many equally good solutions exist (30)
- Many opinions exist (22)
- Values influence decisions (18)
- Systems are complicated (10)
- Multiple parties are affected by systems (4)

Task Related—Group Problem-Solving Skills
- Teams generate more solutions (25)
- Teams generate better solutions (15)
- Reaching agreement/consensus is difficult (10)
- Accommodation is necessary (6)
- Teams compete and/or are defensive (6)

Process Related—Interpersonal Skills Issues
- Effective communication skills are needed (10)
- Some try to force opinions (6)

Should the exercise be used again?

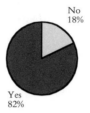

No
18%

Yes
82%

After hearing the discussions, did you
want to change your system?

No
42%

Yes
58%

Fig. 2. Student responses after the exercise

An analysis of the reasons that students provided for why the assignment should be used again identified specific benefits related to both the group process and the later presentations and discussions. The students indicated that the group decision process exposed them to new ideas and perspectives, with 58 percent (36 of 62) noting that they also would consider changing some characteristic of their system in response to what they learned during the presentations and discussions of alternate systems.

The evaluator's overall impression was that the exercise enhanced the educational process by providing a medium through which students who normally did not participate were made comfortable. In addition, they were encouraged to develop interpersonal and group problem-solving skills, including an understanding of diversity issues arising from differences in backgrounds and values. These results are consistent with the positive learning outcomes associated with exposure to and discussion of diversity issues as reported by Astin (1993a, 1993b), Gurin (1999), and Chang (1999).

Perceptions and Student Diversity

A comparison of the groups' recommended designs showed that the systems contain some similarities, but it also showed differences that demonstrate how personal experiences, diversity factors, and values are incorporated in applying discipline knowledge. Of particular interest, differences occurred in how the students should be paid and when they would be paid. The discussion about pay rates and timing showed that students made assumptions and judgments about the type of students being paid, how the payment would be used, the need for the money, and who should receive it.

After all of the systems were described and discussed, it also became apparent to 48 percent (30 of 62) of the participants that there is no one way that would be best and that various systems could be used (see table 2). The discussions of the proposed systems gave recognition to several important issues: first, the importance that must be given to recognizing the characteristics of the final system users; second, the need to recognize that system developers' own experiences may bias assumptions they make in their work; and third, the fact that diverse backgrounds, experiences, and perspectives of others can be much different from their own.

Classroom Discussion

In the classroom discussions of the designs, diversity between and within groups was apparent. The responses brought out issues and assumptions that related to culture and ethnicity, socioeconomic class, disability, and generation/age. There was no evident difference related to gender. Some of the comments provided by the students follow. They demonstrate the variety of perspectives and backgrounds within the classroom. Although some comments were direct, subtle biases became apparent when reasons were provided for the designs. Stereotypical assumptions seemed to be applied to lower-income or inner-city neighborhoods with "junky kids." Some students expressed experiencing discrimination in the resources provided to their neighborhood schools by the school district administration or discrimination within the classroom by their teachers. These experiences and beliefs affected the ways the systems were designed, but that fact was not always apparent until these items were reported during the discussion session. Table 3 shows the aspects of the recommended systems that had differences reflecting diversity issues during the class discussion.

Specific Comments and Insights. During the discussion of whether or not high school students should receive cash or certificates for compensation, another person proposed that video machines in the lunchroom and payment in the form of credits might be best. This prompted one student to break his silence and say:

Don't you realize that some students drop out to work and help support the family? They need the money. The money will be used for food. They don't want to get paid with video machine credits!

At this point there was a moment of "reflective observation" (one of the poles in Kolb's [1981] experiential learning model)—a teaching moment for diversity issues.

Cultural and Ethnic

- "This system might not work internationally. No one from my country would consider this. We have to work hard. It is expected."
- "There are cultural differences to consider. Students need to go to school because they should think that school is good for their future and their country."

TABLE 3.   Aspects of Recommended Systems That Considered Diversity Factors

Group	How Should the Students Be Compensated?	How Are the Payments Made?
A	Attendance, but must have a minimum grade of C.	Credits for gift certificates from local stores/catalogs. Quarterly payment with report card.
B	Base rate on attendance. Bonus incentive on GPA.	Paycheck delivered with report card at end of quarter. Bonus at end of semester.
C	Attendance with a separate base rate for each class year. Bonus for a GPA > 3.5. Minimum GPA of 2.0 required.	Electronic Funds Transfer with ATMs to be put at school. Payment made quarterly.
D	Attendance (allowed five sick days with a valid medical excuse) and grades. District policy sets standard pay rates.	Vouchers for use at area stores. Biweekly payment for attendance. Semeter bonus when grades come out.
E	Attendance and exam score (only passing is required).	Checks distributed in homeroom. Can be cashed in the campus student store. Paid every two weeks.
F	Attendance, but must maintain a 2.0 GPA. Partial payment for good citizenship.	Paid by check using the school's regular payroll system at the end of the semester.
G	Attendance.	Money accumulates in a savings account over four years. Paid at graduation for college.

Diversity Areas Recognized during Class Discussion of Recommendations
Cultural/ethnic   Socioeconomic class
Generational/age   Disability

- "The money should be given to the parents. They need to know the amount. They may not want their children to have any money."

Disability

- "Don't base on GPA because it discriminates against those with learning disabilities. It penalizes those with dyslexia because they can't complete exams under certain conditions even though they know the material."

Socioeconomic Class

- "If you are going to give store certificates you need to include food stores. Low-income families need money to support the family."

Implied Stereotypes, Multiple Diversity Factors, Generational or Value Differences

- "Shouldn't pay for just attendance. We should only pay for good grades. We don't want junky kids to stay there!"
- "The School District needs to set a standard policy for equity and to avoid discrimination. Resources aren't distributed fairly."
- "Only those attending college should get money."
- "No cash should be given because it would be used for beer/ drugs."

Conclusions and Recommendations

Wide diversity has become the norm in undergraduate education, and there is growing evidence of the positive effects that diversity experiences can have on student learning outcomes. Collaborative learning pedagogy is well suited for today's classrooms. It can meet the needs of students with varied learning styles, and it can promote the development of positive outcomes that are associated with diversity experiences. One of the ways that collaborative learning techniques do this is by providing more opportunities for positive discussion and interaction between individuals of diverse backgrounds.

Faculty members considering the use of collaborative learning need to ask themselves a series of questions: What are my objectives for the class and what are my goals for assignments? How can I employ cooperative learning techniques in meeting these objectives and goals? What type of cooperative learning groups should I use (formal, informal, or cooperative base groups)? What cooperative learning technique is appropriate (think-pair-share or another of the many techniques described in the literature)? What should be the duration of a group (permanent or temporary)? What is the appropriate size (dyad, triad, octet, etc.)? How do you form the group (randomly, through instructor assignment, through self-selection, or with some combination of these methods)?

This chapter has provided insights to these questions and demonstrated the development of a cooperative learning exercise, but the answers to these questions depend on a number of variables, beginning with the instructor's goals and objectives. Instructors interested in using collaborative techniques can obtain a basic familiarity from resources cited in this chapter. Designing assignments that use group processes with open classroom discussion will meet the needs of our increasingly diverse student population and improve student learning outcomes. In addition, it will obtain the other positive effects that Astin (1999) identifies—increased cultural awareness and commitment to promoting racial understanding. By gaining an understanding of diversity issues that arise from differences in backgrounds and values, students can then practice in the classroom the skills that are needed to work together in our increasingly diverse society.

Additional Resources

Books

Bruffee, K. A. (1999). *Collaborative learning: Higher education, interdependence, and the authority of knowledge* (2nd ed.). Baltimore, MD: John Hopkins University Press.

    A comprehensive book on collaborative learning that examines the nature of knowledge. The first part discusses and defines collaborative learning. It also explains the difference between collaborative and cooperative learning. The second part explores the nature and authority of knowledge. Appended are materials on classroom design and collaborative learning research.

Johnson, D., & Johnson, R. (1989). *Cooperation and competition: Theory and research.* Edina, MN: Interaction.

    A comprehensive review of all the research conducted on cooperative, competitive, and individualistic efforts. Each chapter is a separate meta-analysis of all studies available at that time.

Johnson, D., Johnson R., & Smith, K. (1998). *Active learning: Cooperation in the college classroom.* Edina, MN: Interaction.

This book is a comprehensive overview of how to use cooperative learning at the college level. It includes an examination of formal cooperative learning lessons, informal cooperative learning groups, and cooperative base groups in college classrooms. There are numerous specific lesson structures.

Web Sites

<http://www.eriche.org/crib/collaborative.html>. *Critical Issue Bibliography (CRIB) Sheet on Collaborative Learning*. The Educational Resources Information Center ERIC Clearinghouse on Higher Education. ERIC CRIB sheets are updated annually to reflect the most recent and/or significant publications on the topic.

<http://www.psu.edu/celt/clbib.html>. A selected and annotated bibliography on collaborative learning provided by the Penn State Center for Excellence in Teaching and Learning.

7
Identifying and Accommodating Students with Disabilities

Carl Fielden

Recent federal legislation and enlightened pedagogy, as well as emerging assistive and instructional technologies, have opened up unprecedented opportunities for students with disabilities to attend postsecondary educational institutions (Dukes & Shaw, 1998). As the demographic landscape of postsecondary educational institutions evolves to include students with disabilities, faculty and staff are becoming increasingly challenged to provide sound instructional and support services to meet the demands of this growing segment of the student population, frequently without the benefit of readily available and useful information resources.

Historically, people with disabilities have been underrepresented in higher education settings and, consequently, the workforce. This is, to some extent, a reflection of the reduced opportunities disabled students have had in the past to participate fully in employment-related postsecondary educational programs. For instance, the 2000 National Organization on Disability/Harris Survey of Americans with Disabilities (National Organization on Disability, 2000) reveals some shocking statistics related to the employment and educational attainment of people with disabilities.

- Only 12 percent of people with disabilities have graduated from college, versus 23 percent of people without disabilities.
- Only 32 percent of people with disabilities between the ages of eighteen and sixty-four work full- or part-time, compared to 81 percent of people without disabilities.

- Over two-thirds of people with disabilities who are of working age but are unemployed report that they would prefer to work.
- Twenty-nine percent of adults with disabilities live in a household where the total annual income is fifteen thousand dollars or less, compared to 10 percent of people without disabilities.

However, one encouraging statistic is the increase in the number of students with disabilities who complete high school. Today, 77 percent of students with disabilities complete high school, compared to 61 percent in 1986 (National Organization on Disability, 2000). The National Organization on Disability attributes this increase to federal legislative efforts concerning people with disabilities (e.g., the Americans with Disabilities Act of 1990 and the Individuals with Disabilities Education Act of 1975), growth in the economy, and greater access to technology.

As more students with disabilities graduate from high school, it is likely that more of them will attend postsecondary educational institutions. Indeed, this has been the intent of regular and special education partnerships, due largely to federal legislation that has influenced the quality and quantity of services provided to students with disabilities at both the K–12 and postsecondary levels. The Individuals with Disabilities Education Act of 1975 (IDEA) mandates, among other things, that students with disabilities in public schools at the K–12 level receive a free and appropriate education in the least restrictive environment possible. The current application of IDEA emphasizes including disabled students as fully as possible in regular classroom settings, so that in theory, if not in fact, they receive the same instruction as their nondisabled peers (Eichinger & Woltman, 1993; Haas, 1993). Consequently, more students with disabilities than before are acquiring the academic literacies required to graduate from high school and enter and succeed at the college and university levels. However, as will be noted later, students with disabilities in general are not as academically prepared for postsecondary education as their nondisabled, college-bound peers (Horn & Berktold, 1999).

At the postsecondary level, the Americans with Disabilities Act of 1990 (ADA), in addition to other federal and state legislation, has influenced the type and quality of academic accommodations universities and colleges provide to students with disabilities. On the legal front, litigation has assisted with the interpretation and implementation of the ADA, such that guidelines now exist regarding what services and technologies public agencies, including postsecondary educational institutions, should provide to enhance disabled students' access to instructional curricula, programs, and media (Office for Civil Rights, 1998; Smith & Jones, 1999).

Assistive technology in particular has enabled many more disabled students than before to attend postsecondary educational institutions. A growing body of literature focused on assistive computer technology attests to its success in providing disabled students access to information (see, e.g., High Tech Center for the Disabled, 1999; Lisieki, 1999) and assistance in acquiring academic skills and literacies (Anderson-Inman, Knox-Quinn, & Szymanski, 1999; Bryant, Bryant, & Raskind, 1998; Lewis, Ashton, Fielden, Kieley, & Haapa, 1999; Merbler, Haladian, & Ulman, 1999; Raskind, Higgins, Shaw, & Slaff, 1998). In addition to assistive technology, computer-mediated communication and other distance learning media are being investigated as to their usefulness in providing instructional access to students with disabilities. Preliminary studies suggest that distance learning media can facilitate access to, and transcend barriers and biases found in, the traditional classroom (Day & Batson, 1995; Kinner & Coombs, 1995), though technological barriers still exist for students with disabilities when they use some distance-education media (Gold, 1997).

Law, technology, and pedagogy have converged to form a complicated morass concerning the provision of services to students with disabilities. Students with disabilities often come to the postsecondary level acquainted with their rights under the ADA. They expect to receive certain academic accommodations and access to technology. Faculty and staff are often unaware of their responsibilities under the law to provide the accommodations and technology these students expect. Then there is the matter of pedagogy. Few faculty have been trained to teach students with disabilities and to design or modify instructional materials or procedures when necessary to make them accessible to students with special needs; hence, the focus of this chapter is on accommodating the instructional needs of students with disabilities in postsecondary educational settings.

While much has been written on the subject of children and disabilities, particularly instructional practices in public elementary and secondary schools, comparatively little has been written on the same topic regarding students with disabilities at the postsecondary level. Consequently, before presenting ideas and strategies for assisting students with disabilities at the college and university levels, it would be useful to (1) present the national demographics regarding students with disabilities; (2) identify characteristics of common, specific disabilities and the educational implications associated with them; and (3) assess the disabled students' overall readiness of students with disabilities for post-secondary study.

Accommodating Students with Various Disabilities

Nationally, students with disabilities comprise a small, but quite diverse, segment of the population at American colleges and universities (Horn & Berktold, 1999; Pacifici & McKinney, 1997). During the 1995–1996 academic year, as part of the National Postsecondary Student Aid Study, twenty-one thousand students completed a survey in which they were asked whether they had any disabilities, including problems with vision, speech, hearing, or mobility. Six percent of the respondents replied affirmatively. Of those who did indicate they had a disability, 29 percent reported having a learning disability, 23 percent reported having an orthopedic disability, 21 percent reported having another health-related disability, 16 percent reported that they were deaf or had a hearing impairment, 16 percent reported having a vision impairment that was not correctable, and 3 percent reported having a speech impairment (National Center for Education Statistics, 1998, cited in Horn & Berktold, 1999). In many cases, a student's disability may have little effect on his or her academic performance; in other cases, a disability can pose what may seem insurmountable challenges for a student. Faculty, now more than at any time in the past, are compelled—if not for altruistic reasons, then by institutional requirements—to accommodate the academic needs of students with disabilities who have not participated in higher education to a large extent. This process of accommodating diverse students with disabilities can be made less daunting if one knows something of the characteristics of common disabilities and their educational implications. The following section will group and define common disabilities and discuss their characteristics and potential educational implications. In a subsequent section, I will discuss strategies faculty can employ to accommodate students who have these disabilities.

Mobility/Orthopedic Disabilities

Cerebral Palsy

Cerebral palsy is a term that describes a group of neuromuscular disorders affecting motor functioning (Tyler & Colson, 1994). The three main types of cerebral palsy include spastic, characterized by rigid or difficult movement; athetoid, which involves involuntary and uncontrolled movements; and ataxic, which typically includes a marked unsteadiness and difficulty with fine motor control. Some individuals may exhibit characteristics of all three types of cerebral palsy (Tyler & Colson, 1994). Cerebral palsy is considered a nonprogressive congenital disorder, since most cases occur in utero and result from oxygen deprivation during an infant's developmental or birth processes. Less commonly, postnatal head injury or infection can result in "acquired cerebral palsy" (Tyler & Colson, 1994; United Cerebral Palsy, 2000). The prevalence of cerebral palsy is estimated to be two per one thousand live births (Shapiro & Capute, 1994, cited in Tyler & Colson, 1994).

Students with cerebral palsy often have another disability concomitantly, such as a learning disability, a seizure disorder, or a communication disorder (Tyler & Colson, 1994). Due to difficulties with fine motor control, students with cerebral palsy may have difficulty writing or typing or, if the vocal muscular is involved, difficulty speaking intelligibly (United Cerebral Palsy, 2000).

Multiple Sclerosis

Multiple sclerosis is an insidious, chronic degenerative disease that attacks the myelin sheath surrounding the nerve fibers of the spinal cord and brain (Bishop, Tschopp, & Mulvihill, 2000). As the myelin sheath is destroyed, electrical impulses are slowed as they move along the nerve tracts. Ultimately, scar tissue replaces the myelin sheath, which results in a further reduction of neural activity (Bishop et al., 2000).

The functional limitations that can occur as a result of multiple sclerosis vary between individuals, depending on the location and extent of the scarring that takes place (Bishop et al., 2000). Symptoms may include impaired mobility, tremors of the limbs, slow and deliberate speech, and visual dysfunction (Bishop et al., 2000), as well as memory failure (Allen, Goldstein, Heyman, & Rondinelli, 1998). Stress appears to be an exacerbating factor for many who have the disease (Schwartz et al., 1999), and people who have multiple sclerosis may experience periods of recovery or stabilization following periods of decline (Flick-Hruska & Blythe, 1992). Multiple sclerosis strikes women more often than men, with the age of onset typically falling between twenty and forty years. The prevalence of multiple sclerosis in the United States ranges from thirty to one hundred per one hundred thousand persons (Bishop et al., 2000).

Spinal Cord Injuries

Spinal cord injuries are another common mobility/orthopedic disability. Motor vehicle crashes account for the majority of spinal cord injuries in the United States, followed by gunshot wounds, falls, and recreational sporting accidents (National Spinal Cord Injury Statistical Center, 2001).

Spinal cord injuries are described in terms of the level and extent of the injury, which determines the amount of mobility and dexterity an individual will have postinjury as well as the likelihood of concomitant illnesses and disorders. Tetraplegia, the most frequent type of spinal cord injury, occurs when one of the eight cervical sections of the spinal cord is injured. Paraplegia occurs when an injury occurs to the thoracic, lumbar, or sacral areas of the spinal cord (National Spinal Cord Injury Statistical Center, 2001). The annual incidence of spinal cord injury is approximately forty cases per million population in the United States (National Spinal Cord Injury Statistical Center, 2001).

The educational limitations posed by a spinal cord injury vary. Depending on the extent and level of injury, a student may be able to participate fully in class activities, whereas a student with a more severe injury may experience frequent absences due to hospitalization for respiratory and circulatory complications.

Deafness/Hearing Impairments

Hearing impairments are common, increasing with age, and comprise the largest group of chronic physical disabilities in the United States (Danek & Seidman, 1995). According to Danek and Seidman (1995, p. 195), "There are no universally accepted definitions of the terms 'hearing impaired,' 'deaf,' and 'hard-of-hearing.'" Deafness and hearing impairment can be distinguished by the degree of functional limitations posed by hearing loss (Danek & Seidman, 1995; Knoblauch & Sorenson, 1998), though a number of people who are deaf view themselves as participants in a cultural-linguistic group rather than as people with a disability (World Federation of the Deaf, 2000). In regard to the prevalence of hearing disabilities, U.S. Census data from the 1997 Survey of Income and Program Participation indicate that 0.4 percent of disabled Americans fifteen years and older reported severe difficulty hearing conversation, whereas 3.4 percent reported less-than-severe difficulty hearing conversation (U.S. Census Bureau, 1997).

Clinically speaking, deafness is a hearing impairment so severe that a person cannot understand what is being said, even with a hearing aid (Knoblauch & Sorenson, 1998). Deafness can occur before birth due to malformation or severe damage to the auditory nerve or after birth as a consequence of infection, high fevers, or accident. People who are deaf depend on visual cues to facilitate communication, so they may miss many of the things that are communicated by voice.

A hearing impairment, conversely, can be temporary or permanent, but it is not as severe as deafness. Nonetheless, hearing loss can certainly affect the quality and quantity of information one acquires. For example, human speech normally occurs between the frequencies of 500 and 200 hertz. Hearing loss within these frequencies can seriously affect one's ability to communicate (Danek & Seidman, 1995).

As might be expected, the written expression of students who are deaf and hard of hearing may be affected adversely by their limited exposure to the full range of spoken verbal syntactical and grammatical cues that hearing people perceive. Furthermore, the speech of students who are deaf (if they can or choose to speak) or hearing impaired may appear unnatural or at times difficult to understand.

Visual Disabilities

Visual disabilities are relatively common in the general population, with nearly 4.3 million Americans reporting some form of visual impairment (Thompson, Bethea, Rizer, & Hutto, 1997). In the United States, blindness is defined as "central visual acuity of 20/200 or less in the better eye after best correction or a residual field of 20 degrees or less in the better eye" (Panek, 1995, p. 217). Visual disabilities are often discussed in terms of their level of severity, ranging from one's ability to "perform visual tasks without special aids" (Panek, 1995, p. 225) to total blindness, which increases an individual's dependence on other senses.

Visual disabilities result from pre- and postnatal causes, including heredity (e.g., retinitis pigmentosa), injury, and disease (e.g., macular degeneration, diabetic retinopathy) (Panek, 1995). Furthermore, a person's vision can fluctuate on an individual basis, so educational limitations and subsequent academic accommodations are made on an individual basis as well.

Accommodating students with visual disabilities can be challenging. Some students with mild disabilities may require only preferential seating in the classroom; other students may require complex assistive computer hardware and software to fully participate in class activities. Furthermore, some students with visual disabilities, particularly those who are blind, may experience difficulty keeping up with the reading demands of the college or university curriculum, since their literacy skills may not be as developed as those of their sighted peers, due to the de-emphasis of Braille instruction in the United States, noted as recently as the late 1980s (Schroeder, 1989; Stephens, 1989; Swenson, 1988), and to limitations that being nonsighted impose on an individual's ability to interact with text to the degree to which a sighted person can (Ely, 1989). Indeed, skilled writers have in mind a general notion of the propositional structure of the text they are writing (see, e.g., Kintsch, 1998), which is based on their knowledge of text genres (Johns, 1997; McCutchen, 2000). By implication, writers whose access to divergent text structures is limited will consequently find their acquisition of, and facility with, text structures thwarted to some extent.

Learning Disabilities

Students with learning disabilities represent the largest population of students with disabilities on college and university campuses (Kerka, 1998). The estimated prevalence of learning disabilities ranges from 5 to 20 percent of the population (Gadbow & Dubois, 1998, cited in Kerka, 1998; Lerner, 1989). Though most of the research in the field of learning disabilities concerns children, a growing body of research has begun to focus on adults with learning disabilities in postsecondary and vocational settings. What is known is that learning disabilities persist for a lifetime (Roffman, 2000); that is, contrary to former beliefs and educational practice, children do not outgrow learning disabilities.

Several definitions of learning disabilities have been articulated over the past twenty-five years. The first definition of learning disabilities, one that was incorporated into subsequent definitions, was stated in the Education for All Handicapped Children Act of 1975 (cited in Vogel, 1998, p. 7).

> The term "specific learning disability" [SLD] means those children who have a disorder in one or more of the basic psychological processes involved in understanding or in using language, spoken or written, which disorder may manifest itself in an imperfect ability to listen, think, speak, read, write, spell, or to do mathematical calculations. The term includes such conditions as perceptual handicaps, brain injury, minimal brain dysfunction, dyslexia, and developmental aphasia. The term does not include a learning problem which is primarily the result of visual, hearing, or motor handicaps, of mental retardation, or emotional disturbance, or of environmental, cultural, or economic disadvantage.

Since 1977, other learning disability definitions have followed, but it is the 1986 definition provided by the Association for Children with Learning Disabilities (cited in Vogel, 1998, p. 8) that appropriately accounts for the persistence of learning disabilities into adulthood.

Specific Learning Disabilities is a chronic condition of presumed neurological origin which selectively interferes with the development, integration, and/or demonstration of verbal and/or non-verbal abilities. Specific Learning Disabilities exists as a distinct handicapping condition and varies in its manifestations and in degree of severity. Throughout life, the condition can affect self-esteem, education, vocation, socialization, and/or daily living activities.

The characteristics of learning disabilities have been well documented in the literature and manifest themselves in six domains: oral language, reading, written language, mathematics, study skills, and attentional difficulties (Vogel, 1998). For example, students with learning disabilities in the oral language domain may experience difficulty with expressive and receptive language, possess poor phonemic awareness, display vocabulary weaknesses, and demonstrate difficulties with grammar and syntax (Lerner, 1989; Vogel, 1998). The reading difficulties experienced by some students with learning disabilities center around reading comprehension, decoding, reading rate, retention, and sensitivity to text structure (Englert & Thomas, 1987; Vogel, 1998). Students with learning disabilities that affect mathematical performance may have difficulties mastering basic math facts, recalling the sequence of steps in mathematical operations, copying problems and aligning numbers in columns, and possibly writing numbers in the correct sequence. In some cases, number and symbol reversal may be a problem, along with spatial awareness (e.g., the student may confuse right and left or have difficulty with time and compass orientation) (Lerner, 1989; Roffman, 2000; Vogel, 1998). Students with learning disabilities who have difficulties with study skills may experience difficulty organizing papers, taking notes, initiating course assignments, and memorizing course information. They may have difficulty taking tests, due to their having a lack of effective test-taking strategies (Vogel, 1998). Students with attentional problems may have difficulty responding to and maintaining conversations, because they may become distracted in the course of the conversation. Consequently, they may change the topic of conversation suddenly or inappropriately, possibly engaging in another activity during the conversation (Vogel, 1998).

Early learning disability studies have shown that deficits in written expressive language appear to be more prevalent than those in the other areas just discussed (Gregg, 1983; Vogel, 1998; Vogel & Konrad, 1988). Regarding the written expression of students with learning disabilities, a number of studies have shown that students with learning disabilities have both higher- and lower-order difficulties with writing (Newcomer & Barenbaum, 1991, cited in Wong, 2000), suggesting that they lack an understanding of the syntactical and text structures (Englert & Raphael, 1988; Englert & Thomas, 1987; Thomas, Englert, & Gregg, 1987) that help readers and writers represent relationships between ideas in story narratives and expository texts. In addition, students with learning disabilities seem to possess insufficient strategies for generating and monitoring the production of text (Englert & Mariage, 1991; Englert & Raphael, 1988; Singer & Bashir, 2000; Wong, Wong, & Blenkinsop, 1989), as well as for revising text (Graham & MacArthur, 1988; Graham, MacArthur, & Schwartz, 1993; MacArthur, Graham, & Schwartz, 1991).

Learning disabilities are diagnosed using norm-referenced, psychometric testing instruments. The purpose of such testing is to assess whether a significant discrepancy exists between a student's level of intellectual functioning (aptitude) and his or her performance (achievement) in an academic skill area. A statistically significant discrepancy between a student's aptitude and achievement can indicate a learning disability. However, as McCue (1993, p. 56) suggests, "the clinical identification of processing deficits is a more relevant objective of the assessment process than is discrepancy measurement, particularly in adults." Therefore, thorough learning disability testing also seeks to identify the processing deficits that may limit a student's academic functioning (McCue, 1993). Such testing includes the administration of assessment instruments that address the content areas of attention, memory, reasoning and problem solving, executive functions, language functions, functional literacy, and perceptual motor skills (McCue, 1993).

Attention Deficit Hyperactivity Disorder

Although learning disabilities and attention deficit hyperactivity disorder (ADHD) are often combined, they are not one and the same. Indeed, ADHD is classified as an independent disorder in the fourth edition of the *Diagnostic and Statistical Manual of Mental Disorders* (American Psychiatric Association, 1994). According to that manual, "the essential feature of Attention Deficit/Hyperactivity Disorder is a persistent pattern of inattention and/or hyperactivity-impulsivity that is more frequent and severe than is typically observed in individuals at a comparable level of development" (p. 78). Furthermore, some symptoms of ADHD must have been present before age seven, some impairment from the symptoms must be present in two settings, there must be evidence of "interference with developmentally appropriate social, academic, or occupational functioning" (American Psychiatric Association, 1994, p. 78), and the behavior cannot be accounted for by another mental disorder.

It is estimated that ADHD occurs in 3 to 5 percent of schoolchildren (Barkley, 1990, cited in Brown, 2000). Furthermore, more males than females are diagnosed with ADHD (Brown, 2000). Though once considered to be a childhood disorder, ADHD has been shown to persist into adulthood (Turnock, Rosen, & Kaminski, 1998). Characterized by inattention, hyperactivity, and impulsivity, it is often associated with other disorders (Richards, Rosen, & Ramirez, 1999). Students with ADHD are reported to have low motivation to succeed in academic environments (Brim & Whitaker, 2000). In addition, students with ADHD may have impaired executive functioning systems, which are involved in formulating goals, as well as planning how to achieve those goals (Ylvisaker & DeBonis, 2000). It is more than coincidental, then, that college students with ADHD tend to have more academic problems than their nondisabled peers, often receiving lower grades and dropping out of classes at a higher frequency (Turnock, Rosen, & Kaminski, 1998).

Overall, national trends indicate that students with disabilities are less prepared for postsecondary education than their nondisabled peers. The 1988 National Education Longitudinal Study (National Center for Education Statistics, 1994, cited in Horn & Berktold, 1999) surveyed a representative sample of eighth-grade students and followed their educational progress every two years. Data collected on the study participants revealed that 57 percent of students with disabilities intended to complete a bachelor's degree and that an additional 29 percent planned to enroll in postsecondary courses of some sort. However, following high school, only 66 percent of students with disabilities had in fact enrolled in postsecondary institutions, compared to 75 percent of their nondisabled peers. Horn and Berktold (1999) suggest that this disparity was due to differences in academic preparation. In high school, students with disabilities who participated in the National Education Longitudinal Study took more remedial classes than advanced placement classes. The study also showed that students with disabilities were less likely than their nondisabled peers to be minimally qualified for admission to a four-year college or university. Students with disabilities who enrolled in postsecondary institutions tended to have lower scores on the Scholastic Aptitude Test (SAT) and were more likely to be enrolled in remedial classes than their nondisabled counterparts. Finally, the study noted that by 1994, 47 percent of students with disabilities who had enrolled in postsecondary institutions had left without completing a degree or credential, compared to 36 percent of study participants who were not disabled.

Students with disabilities are in many ways an at-risk population in postsecondary educational settings. While federal disability law protects students with disabilities from being discriminated against in the admissions process, they are likely to leave higher education without achieving their goals unless aggressive measures are put in place to enhance retention. Hence, there is a the need for active collaboration between faculty, student services personnel, and students with disabilities.

Legal Issues and Accommodation for Academic Institutions

Most public postsecondary educational institutions have a Disability Support Services office or at least a Section 504 officer or ADA compliance officer (Lissner, 1997). Section 504 of the Rehabilitation Act of 1973 mandates that no otherwise qualified individual with a disability will, solely on the basis of his or her handicap, be excluded from participating in and receiving the benefits of any program receiving federal financial assistance. A Section 504 officer (alternatively called an ADA compliance officer) ensures that in the absence of an established Disability Support Services office, federal law will be complied with in regard to providing academic accommodations to students with disabilities.

The Americans with Disabilities Act of 1990, which, among other things, expanded the applicability of disability law to all public institutions, including institutions of higher education, is a companion law to Section 504 of the Rehabilitation Act of 1973. The ADA defines major concepts that have a bearing on an educational institution's responsibility to provide reasonable academic accommodations to students who are academically qualified to meet the entrance requirements for admission to an academic program. First, the ADA defines an individual with a disability as a person who "(a) has a physical or mental impairment which substantially limits a major life activity; (b) has a record of such an impairment; or (c) is regarded as having such an impairment" (Simon, 1999, p. 2). Second, the ADA defines who is "otherwise qualified" to include "(a) students who can meet the technical and academic qualifications for entry into the school or program; (b) members of the public who have a disability; (c) an employee with a disability who can, with or without a reasonable accommodation, perform the essential functions of the job; (d) persons who are discriminated against because of their association with persons with disabilities" (Simon, 1999, p. 2).

Postsecondary educational institutions are required to make reasonable accommodations so students with disabilities are extended an equal opportunity to participate in the institution's courses, programs, and activities, including extracurricular activities (Simon, 1999). Academic accommodations typically include, among other things, the provision of extended time for exams, a quiet testing environment, the opportunity to tape-record class lectures, note-taking assistance, printed materials provided in alternate formats (e.g., Braille or audiotape), large-print text, books provided on cassette tape, and the use of assistive computer technology. In some instances, administrative accommodations may include course substitutions and waivers. Institutions are also required to provide auxiliary aids and services such as qualified interpreters of sign language and readers. Postsecondary institutions are not required to provide personal services such as attendants, glasses, or tutors (Simon, 1999). (However, if a college or university does provide tutoring to other students, then it must ensure the tutoring program is accessible to students with disabilities.) The law does not require an institution to provide accommodations that would fundamentally alter an educational program or the essential academic requirements of a program of study (Simon, 1999).

Institutions are required to have in place policies and procedures for handling accommodation requests, as well as grievance procedures for resolving conflicts concerning the accommodations provided. In addition, institutions must have in place a means for determining whether accommodations are needed and procedures for providing the accommodations (Simon, 1999).

Students and faculty also have legal obligations. For instance, students must provide an "adequate notice of disability" (Simon, 1999, p. 5), in a timely fashion, whereupon the institution has an obligation to accommodate the student appropriately. However, students are not obligated to request accommodations for their disability, but if they intend to use an accommodation, they must submit documentation of their disability before accommodations are required to be granted. Faculty have obligations as well. For example, a faculty member may not refuse to provide a student with an accommodation, such as extended time on an exam, or to allow a student to tape-record a lecture, nor can he or she require a student to justify an accommodation (Simon, 1999).

In 1998, Congress amended the Rehabilitation Act of 1973 to ensure that federal agencies make their electronic and informational technology and materials accessible to people with disabilities. Section 508 was enacted to eliminate technological access barriers to information and to encourage the development of new technologies that will provide unrestrained access to information available to nondisabled people.

Section 508 addresses standards for software applications and operating systems; Web-based intranet and Internet information and applications; telecommunications products; video and multimedia products; self-contained, closed products, such as information kiosks, calculators, and fax machines; and desktop and portable computers. For instance, software products must be accessible to people who use screen-reading software (primarily people with visual disabilities) to speak the text present on a computer screen; the dialogue on videos will have to be captioned for people who are deaf or hearing impaired; likewise, Web-based information will have to be designed according to the access guidelines developed by the Web Accessibility Initiative of the World Wide Web Consortium. These access guidelines provide standards for designing Web pages that are accessible to people who use screen readers. The law requires at this time that electronic and information technology purchased or used by *federal* agencies must be accessible to people with disabilities. Should Section 508 be applied to the states, faculty will be required to design their instructional materials so they are accessible to people who use assistive technology or alternative means to obtain informational and educational material.

Pedagogical Implications: Assisting Students

Setting aside the possible future technological implications for making educational materials and processes accessible to people with disabilities, a number of strategies exist to make course materials and information accessible to students with disabilities currently. This section introduces some of these strategies, which are linked to instructional needs called out by specific disabilities.

Students with Mobility/Orthopedic Disabilities

Students with mobility or orthopedic disabilities often only require a few adjustments of furniture or equipment in the classroom to accommodate their academic needs. For example, classroom furniture should be moved to provide easy access for someone who uses a wheelchair. People with physical disabilities who are required for medical reasons to minimize the distances they walk can be given preferential seating to minimize their need to move around the classroom in search of a seat.

In a laboratory setting, equipment should be placed where it is in reach of someone who uses a wheelchair. Adjustable tables can be placed in computer labs so they can be raised or lowered to fit a wheelchair under them. Equipment such as printers, scanners, fax machines, and copy machines should be placed so that someone in a wheelchair can use them independently. This means that a person in a wheelchair should be able to easily reach the operating buttons, paper trays, and other essential components.

Students Who Are Deaf or Have Hearing Impairments

As discussed earlier, students who are deaf or who have limited hearing are at a distinct disadvantage in an academic setting where speech is the primary mode of communication. Even when a student who is deaf or hearing impaired can read lips, he or she may only catch 30 percent of the information supplied in such a setting (Chang, Richards, & Jackson, 1996). Therefore, the instructor should face the student directly and speak clearly. It is not necessary to unnaturally enunciate words. Also, the instructor should avoid talking while writing on the chalkboard.

As with students with mobility limitations, students who are deaf or hearing impaired should be allowed to sit as close to the instructor as possible, to maximize their opportunity to accurately lip-read. Another consideration is lighting. The instructor should not stand with his or her back too near a window or other light source, since this makes lipreading difficult, due to the diffuse lighting.

Note-taking is difficult for a deaf or hearing-impaired student who is trying to focus on a speaker's lips. Faculty can facilitate the student's learning by providing lecture notes. In addition, using visuals such as graphs and charts facilitates understanding for a student who is deaf or hearing impaired (Chang et al., 1996). Listing on the board topics that will be covered in the lecture will assist the deaf or hearing-impaired student to follow the topic. Since deaf or hearing-impaired students may miss the oral delivery of instructions, instructors should write down the due dates of assignments, tests, and projects.

Computer-mediated communication is another avenue through which information can be communicated. Instructors can send assignments and correspondence via email. Advocates for email conferencing tout its benefits of transcending time, space, and distance (Warschauer, Turbee, & Roberts, 1996). In the writing classroom, computer-mediated communication also seems to influence writers' consideration of their audience, highlighting the role revision plays in writing practiced as a social activity (Garner & Gillingham, 1996). For example, Mabrito (1991), who studied high- and low-apprehensive writers, found that high-apprehensive writers—that is, students who were apprehensive about writing in general—made more suggestions for revisions during electronic exchanges between peers than in face-to-face encounters with fellow students. Also, this same cohort of student writers reported that they relied more on peer feedback submitted via email than on feedback provided in face-to-face encounters.

Students Who Are Blind or Visually Impaired

Students with visual disabilities depend extensively on their hearing. Therefore, faculty should read aloud what they write on the board. It is also necessary to describe everything that is important (Chang et al., 1996). Preferential seating should be given to students with visual disabilities, so they can sit in an optimal location to hear the class discussion.

The physical layout of the classroom or lab is also very important. The instructor should ensure that the student who is visually impaired has easy access in, out, and around the classroom, and if it is necessary to move equipment or furniture, the visually impaired student should be told where it has been moved.

As with students who are deaf or hearing impaired, computer-mediated communication can be used to prompt class discussions, disseminate assignments, and develop students' writing fluency and self-empowerment in the context of an electronic writing community. Especially noteworthy has been research that has shown the potential of computer-mediated communication technologies to usurp traditional group dynamics that tend to disenfranchise those who are not granted privileged status in or are less articulate in oral discourse (Krupnick, 1985; Selfe, 1990).

For instance, Selfe (1990, p. 127) has observed of her computer-mediated composition classes:

> In the electronic environment of my class, those quieter members and those who wanted to mull over their responses before they contributed were no longer silenced or marginal in our discussions. They spoke as loudly, as articulately, and as frequently as anyone else.

Students Who Have ADHD or Learning Disabilities

As with the disabilities already discussed, seating is also an important consideration for students who have ADHD or learning disabilities. In this case, care should be taken to minimize distraction.

To enhance students' memory for the course content, faculty should consider using graphic organizers to represent key concepts and relationships (Ijiri & Kudzma, 2000). Several recent studies have shown that advance organizers that employ graphic representations of text can facilitate students' comprehension and subsequent recall of text (see, e.g., Englert & Mariage, 1991; Vallecorsa & Debettencourt, 1997).

Instructors should also try to teach to a variety of modalities (e.g., visual and tactile as well as oral), since the learning disability and ADHD literature indicates that students with these disabilities may have processing deficits in several areas (Lerner, 1989; Tyler & Colson, 1994). In addition, frequent summary and review of course concepts may enhance students' memory for the information (Ijiri & Kudzma, 2000).

The literature on the composing strategies of students with learning disabilities and other basic writers clearly shows that they need and can benefit from instruction in self-regulatory metacognitive strategies involving goal setting, generating and organizing content using text structure, and revising (Graham & Harris, 2000; Graham, MacArthur Schwartz, 1993; MacArthur, Graham, & Schwartz, 1991).

Conclusions

Students with disabilities are often faced with significant challenges at the postsecondary level. Some of these challenges are brought on by the nature and extent of their disabilities, whereas others are imposed by elements within the academic setting. Likewise, students with disabilities present tremendous challenges—and opportunities—for faculty to explore new and effective strategies to enhance their students' learning. Faculty can play an essential role in facilitating disabled students' entry into and success in college and university settings, particularly when they have an understanding of their students' disabilities as well as their students' capabilities.

Additional Resources

Books

The Alliance for Technology Access. (2000). *Computer and Web resources for people with disabilities* (3rd ed.). Alameda, CA: Hunter House.

   Intended for a novice audience, this book is a comprehensive source of information on assistive hardware and software products for people with disabilities. Indeed, the authors state that the book was "written for a community that has not yet discovered the power of technology" (pp. 2–3). The text walks the reader through the process of intelligently selecting appropriate assistive products that provide computer access to a wide range of people with varying degrees and types of disabilities. Included in this discussion are product descriptions and vendors.

Paciello, M. G. (2000). *Web accessibility for people with disabilities.* Lawrence, KS: CMP Books.

This is an excellent reference for people who are conversant in the language and techniques of Web design but may be novices to the field of accessible Web design—or, better, universal design. After first discussing pertinent legislation and legal precedents, the text guides the reader through techniques for designing Web sites that are universally accessible. The text also discusses emerging technologies that will have a bearing on the future accessibility of computer hardware and software. Included as well is a comprehensive list of Web accessibility resources, including products and informational Web sites.

Organizations and Web Resources

Adaptive Technology Resource Centre (ATRC). The ATRC (<http://www .utoronto.ca/atrc>) is actively engaged in researching techniques for making a wide variety of media accessible to people with disabilities. Particularly noteworthy is the ATRC's development of a free evaluation program called A-Prompt that Web designers can download to assess the accessibility of their Web sites.

American Foundation for the Blind (AFB). The AFB (<http://afb.org>) provides a wide variety of resources (e.g., information on blindness, a directory of services, and a "bookstore") to people who are blind or visually impaired or who assist those who are.

Association on Higher Education and Disability (AHEAD). This organization serves as a clearinghouse of information regarding disability policies in higher education. AHEAD (<http://www.ahead.org>) sponsors training, workshops, and publications to assist professionals in higher education who provide support services to students with disabilities.

Deaf Linx. Deaf Linx (<http://www.deaflinx.com>) is a Web site devoted to disseminating information for and about the deaf community. The site provides a wide range of resources that range from education and employment issues of people who are deaf to reports of recent medical interventions.

Learning Disabilities Association of America (LDA). The LDA (<http://www .ldanatl.org>) is a national organization with strong state and local chapters. The national office serves as a clearinghouse for information about learning disabilities, including reports of research on learning disabilities and effective support strategies in higher education settings.

National Organization on Disability (NCOD). The NCOD (<http://nod .org>) provides links to a wide range of information resources and services concerning the employment, education, and health care of individuals with disabilities.

Trace Research and Development Center. The Trace Research and Development Center (<http://www.trace.wisc.edu>) has been on the cutting edge of research in assistive technologies for over thirty years. A primary focus of the Trace Research and Development Center has been on the design of accessible documents. Currently, however, the center is involved in major projects involving universal design and access to mainstream computing systems. This Web site features a number of documents offering guidelines for designing accessible electronic media.

United Cerebral Palsy Associations. The United Cerebral Palsy Associations Web site (<http://ucpa.org>) is a clearinghouse of information about cerebral palsy, including health care and educational issues, as well as products and services that improve access for people who have this disability.

8
Linguistic Diversity and Instructional Practices

Ann M. Johns

The issue of linguistic diversity in North American universities, particularly as it relates to pedagogical practices, is so complex that it becomes a daunting task to discuss it in a single chapter. It is so daunting because a comprehensive discussion would include the essential interactions that the term implies, among language, culture, and ideology; motivations to achieve in a second language or dialect and student learning; age of entry into an English-speaking country and second language fluency and accuracy; issues of socioeconomic status, language learning, and literacy; and students' previous teaching and learning experiences and their academic literacies in their first languages. Thus, this chapter only begins to discuss the issues at hand.

Who Are Our Linguistically Diverse Students?

Complicating our understanding of linguistic issues in the classroom is the classification system established by the U.S. Census and adopted by many educational institutions and legislators as well. Though convenient for general reporting, the vague, broad-brush census categories such as "Asian," "Hispanic," or "African American" are not useful for distinguishing among individual students, or even student groups, in our classrooms.[1] For example, in many parts of North America, the "African American" census category now includes a growing contingent whose families have recently arrived from Somalia or Ethiopia in eastern Africa, students very different from the young people descended from West Africans whose ancestors were forcibly brought to the United States in the seventeenth to nineteenth centuries.

Deconstructing One Census Category: "Hispanics"

Focus on linguistic diversity and culture within a single census category, "Hispanics," may illustrate why we educators need to be increasingly alert to variation.[2] "Hispanics"[3] now make up 12.5 percent of the U.S. population, and, not surprisingly, they have a variety of linguistic, educational, migratory, class, and literacy backgrounds. In the section that follows, I attempt to identify some of these distinctions within "Hispanic" groups and to relate these differences to educational issues. But first, I pass on a word of caution from Cohen and Horowitz (2002, p. 45).

> There is agreement that what distinguishes [linguistically diverse] students the most is how different they may be from one another, whether the factors are internal to the learners or conditioned by the external context in which they have learned languages. There are urban, rural, migrant, and immigrant bilinguals who come to schools with different kinds of daily experiences with language. In addition, there are a minority of distinct groups nestled within each of these groups.

Given that caveat, the categories presented in the following discussion must be considered both general and internally varied.

The smallest group of "Hispanics" in most of our colleges and universities are the international students from Spanish-speaking countries such as Spain and Mexico. They tend to be well-educated in their first languages, from high socioeconomic classes, and much like educated Western European international students in terms of their academic interests and concerns. Their spoken and written English is often accented, but they tend to be proficient readers with already determined academic interests and motivations in disciplines across the curriculum. They are familiar with the genres of academic institutions and with the metalanguage of English grammar (nouns, verbs, etc.) due to their training in their home country in English as a foreign language. A considerable number of these international students remain in the United States, and quite a few eventually become part of our universities' "Hispanic" faculties, though they are quite different socioculturally from our other "Hispanic" students.

A second, much larger cohort of "Hispanic" students in North American educational institutions consists of what most practitioners are now calling "Generation 1.5" (Harklau, Losey, & Siegal, 1999;

Roberge, 2002), sometimes included among the ELL (English language learner) or LEP (limited English proficient) students by K–12 educators. These young people are foreign born and educated partially in their home countries and partially in the United States. Students fitting this description often talk about being "ni de aqui, ni de alla," neither of the United States nor of Mexico (or Cuba, Colombia, Puerto Rico, etc.). Generation 1.5 (Gen. 1.5) students tend to have weak academic preparation in their first languages, particularly in reading and writing, and thus may be unable to effectively transfer first language literacy skills into English (see, e.g., Cohen & Horowitz, 2002, on literacy skills transfer).

Some recently arrived Gen. 1.5 students speak and write in accented English. Others, particularly those who arrived in the United States before puberty, may speak unaccented English and control what Cummins refers to as "basic interpersonal communication skills" (BICS) as well as do monolingual English speakers. Yet transfer from Spanish ("negative interference") can continue to take place in their literacy practices (reading and writing). Thus, they may not have "cognitive academic language proficiency, or CALP" (Cummins, 2000)—the grammar, concepts, and vocabulary essential to academic success in English. It is important to note here that it requires at least six years of concentrated instruction in academic English for students to achieve CALP. However, some students do not attain proficiency even after twelve years of education in this country, due to a number of educational, linguistic, cultural, and motivational factors (Scarcella, 1996).

Other issues also play into the Gen. 1.5 students' motivations and abilities to perform. Many have adult responsibilities within their families: driving their parents and siblings to various appointments and activities, translating for parents and relatives, working many hours to assist their families to survive, and caring for a younger sibling or grandparent. Another important issue that influences these students and their schooling is identity, as my diverse freshmen students discovered about themselves and about diverse students in the local high school when they began to explore issues of identity and persistence of first cultures (Johns, 2001b). Gen. 1.5 students are often torn between their first cultures and the more traditional expectations of their parents, on the one hand, and the well-documented attractions of the American culture all around them, on the other. Our bookstores contain many memoirs and autobiographies of young people in America wrestling with who they are and the demands of their first and second cultures (e.g., Chang, 1998; Rodriguez, 1982). Students' identities, or identity conflicts, are manifested in their speech, dress, construction of selves in their writing (i.e., "voice"), or behavior in our classrooms and in their communities (Ivanic & Camps, 2001).

A third group of "Hispanic" students consists of the second generation, the children of immigrants who have experienced no first-culture education. These students are almost always English dominant, though they, too, may not have attained CALP during their K–12 education. Many do not speak Spanish well (or at all), and they generally do not read or write in standard Spanish, though they may use a border version of the spoken language, sometimes called "Tex-Mex" or, in southern California, "Calo." A number of these students call themselves Mexican American (or Cuban American, etc.), demonstrating more of an attempt at assimilation than occurs among the Gen. 1.5 group, a number of whom still refer to themselves as first-country nationals (e.g., Mexican, Cuban). Others attempt to return to their cultural and linguistic roots through "heritage" Spanish classes and involvement in student political organizations such as MEChA (Movimiento Estudiantil Chicano de Azlan). Thus, issues of identity, voice, and culture can be fully as important for this second-generation group as they are for Gen. 1.5 students.

Other Issues Relating to Students, Diversity, and Language

I have discussed three, rather general "Hispanic" student categories at some length in order to dispel any notion derived from the U.S. Census, or from our university administrative codes, that students of "Hispanic" heritage, or individuals from any of the other census clusters, come to our classrooms with relatively homogeneous linguistic, cultural, socioeconomic, or literacy experiences. More extreme distinctions could be cited for other groups conflated by the U.S. census. For example, the major linguistic and cultural differences between South Asians (e.g., Indians and Pakistanis) and North Asians, Japanese, Chinese, and Koreans must be considered—along with their varied sociocultural, linguistic, and immigration patterns. Among some Asian groups such as Chinese, Japanese, and Koreans, there are also differences in writing systems that impact both reading and writing across languages.

Other sources of linguistic and cultural difference in our classrooms relate to the varieties of English that our native-speaking students have acquired. Wolfram, Adger, and Christian (1999) note that certain American English dialects have prestige and others do not. These differences influence access to, and success in, school and college. Often, students who speak nonstandard forms of English (e.g., "Ebonics,"

Chicano English), with different grammatical patterns, pronunciation, and vocabulary as well as different ways of social interaction, are stigmatized by teachers and other students, though, in fact, the dialects spoken are coherent and regular, with analyzable linguistic systems (see Baugh, 2002). Wolfram, Adger, and Christian (1999, p. 23) tell us:

> The attitudes of teachers and other educators, as well as other students, can have a tremendous impact on the education process. Often people who hear a vernacular dialect make erroneous assumptions about a speaker's intelligence, motivation, and even morality. This kind of dialect-based stereotyping can affect even those who value cultural difference because dialect prejudice can be very subtle and can operate on an unconscious level.

How can we learn about these issues as they relate to our students? What can we do to enhance and draw from our students' linguistic and cultural experiences? How can we encourage their success? How can we help our students to understand and use their own cultures and languages—as well as the cultures and languages of the college or university? In the next section, I briefly explore these questions.

Pedagogical Possibilities

Here, I address some issues of linguistic and cultural diversity related to all disciplines and classrooms. Additional assistance can be found in the Additional Resources section of this chapter and in other chapters and the bibliography of this volume.

Discover Who Our Students Are

Who enrolls in our classes? How do our students identify themselves culturally, linguistically, educationally, or ideologically—or in terms of the content and values of our classes? There are several ways to discover the answers to these questions; a number of the ways are technological, for example, bulletin boards or anonymous questionnaires administered through a classroom management system. However, to obtain the information quickly, it may be just as easy to ask students to complete a bio-data sheet during the first week of class. This sheet can be used for a number of purposes: forming groups, assessing students' prior knowledge, investigating students' interests or vocational goals, and determining their linguistic and cultural backgrounds. Included in the last category might be such bio-data questions as the following:

1. Were you born in another country? If so, where?
2. When did you migrate to the United States?
3. If you were to use five words to identify yourself to others, what would they be? (Here, students often use identifiers such as *Chicano*.)
4. What high school did you attend? Did you study a language other than English there?
5. What is your first language? Do you read and write in this language? If so, how well? *What* do you read, or write, in your first language?
6. If English is not your first language, how would you assess your ability to read difficult academic materials in English? To write research papers?
7. Since you entered (name of university), have you written a research paper? If so, in what class?
8. Are you a member of a club or organization that relates to your ethnicity? Are you planning to take "heritage" language classes to improve your ability in your first language? Did you study the content of this class in your home country?

If especially designed for the goals of each class, a bio-data sheet such as this can give us a quick overview of the students, their needs, their course-related interests, and their linguistic backgrounds.[4]

Determine How Students Can Exploit Their Own Learning Styles and Languages and the Knowledge They Bring to the Classroom

As instructors, we can draw from students' own cultural and linguistic experiences and constructions, or their own discoveries during the term, to enhance their learning and to inform other students. As we prepare our curricula and assessments and the students' bio-data sheets, we need to ask ourselves

- How might the students use their prior knowledge to complete assignments?
- How can students' knowledge and background enhance other students' learning (e.g., through group interactions, presentations, or poster sessions)? (See, especially Wlodkowski & Ginsberg, 1995, on this topic.)
- How can assessment practices encourage students to exploit what they know or how they know it, to demonstrate achievement in the class? (See, e.g., Angelo & Cross, 1993.)

Here is one example from my own experience of drawing from students' knowledge when working with course concepts and content. In the freshman learning communities experience at my university (Freshman Success), in which a literacy (reading/writing) class is linked to a general education (GE) class, my colleagues and I draw from the GE disciplines such as anthropology, economics, biology, geography, and history to encourage students to use their own life experiences as data. We design papers in which the students apply disciplinary concepts to complete research on their families and communities or on other communities through service-learning projects, and they interweave these concepts and data into their papers and presentations (see, e.g., Johns, 2001a). My colleagues and I believe that it is only through drawing from what they know or can investigate with confidence that students can thoroughly understand the language, concepts, and discipline studied and how it all relates to their lives. This relationship between life experience and disciplinary learning is important for all students (see Light, 2002), but it is particularly important to linguistically and culturally diverse students who often find college to be abstract and removed from their everyday experiences.

Help Your Students to Understand That Your Discipline Is Embedded in Specialized Language and Symbols and in a Distinct Culture

Our disciplinary practices are cultural practices, developed over time as we became initiated through education and experience. What we value in terms of language and concepts, approaches to research, and ways of speaking and writing is determined by the particular disciplinary cultures to which we show allegiance. Jay Lemke (2002, pp. 27–28), one of the great names in education and applied linguistics, tells us:

> To think like a physicist (or biochemist or chemical engineer), to write like one, to make sense of technical genres as do those who create them authoritatively, students need to understand the larger value assumptions and subcultural conventions of the scientific community. [Among other things] they need to understand how the texts of technoscience not only serve internal functions within the community, but how they link the community to its larger social, economic, and political functions in wider society.

In his explanation of the relationships between cultural values and texts, Lemke points out that in the sciences and engineering, as well as in some other disciplines, written language alone cannot describe, for example, "complex shapes, shades of color or degrees of temperature" (p. 27). Thus, visual representations are central to argumentation, narration, and description in these disciplines. Lemke provides for readers (and for his students) some examples to show the central role of visual representation in certain disciplines.

- In one seven-page research report, 90% of one page was taken up by a complex diagram.
- The main experimental results of a two and one half–page report were presented in a set of graphs. The main verbal text did not repeat this information but only referred to it and commented on it.
- In most theoretical physics articles, the running verbal text would make no sense without the integrated mathematical equations. (p. 27)

However, written language can be more of a challenge to linguistically diverse students than is visual representation. Constantly, they confront disciplines in which language and meaning are construed through certain specialized syntax and word choice. In a study of chemical engineering students writing lab reports, for example, Schleppergrell (2002) found that linguistically diverse students had great difficulty making themselves understood by scientists in their writing at the sentence level, not because they made common grammatical errors, but because they did not understand how to express themselves in the syntax of the sciences. One of our responsibilities, then, is to make students aware of how experts in our disciplines talk and write, in addition to the ways that they state hypotheses, make arguments, and draw conclusions from data.

I now turn to another example from my own teaching experiences. One of my jobs as a literacy teacher is to help students to explore the language, genres, and values of their chosen disciplines. Thus, I assigned my freshman students the following tasks.

(a) Investigating the department of their major on the university Web site and identifying a faculty member in their major of choice
(b) On the Web or in the library, finding published professional writing by this faculty member and making a copy of this text, including visuals
(c) Interviewing the faculty member about this example of professional writing: its formal structure, its vocabulary, its use of visual representation, etc.

(d) Exploring with the faculty member his or her writing processes as the manuscript was being written and published

The students discover that there are a wide variety of texts, text processes, and visual representations in faculty professional writing, and according to the students' faculty informants, each of these demonstrates not only writing purpose but the social construction of knowledge and language within the writer's discipline.

What, then, does your discipline value? Visual representation of information? A certain type of text structure, such as IMRD (introduction, methodology, results, discussion)? An understanding and ability to apply certain concepts? Certain types of sentences—or verbs? The more you can make your discipline and its language, texts, and values (i.e., its culture) transparent to students, the more they may understand and appreciate their reading and writing assignments, group work, lectures, service learning, or other pedagogical activities.

Interactions between Our Linguistically Diverse Students and Ourselves

The most difficult challenges that we face as we teach linguistically diverse students are our own biases, our own social constructions of learners and their languages and of ourselves as their teachers. We are special audiences for our students, and we have requirements, language demands, values, and assessments that are discipline and class-specific. Our requirements, our biases, our preferred ways of judging texts or assessing students should be transparent and carefully considered, especially for students who are linguistically and culturally diverse.

In this section, I turn to more negative faculty responses to linguistically diverse students and offer suggestions for reconsideration.

Examine Your Own Biases about Linguistically Diverse Students

How do our own biases and expectations intersect, or clash, with those of our diverse students? As we work with students with different linguistic and cultural backgrounds, we need to ask ourselves some questions.

Faulty Critical Thinking

One questions we need to ask ourselves is, "Why am I responding so negatively, or positively, to this student's efforts at critical thinking?" A discussion of critical thinking as a cultural construct has appeared relatively frequently in applied linguistics literature. Atkinson (1997, p. 89), for example, after examining a variety of approaches to critical think-ing in North American pedagogy, concludes:

> Critical thinking is *cultural thinking.* Thus, I have suggested that critical thinking may well be in the nature of social practice—dis-coverable if not clearly self-evident only to those brought up in the cultural milieu in which it operates, however tacitly, as a socially-valued norm. [The literature points to] vastly different understand-ings across cultures of three notions directly implicated in critical thought: individualism, self-expression, and using language as a tool for learning.

Because critical thinking is a social construct and not, as some tend to believe, a cluster of universal abilities, assessing what our students view as critical thinking (based on their first cultures and languages or their earlier education) and modeling what we believe to be critical thinking in our classrooms are essential moves, especially for those who are not mainstream standard English speakers. Before we complain that our students "can't think," we need to consider what kinds of thinking our classroom demands and give students opportunities to practice that thinking in writing and in groups before making a graded assessment. Does your course work require synthesis? Explain what this means and model your efforts to synthesize information. Does it require sum-mary? Show students what a good summary looks like in your class. Does it require annotation? What should be annotated?

Student Error

Another question we need to ask ourselves is, "Why do I find certain errors made by students offensive?" Studies of faculty responses to errors in writing by second language students (e.g., Vann, Myer, & Lorenz, 1984) show that some types of errors (e.g., of verb tense) are considered by many faculty to be more offensive than others (e.g., mis-use of the English definite article, *the*). We need to examine our nega-tive responses to errors, discuss the most offensive errors with our stu-dents, and encourage students to edit (or to obtain editing assistance) as these errors are made.

For some faculty, it has been a long time since they studied English grammar, so they may have difficulty identifying what the errors are called (e.g., comma splice, subject-verb disagreement). If you feel that you or the students need some updating, you might visit your English department or writing center and ask an expert to come to your class to discuss errors or to identify the errors in your students' work, or you might consult one of the many handbooks available on the market (see, e.g., Raimes, 2001). You may find out, in the process, that the students whom you believe to be the least proficient writers make the same errors over and over and that these can be easily corrected if identified.

As instructors, we also need to decide which kinds of assignments should be graded for error and which should not. For example, in-class written examinations might be assessed for content, organization, and reasoning only, whereas out-of-class written work could be graded for sentence-level errors as well. Leki points out in *Understanding ESL Writers* (1992, pp. 111–112):

> A learner's progress [in acquiring a second language] is not stable but is characterized by movements backwards and forwards along the path toward the second language, as new input, previously too complex to take in, is analyzed and processed. . . . This analyzing and processing causes previously in-place interlanguage features to shift.
>
> Sometimes, under certain conditions, a seemingly acquired second language form is dropped in favor of an error. . . . This phenomenon occurs in a variety of situations: if the learner must suddenly deal with new or difficult subject matter in the second language, experiences anxiety, lacks practice in the second language, or slackens attention.

Faculty Assignments and Assessments

When I directed a teaching and learning center at my university, I often heard faculty say that linguistically diverse students "can't write." They often attribute this apparent deficit to inappropriate bilingual education, too much whole-language training, laziness, or other factors external to their classrooms. As responsible teachers, we need to determine what "can't write" means to us (sentence-level error? inability to structure paragraphs? faulty argumentation?) and to assist students in getting help from tutors or literacy teachers. We also need to design assignments that are clear, explicit, and well modeled, so that all students, second language or not, understand what they are to do and what a successful paper (or other assignment) might look like.

Wlodkowski and Ginsberg, whose outstanding volume *Diversity and Motivation: Culturally Responsive Teaching* (1995) should be read by all faculty with diverse classrooms, make the following recommendations for writing (and other) assessments that are administered in a diverse classroom (pp. 237–243).

- The assessment process should be connected to the learner's world, frames of reference, and values. [One of the important arguments made by Leki (1992) and others about linguistically diverse students is that they tend to write more proficiently when they care about and understand what they are writing. This has certainly been my finding. See, e.g., Johns 1997, 2001b.]
- Demonstration of learning should include *multiple ways* to represent knowledge and skills. [As noted in the discussion of linguistic diversity at the beginning of this chapter, students vary considerably in terms of their reading, writing, and speaking abilities. Given this variance, students should be tested for learning in a number of ways—through poster sessions, visual representations, oral presentation, and out-of-class formal and informal assignments, as well as the standard in-class multiple-choice and essay examinations.]
- Self-assessment should be essential to the overall assessment process. [Angelo & Cross (1993), among others, suggest a number of methods by which students can assess themselves during the learning process. For example, faculty can ask students what they learned from writing a paper or from a recent lecture; they can ask students to write about how they studied for and took an examination—and how they might change their approaches for future examinations. More important, they can ask students how they can best demonstrate what they have learned in the class.]

When we have linguistically and culturally diverse students in our classes, we will want to reconsider the use of self-assessment. Wlodkowsi and Ginsberg (1995, pp. 240–241) note that many diverse students may feel uncomfortable about self-disclosure or candor about their academic accomplishments—or failures. Thus, we can use our student self-evaluations as personal assessments rather than as something that students share either with their classmates or the instructor. The uses of technology often provide a more comfortable way for these students to assess themselves. I have found that using a classroom management system such as Blackboard or WebCT or just encouraging email responses provide for some students a comfortable avenue for self-assessment and expression not found in face-to-face groups, particularly in a large lecture class.

Plagiarism

Finally, there is the issue of plagiarism and the diverse student. The concern for what is seen as plagiarism is certainly widespread and valid, for "plagiarism undermines the authority of the teacher and the text" (Pennycook, 1996, p. 215; see also Johns, 2001b). If, in fact, plagiarism is a concern in your classes, then you need to discuss with all of your students, particularly those who are diverse, what you consider plagiarism to be and what the penalties for plagiarism are. The more specific you can be through use of examples, the more complete will be the students' understanding of what plagiarism means.

This explanation of plagiarism is particularly important to linguistically diverse students, because they may be uncomfortable with writing in English (and therefore find it easier to use as a crutch someone else's text) or, more important, because in their first cultures, copying may be an acceptable or even honored practice. In her fine discussion of writing among modern Chinese students, Matalene (1985) makes the point that by copying great writers, the Chinese "honor the ancients," a very different view from that of my faculty colleagues.

With technology, we have access to Web sites posted by our libraries and information technology services about the nature of plagiarism, with examples that show students when they will have crossed the line. Consult your library or direct your students to the appropriate Web site.

Enhancing All Students' Learning Opportunities

Other authors in this volume discuss ways in which students can apply classroom concepts and approaches in the world (see, e.g., Washington, Weber, & Young), so this section will focus on integrating the linguistically and culturally diverse student into a classroom in which learning by all students can be optimized. (For more complete discussions, see also Carrasquillo & Rodriguez, 2002; Roberts, 1994; Schleppergrell & Colombi, 2002; Wlodkowski & Ginsberg, 1995.)

Assist Students in Setting Goals for Achievement in Your Class

Why do students enroll in our classes? One reason, certainly, is that the classes are required; however, even in required classes, students can set goals for themselves as well as working within the goals you set for them. On the bio-data sheet discussed earlier, you might ask the following:

- Look at the class readings or textbook. What topics are of particular interest to you? What life experiences can you bring to the study of these topics? What would you like to learn about these topics? How might you use your learning in this class in your profession or life experience?
- What goals do you have for yourself as a learner? For example, what grade do you plan to earn in this class? What will you do to earn this grade? What will you have to work on (e.g., improving your writing in English or gathering the courage to consult with your instructor)?
- What do you consider your strengths as a learner, particularly for this class?
- What do you still need to work on?

Make Your Goals and Expectations Clear

As I noted earlier, any well-crafted classroom requires that the objectives for students and the specific processes for assessment be made clear. However, for linguistically diverse students, in particular, it is very important that students understand the following:

- What is required of them in terms of an assignment and what a good example of a student assignment response looks like. (This understanding could be facilitated by, for example, posting models of good papers on a Web site, discussing what is valued in the assignment, and making clear what plagiarism means in the class.)
- How assignments and other assessments will be scored, that is, what criteria will be used to grade students' work. (If you plan to grade organization of a text and sentence-level error, make that clear to the students. Some students believe that editing and error are, or should be, graded only in English classes.)
- What other expectations you have—for example, how you will grade participation.

Encourage Positive Group Interaction in the Classroom

It has become increasingly clear to educators that the old methods of lecture and assessment do not lead to optimal learning in most classes, particularly among some diverse students (see Light, 2002). However, creating group interaction, particularly among students from a variety of ethnic and linguistic backgrounds, is challenging, because students tend to associate with others who are like them, whose languages and cultures are familiar. Johnson, Johnson, and Smith (1998) provide many general suggestions, and discuss the pitfalls, in cooperative learning and other approaches to group work. (See also Venable, in this volume.) Here are some specific suggestions for instructors in multilingual classrooms.

- When creating groups, particularly for long-term assignments or other extended work, select the student groupings yourself—don't rely on student self-selection. If possible, place linguistically diverse students who still face difficulty with oral English with at least one individual who is sympathetic and will work diligently with these students. If students have difficulty with reading and writing, make sure that your assignment includes other possibilities for their group involvement.
- Rotate student roles (facilitator, note taker, timer, reporter) within the group, so that one or two of the four or five students in the group do not dominate.
- Assign to groups projects that can draw equally from linguistically diverse and native-speaking students—real-world tasks or issues with which the diverse students have had experience or tasks that require technological or diverse student background knowledge.
- Create situations in which the diverse students teach the others and vice versa. One example would be jigsaw reading, a practice that requires each student to be responsible for part of the text. Another would be student presentations to others in the group about their families or cultures as they relate to course content.
- Structure group sessions in which there are problem-solving exercises to build group cohesion, activities that do not require advanced knowledge of one culture or one linguistic register.
- Establish positive interdependence through situations in which individual members of the group cannot succeed without each other.
- Provide methods for individual accountability within the group and opportunities for group members to assess themselves as individuals and to assess other members of the group. Make these assessments part of the project grade.

In addition to group work, members of your class can also be paired to complete out-of-class research or other activities. For example, I assigned pairs of students with different linguistic and cultural backgrounds to make observations for their research and report their findings to the class. In some cases, the students who still had some difficulty with formal speaking presentations did not want to present a long oral report; instead, they designed the overheads that were central to the presentations. Another method for pairing students involves asking them to prepare questions about the previous lecture or about a reading. Having preparation time gives the second language student an opportunity to think through both the meaning and the syntax of their questions. (Note: Forming questions in English is *hard*!)

Assess the Success of Your Attempts at Inclusion

In addition to keeping track of how the groups are doing, culturally and linguistically as well as pedagogically, it is important to pause and to discover what students are learning from the class and particularly whether the linguistically diverse students are grasping the material. There are many suggestions for making these formative assessments (see, e.g, Angelo & Cross, 1993). Here are a few from a favorite teaching text (Davis, 1993, pp. 56–57).

- Have students write an unsigned "minute paper." Toward the end of the class, ask students to answer questions on paper such as "What is the most significant thing you learned today?" or "What questions do you still have about this topic?"
- Ask students to list in writing (or discuss in their groups) key concepts or ideas from a lecture or reading.
- Ask students to define and/or apply to their own experience a key concept.
- Collect students' lecture notes at random.
- And come early and talk to those students who are not participating frequently in an attempt to relax them—and discover why they are not taking part.

Conclusion

It would be much easier for all of us to teach students who are like us, who share our cultural and linguistic experiences and appreciate our disciplines as we do. However, in this diverse world, we need to sacrifice ease for complexity, implicit teaching for explicit discussions of requirements and content and for considerations of difference in giving assignments and creating groups. The challenges are great, but the rewards can be even greater.

Notes

1. Admittedly, these general categories do have some value for administrative reporting and assessment of success. It might be important to know, for example, that the graduation rates in 1998 for "Hispanics" who enrolled in college were 48 percent; for Asian Americans, 66 percent; and for American Indians and African Americans, 37 percent. Differences within the "Hispanics" category are important to note as well, particularly as they relate to college graduation rates among the entire "Hispanic" population in the United States: Mexican American, 5.1 percent; Puerto Rican, 8.6 percent; Cuban American, 13.9 percent; Central and South American origin, 11.8 percent (Hixon, 2002).

2. See Carrasquillo and Rodriguez (2002) for a much more complete discussion of a number of "language minority" student groups: Asians and Pacific Islanders, Arabs, Russians, Haitians, and American Indian, Eskimo, and Aleut students.

3. The term *Hispanic* is itself problematic. Though it is the term used by the U.S. census, many members of the populations whom it identifies view *Latino* as a more neutral term. Our students identify themselves in more specific ways: as Chicano for politicized Latinos north of the border; as Mexican, Cuban, Colombian, and so on; or as Cuban American and so on.

4. For a more complete discussion of bio-data sheets and other needs assessments, see Johns, 1994.

Additional Resources

Books

California Teachers of English to Speakers of Other Languages. *California pathways: Second language students in public high schools, colleges, and universities.* (1997). Glendale, CA: Author.

> Though addressed to educators in one state, this volume nonetheless covers universal issues, including the difficulties students have acquiring academic English, factors affecting English language development, and resources for instructors. The mailing address for California Teachers of English to Speakers of Other Languages (CATESOL) is 1146 N. Central Avenue, #195, Glendale, CA 91292.

McLeod, S. H., Miraglia, E., Soven, M., & Thaiss, C. (Eds.). (2001). *WAC for the new millennium: Strategies for continuing writing-across-the-curriculum programs.* Urbana, IL: National Council of Teachers of English.

One chapter in this volume, "ESL Students and WAC Programs: Varied Populations and Diverse Needs" (Johns, pp. 141–164) addresses the issues in this chapter directly by reviewing the research on second language acquisition, error, and contrastive rhetoric and then suggesting ways in which faculty across the curriculum can use this research to understand and work with their students. Other chapters of interest might be "Writing Intensive Courses and WAC" (Townsend), "The Politics of Literacy across the Curriculum" (Villanueva), and "Writing across the Curriculum and Service Learning: Kairos, Genre, and Collaboration" (Jolliffe).

Roberts, H. (Ed.). (1994). *Teaching from a multi-cultural perspective*. Thousand Oaks, CA: Sage.

This volume was designed for faculty across the curriculum, and it contains seven chapters by faculty and administrators with practical advice on curricula, approaches to teaching, and assessment. Chapters include "Treating All Students Equally" (Lou), "Languages and Cultures in the Classroom" (Johns), and "Equity in Classroom Assessment" (Harris).

Schleppegrell, M. J., & Colombi, M. C. (Eds.). (2002). *Developing advanced literacy in first and second languages: Meaning with power*. Mahwah, NJ: Lawrence Erlbaum.

Though written for literacy instructors at the university level, this volume contains several specialized chapters that would undoubtedly be of interest to faculty in other disciplines. These include "Multimedia Semiotics: Genres for Science Education and Science Literacy" (Lemke), "Challenges of the Science Register for ESL Students: Errors and Meaning-Making" (Schleppegrell), "Writing History: Construing Time and Values in Discourses of the Past," (Martin), and "African American Language and Literacy" (Baugh).

Sigsbee, D. L., Speck, B. W., & Maylath, B. (Eds.) (1997). *Approaches to teaching non-native English speakers across the curriculum* (New Directions for Teaching and Learning No. 70). San Francisco: Jossey-Bass.

Takaki, R. (Ed.). (1994). *From different shorts: Perspectives on race and ethnicity in America*. New York: Oxford University Press.

This is a collection of scholarly essays written in debate format, covering issues such as student achievement and the best explanation(s) for racial inequality. It is an excellent text for a faculty discussion group.

Wolfram, W., Adger, C. T., & Christian, D. (1999). *Dialects in schools and communities*. Mahwah, NJ: Lawrence Erlbaum.

In this comprehensive volume, dialect is defined as "a variety of language associated with a regionally or socially defined group of people." The authors discuss specific issues relating to schools, for example, cultural styles in the classroom, teacher and cultural attitudes toward dialects, and the relationships between reading and writing and dialect speakers. They also provide a list of common grammatical features in the vernaculars of English. This book is a must for teachers with a considerable number of African American English speakers or Chicano English speakers.

Web Sites and Volumes to Share with Students (to help them with their writing)

<http://owl.english.purdue.edu/lab/index.html>. The Purdue Online Writing Lab offers extensive online assistance for all students writing academic papers.

<http://www.rpi.edu/web/writingcenter/online.html>. The Rensselaer Polytechnical Institute Writing Center helps writers with style (parallelism, sentence length, word choice) and punctuation, as well as with citation practices.

Raimes, A. (2001). *Keys for writers* (3rd ed.). Boston: Houghton Mifflin.

Every student needs a writer's handbook, of which there are many. This volume is particularly good for linguistically diverse students, because Raimes is a former ESL teacher.

9
Faculty and Student Diversity: A Case Study

Minjuan Wang and Terre Folger

College classrooms are becoming more complex in several ways. Changes in the professoriat and student population and rapidly developing technology contribute greatly to this complexity. With regard to faculty, Finkelstein, Seal, and Schuster (1999) suggested that major changes are occurring in the professoriat as more female, foreign-born, and minority scholars are employed on campuses. Based on their analysis of data from the 1993 National Study of Postsecondary Faculty, these researchers reported that new, foreign-born faculty are more likely to be younger than the rest of the faculty cohort. Studying current student populations, Davis (1993) noted that demographic changes in the college applicant pool and college admissions policy effect greater diversity in today's college classes.

Diversity is realized in other ways as well. Goebel (1995) found that students' differences in learning and communication styles relate to gender, class, and ethnicity. This researcher suggested that students from cultures that value individualism perform well in classrooms where individual students are encouraged to interact, and even debate, with instructors. Students from cultures that tend to value community more highly than individual performance may benefit from cooperative learning and collaboration. Chamberlain, Guerra, and Garcia (1999) reviewed the literature on intercultural communication, focusing on teacher-student classroom interactions and exploring ways that teachers can respond to cultural incongruities and reduce cultural clashes between themselves and students from different cultural backgrounds.

Technology must also be considered in the classroom diversity mix. Kellner (1998, p. 211) has written that college faculty face the "chal-

152

lenge of providing people from diverse races, classes, and backgrounds with the tools to enable them to succeed and participate in an ever more complex world." Freedman and Liu (1996) investigated issues fundamental to computer-assisted, multicultural education. Their findings indicate that students with varied ethnic backgrounds have different attitudes about and knowledge of the use of computers, as well as differing cross-cultural communication patterns and learning processes when working with this technology. Not surprisingly, classes in which technology is the subject are also affected by the increasingly diverse student population, as shown in work by Chamberlain et al. (1999), Freedman and Liu (1996), and Kay, Jensen-Osinski, Beidler, and Aronson (1983).

What else goes into the mix? Age is one factor, as midlife or reentry students return to the classroom. Kay et al. (1983) reported that the intergenerational classroom they studied had greater student participation than a comparable single-generation classroom, a finding that is particularly relevant to this chapter.

Our research relates the experiences of Dr. Wang, a junior, female, foreign-born faculty member undertaking her first teaching assignment in a large North American university. Her class "Technologies for Teachers" embodied all of the aspects of diversity just described. The cultural and generational diversity represented there included, by necessity, Dr. Wang's own cultural and generational characteristics as juxtaposed to those of the students. These differences within the classroom affected the learning community and motivated this research. Two contingencies explored are (a) the degree of generational and cultural differences present in her classroom and (b) the effects of diversity on the communication process throughout the semester. What is described here appears to have implications for facilitating both teacher-student and student-student interactions within a culturally and generationally diverse learning environment.

Context

Two important contextual factors considered here are the technology-based course itself and instructor and student diversity. Given this context, Dr. Wang used strategies that she hoped would encourage communication within the classroom. In the remainder of this section, the course and the demographics of both the students and the instructor are described. The sections that follow outline the instructional and assessment strategies employed by Dr. Wang. Finally, the results and pedagogical implications are presented.

Course Description

"Technologies for Teachers" is an introductory, upper-division course that provides hands-on experience with the possibilities and potential of computer technology in education. The goal of this course is empowerment of preservice and in-service teachers to use a wide variety of computer-based technologies both professionally and in the classroom. Conceivably, teachers and preservice teachers leave with a taste of all that is possible for using technology in teaching and with a sample of concrete ideas for infusing technology with pedagogies. This study focuses on two sections of the course (with an identical curriculum) taught during the same semester by Dr. Wang.

The sixteen-week course, taught in three-hour segments, encompassed sixteen modules. Major topics included telecommunications; effective presentations using PowerPoint and Inspiration; desktop publishing; Web development; and ethical, legal, and safe use of technology and media. All modules started with a half-hour instructor presentation, continued with one-hour core classroom activities, and ended with individual portfolio work. Portfolio projects were the capstone assignments and were submitted for review in the seventh, eleventh, and sixteenth weeks. In these portfolios, students presented their technology-integrated lesson plans or multimedia projects (e.g., a Power-Point presentation or WebQuest), either in hard copies or electronically.

Students were also encouraged to participate in the Learning through Cyber-Apprenticeship (LTCA) project, a federally funded grant program that provided opportunities for student teachers to work directly with technologically skilled working teachers in the field. In the LTCA projects, students created technology-based materials to be used in the teachers' classrooms. Students from both sections participated in this project, but at varying levels.

Instructor Diversity

Dr. Wang was born in a small village along the Yellow River in northern China. She attended a premier university in China, receiving her B.A. in literature. Dr. Wang then received a graduate assistantship at an East Coast university in the United States and earned her M.A. in comparative literature. She earned her Ph.D. in information science and learning technologies from a Midwestern university in the United States. During her Ph.D. studies, she embraced a constructivist approach to teaching and learning. At present, she is a relatively new assistant professor at a comprehensive university in California.

As a foreign-born and junior faculty member, Dr. Wang faces many challenges in her classroom. Dr. Wang's own experiences with the Chinese educational system influenced her expectations about the classroom. Facilitating the learning of the culturally and generationally diverse student population required adjusting to her students' interactions with her as a professor and to their expectations of faculty in comprehensive North American universities.

Student Diversity

Table 1 provides the demographic data for the two sections of Dr. Wang's class, referred to here as Section 1 (N = 19) and Section 2 (N = 18). Although both sections included in-service and preservice educators ranging from twenty-three to sixty years in age, the age range in Section 2 was larger (ages 22–60) than in Section 1 (ages 23–33). Section 2 was also more ethnically diverse.

An online incoming student survey (app. A) conducted by an outside evaluator provided information on the students' enrollment and teaching status, entering computer skills, awareness of ethical use of computers, and willingness to integrate computer technologies into classroom. The survey revealed that teaching status was more varied for Section 2 students, a collection of teaching interns, in-service teachers, and preservice teachers. Section 2 students also taught more subjects to a larger range of grade levels (from first grade through high school).

Instructional Strategies

In their excellent volume, Wlodkowski and Ginsberg (1995) suggested strategies to facilitate diverse students' learning that include fairness and

TABLE 1. Demographic Data of the Two Sections

Item	Section 1 (N = 19)	Section 2 (N = 18)
American Indian	0	0
Mexican American	4	1
Asian American	1	2
Pacific Islander	0	0
White non-Latino	10	11
Filipino	1	0
Vietnamese	0	2
Canadian	0	1
European	0	1

respect for all. These authors emphasized the importance of taking into account the expectations and experiences of students from various cultural backgrounds. They noted that "people who feel unsafe, unconnected, and disrespected are unlikely to be motivated to learn" (p. 2). The writers concluded that diversity can be used to unite, or can divide, a group of students in their learning pursuits. Building a supportive learning environment, increasing students' awareness of diversity, and facilitating student-student communication are strategies conducive to success.

Building a Supportive Learning Environment

Student and faculty diversity in Dr. Wang's "Technologies for Teachers" class enriched but also complicated the technology classroom. Because the major goal for the course was students' incorporation of technological tools in teaching and learning, the students' diverse experiences provided opportunities for the class to explore various avenues for technology integration. However, the differences among students in computer skills, learning styles, and English fluency created instructional challenges.

With awareness of her students' diversity in all of these aspects, Dr. Wang endeavored to build a positive learning environment. To address individual differences with regard to technology experience, Dr. Wang balanced whole-class instruction with individualized learning in which she and more proficient students assisted those having difficulties. To accommodate varied learning styles, Dr. Wang reduced direct instruction and allowed individuals to self-pace their learning. She also addressed the students' varied levels of English proficiency by pairing students who were fluent with second language students in the classroom.

Increasing Students' Awareness of Diversity

Hall (1992) noted that individuals from different racial and ethnic backgrounds have subtle variations in the ways they communicate, differences of which those from other cultures may be unaware. In an increasingly diverse learning environment, teachers and learners must recognize differences in order to promote effective communication. In Dr. Wang's course, the opportunity to work and talk with a partner or in a group setting in the classroom permitted a recognition and discussion of these differences.

Dr. Wang discovered that using examples to illustrate a point or an abstract idea has a twofold application in a culturally and generationally diverse classroom. Examples that are culture- and generation-specific to the instructor or class members can be used to hold students' attention and arouse their interest and cultural curiosity. Additionally, using culture- and generation-specific examples can open a forum for questions and experiences regarding communication. Examples that may not be culture- or generation-specific recognize the present commonality and facilitate students' understanding of course materials.

Facilitating Group Collaboration and Communication

Dr. Wang encouraged students in both sections to work in collaborative groups throughout the semester. Some of the activities occurred during class time. Others required students' collaboration after class, in the computer lab or other locations. A group is more likely to be high functioning if members are able to develop a "comfort zone" that holds the group together. In these classrooms, giving students sufficient latitude to form groups through choice and to explore methods of collaboration provided a natural "comfort zone."

The instructor needs to monitor teamwork to assure its productivity. Groups that have conflicting opinions or communication problems need more attention. Instead of eliciting compromise as a solution, students should be encouraged to resolve the conflicts through negotiation and rational debate (Derry, Gance, Gance, & Schlager, 2000; Mercer, 1995). In this way, members of the group will achieve a better understanding of the topics being discussed, and debate as a form of communication can be established and practiced as part of the classroom culture. Although social constructivists (Derry et al., 2000; Mercer, 1995) have argued that negotiation and rational debate are conduits toward active and discovery learning, groups need to make timely decisions and deliver projects within time constraints. The instructor's strategic intervention can help groups reach consensus.

Assessment Methods

Dr. Wang conducted classroom-based research while implementing the strategies just mentioned. In addition to the incoming student survey, the outside evaluator also conducted an online end-of-semester survey (app. B). This survey assessed students' learning gains by asking them to rate their self-perceived technological skills as presented in the course. The survey also elicited students' attitudes about the "Technologies for Teachers" curriculum, including balance of individual work and teamwork, the point values of the different activities, and the potential relevance of the course for others.

A semi-structured reflection survey (app. C) was distributed to the two sections by email during the ninth week of the semester. The survey elicited students' voluntary reflections on intercultural and intergenerational issues. It also asked questions about their perceptions concerning the efficiency and effectiveness of classroom communication and collaboration. The fifteen responses to the email survey produced limited, but interesting, results regarding students' awareness of generational and cultural diversity. Written reflections regarding students' perceptions of collaborative group work related to three major themes: (a) attitudes toward learning tasks, (b) collaborative processes in group work, and (c) expressed desire to continue to work with the group.

Finally, the researcher (also the instructor) used her own participant observation reports that depict data concerning communication and interactions in the classroom. In her notes, she also related data concerning task orientation and student engagement. The structure of the class, a combination of instructor presentation and students' hands-on activities, made Dr. Wang's observations possible. She took notes during the students' in-section group activities and wrote reflective memos of classroom communication after sessions. For sessions that involved group collaboration in completing class projects, Dr. Wang also wrote reflections on the process and results of group work.

Results

Dr. Wang found that *diversity served as a motivator* for the students in Section 2, facilitating *interaction dynamics*. Diversity awareness also impacted the *communication* in the more diverse classroom, influenced *group collaboration,* and affected *learning outcomes*. Excerpts from the collected data evidence these results.

Diversity as Motivator

The context and content of the learning pursuit are central to the results. Unsolicited student email and face-to-face comments provide tangible evaluations of Dr. Wang's success in building a supportive learning environment. Students in both sections felt that the instructor had maintained a respectful classroom environment in which a sense of teamwork and community were attained.

Once a supportive learning environment is formed in a diverse classroom, diversity can function as a motivator to promote students' engagement in learning activities. Beginning in week 3, the classroom atmosphere of the two sections varied. Section 2 was rarely quiet, a finding consistent with the literature on collaborative classrooms. Students frequently asked questions during instructor presentations, moved around the room to search for group activity partners, and interacted with members both within and outside their groups. Conversely, the students in Section 1 initiated fewer interactions during the instructor presentation, chose to stay in their seats and work with others in nearby seats for group activities, and limited their interactions with fellow students to those in their seated group. Consequently, the in-class projects (e.g., a PowerPoint presentation on motivating students, an online lesson plan) produced and submitted by Section 2 evidenced more input from other students in their section. The resulting presentations in Section 2 engaged the interest of more students in the classroom as well. A great majority of Section 2 students' projects and presentations exceeded the instructor's expectations.

An examination of portfolio projects submitted at week 3 also revealed differences between the two sections. Students' learning outcomes, shown in point averages, were higher for the Section 2 students (Wang & Folger, in progress) than for the Section 1 students.

According to previous research (e.g., Chapman, Selvarajah, & Webster, 1999; Laurel, 1991; Wang, Rossett, & Wangemann, 2002), learner engagement in tasks leads to better performance due to increased concentration and motivation. The high frequency of interactions in Section 2 of Dr. Wang's class indicated closer interpersonal relationships among the students and promoted an increased level of engagement in in-class activities.

Increased Diversity Awareness

The contrast of students' interaction dynamics, engagement, and learning outcomes in the two sections suggests that student diversity awareness played an important role. Because of the nonobligatory nature of the instrument, only three Section 1 students and five Section 2 students responded to the email survey on diversity awareness. Four themes emerged from the lengthier responses of the Section 2 students: (a) respect for Dr. Wang's capacity, knowledge, and dedication to teaching; (b) sympathy with the challenges of teaching in a foreign country; (c) enjoyment of the intergenerational and intercultural diversity in the classroom; and (d) appreciation of the instructor's cultural background. The following comments from the survey illustrate that the Section 2 students who responded were culturally curious and very much aware of the generational and cultural diversity of the section.

- "I am 42, and am very aware of the differing generations in any classroom I am in. I am aware that I am old enough to be the mother to many of the students I study alongside. And I am very aware I am much older than many of the people—especially you—that I am actually learning from. I am happy to say I have observed that the university classroom—and our classroom—is filled with people of many generations, many ages. I have become entirely comfortable in each of my classrooms, finding that I am not so "old," but have peers of many ages older and younger than myself. I am also very comfortable learning from someone younger than myself . . ."

- "Derry, my devout neighbor, likes hanging around me. He is much older than I. He also expressed personally that he felt comfortable working with me, because of his limited computer experience. In other words, he feels comfortable enough that we can work together . . ."
- "I am an ABC (American Born Chinese). I am not afraid to speak up and speak out loud and clear. . . . Remember, in America, it's common for people to be critical of issues, to be able to express criticism. . . . It's very democratic and needless to say very American."

Section 1 students' responses were shorter and focused on fewer themes. The two identified themes were (a) Dr. Wang's position as a role model for Asian American students and (b) lack of recognition of classroom diversity. Excerpts from the email responses portray these themes.

- "I too was born in the 70s, so I don't sense any intergenerational gaps between us. If anything I feel more comfortable around you to ask questions and to participate."
- "No, I don't feel there is much of a generation gap. I have not looked closely but I think everyone is within about 10 or 12 years of age."

Impact of Diversity Awareness on Collaboration

For grading purposes, all students were required to submit a one- to two-page reflection on their collaborative process (see app. C). These written reflections were completed and turned in at the end of the semester. The students' reflections were triangulated with the participant-observer data on the collaboration process.

The reflections reveal that Section 2 students' collaborations were motivated more by common interest and that Section 1 students just collaborated in order to complete assignments. Not surprisingly, Section 2 produced a higher quantity and quality of group work, in the LTCA as well as in other projects. The ways in which the groups collaborated and their expressed interest in future collaboration reveals members' attitudes toward each other. Here is some of the relevant data.

Attitudinal Differences

In Section 1, 85 percent of the students took on group projects such as LTCA because they needed more points, and they tended to work with classmates who lived nearby. In other words, the selection of teammates was based on convenience. By contrast, 80 percent of Section 2 students chose to work on the LTCA projects because the topics were interesting. Their selection of teammates was based on expertise and acquaintance. Dr. Wang recorded the following conversation with a group member in Section 2.

> *Dr. Wang:* So how did you decide to work on Greek culture?
> *Tony:* Emily teaches art history and I lived in Europe two years.
>   We are both interested in European culture, and this topic
>   is related to Emily's teaching.

Collaborative Group Communication Processes

Section 2 students reported more meaning negotiation and emotional engagement in their collaborative groups. One student wrote: "at times, we disagree with our ways in cooperative learning. The good thing is that we express our view points loudly and with humor!" This reflects an uninhibited manner of communication, based on a strong social bond. They did not argue about their grades, since "we all participated based upon our own given talents and perspective." By contrast, some of the Section 1 groups were collegial during the work process but were concerned about some of the group members who tended to take advantage of others' work, which students termed "free bus riding."

Continuing Relationships

Section 2 students expressed their desire to sustain a postcourse relationship, seeking opportunities to collaborate in other projects. Linda reflected on her group collaboration on the LTCA project, "we'd like to continue working on the Rainforest WebQuest in the next few months, even though the class has ended and we have got our 'A'(s)."

Impact of Diversity Awareness on Classroom Interactions

Students influenced each other through classroom interaction. In Section 2, this interaction resulted in a higher level of motivation and more positive attitudes toward the course. In addition, groups that had strong morale consolidated and supported individual efforts to achieve goals. According to Dr. Wang's observation of the classroom, Section 2 students interacted more often and at a more complex level during class time. They helped each other to understand course content, recalled commands and procedures, and troubleshot technical problems.

One student reflected on how her group survived the rigors and challenges provided in the course. Her observation follows.

> I know [*sic*] Anna and Lilly over the last two semesters but we really had no reason for real collaboration before this class. The social network was essential to maintain sanity in this class. If not for the challenges, frustrations and travails presented by this course, I believe that we most likely would have remained passing acquaintances. Instead we (like soldiers in combat) developed the "us against the course" attitude. We buoyed each other up and encouraged each other.

In addition, students' reflection on group activities indicated that Section 2 students were more involved in collective reasoning, in that they constantly expressed different opinions and attempted to reach consensus through negotiation and debate. Strong social bonds served as the foundation for the freedom with which they conducted their discussions. From the social constructivist perspective (Derry et al., 2000; Edwards & Mercer, 1987; Mercer, 1995), negotiation and debate are valuable processes for students' knowledge acquisition and cognitive growth.

Impact of Diversity Awareness on Group Collaboration

Cultural and generational diversity in these classrooms could have been an obstacle for effective learning. In Section 2, in particular, the instructor and students used their diversity to develop a supportive learning environment. Dr. Wang provided the opportunity for students to form groups based on their own criteria. As a consequence, some of the groups had members of similar backgrounds, while others reflected the diversity of the section. The groups discovered their own ways of communication and collaboration. One homogenous group member recounted:

> Because we were a bit older than some students, we had the same general disposition and approach so we had that comfort zone. . . . it helped our communication. But basically it was the shared diffi-

culties that required us to stick together for support and sanity through a very challenging course.

In contrast, another group reported that they formed their group based on the strength of each member in designing, developing, researching, or gathering information. The members disregarded age and ethnicity when looking for collaborators. They formed a group that had large intervals among members' ages and represented different cultural backgrounds. Nevertheless, Jennifer said: "I do not recall any incidents where there were miscommunications due to age or cultural differences. Those specifics had no involvement in our work." David's reflection corroborated Jennifer's. His comments provided an additional insight.

> That's the beauty of effective teachers. Communication skills. When you can express your thoughts and have an open non-judgmental mind, you can achieve anything with a group. Culturally I have always worked with Anglos, Asians, African Americans, and Latinos. This is my culture.

David implied that he is a member of a culture that transcends age and ethnicity, a teacher culture based on effective and open communication.

Impact of Diversity on Learning Outcomes

It seems that diversity was not always an obstacle but motivated students' engagement in learning tasks. In Section 2, the students formed groups that were diverse in both culture and age. They admitted that their different learning styles were reflected in how they approached cooperative learning tasks, for example, but they also agreed that being able to express conflicting opinions openly led to resolution. Resolving conflicts regarding learning tasks clarified their thinking and affected the quality of their work. They recognized intergenerational differences as well but were able to arrange a comfort zone so that experience contributed to their projects as much as did expertise. They also recognized the need to go to extra effort in order to communicate clearly. To explain and feel free to explain points of view based on differences impacted their motivation and attitudes toward the learning opportunities provided in class.

Impact of Diversity on Attitudinal Outcomes

The end-of-semester survey assessed students' attitudes about the "Technologies for Teacher" curriculum. Students were asked to rate their technological skills. Table 2 displays the mean ratings for all eight items by the thirty-seven students.

After the preceding discussion, it is not surprising to find that Section 2 students had a more positive ($p < 0.005$) reaction to the course. Section 2 also had significantly higher ratings ($p < 0.05$) for the instructor's knowledge and skills, the relevance of the course to their teaching situation, and the clarity and sufficiency of feedback received. Students' attitudinal outcomes are related to the level of their engagement and the learning outcomes. This relationship, in fact, has been addressed by other researchers (e.g., Chapman et al., 1999; Hamilton & Ghatala, 1994). Hamilton and Ghatala (1994, p. 417) stated,

> A student's attitudes and motivational orientation influence the degree to which she follows classroom rules and regulations, the academic tasks she chooses, the nature of her involvement in those tasks, and how much energy and persistence she puts into them.

Section 2 students' acknowledgment and use of diverse learning styles and talents contributed to their engagement in learning tasks.

Pedagogical Implications for All Classrooms

We believe that this research has far-reaching implications for teaching in multicultural, generationally diverse classrooms. In this section, we will make suggestions for faculty regarding teaching style, group work, learning environments, and student awareness of diversity. Finally, we

TABLE 2. Students' Reaction to the Course (mean ratings)

Item	Section 1 (N = 19)	Section 2 (N = 18)
Instructor's knowledge/skills	3.8	4.7
Relevance to a real or anticipated teaching situation	3.4	4.4
Variety of activities	3.1	3.7
Balance of individual work and teamwork	3.1	3.6
Challenge (Q20e)	4.0	4.3
Alignment with methods sections (Q20f)	2.9	3.5
Point value of different activities or tasks (Q20g)	1.8	2.4
Clarity/sufficiency of feedback received (Q20h)	2.8	3.6
Mean	3.1	3.8

will recount the effect that the instructional experience in a culturally and generationally diverse classroom had on Dr. Wang's future teaching goals.

Motivation and Attitudes toward Learning

Participant observation notes reveal that the two sections of Dr. Wang's class held different orientations toward task completion and learning. These orientations are shown in questions students asked related to the course assignments. Many Section 1 students asked questions about the accumulation of points—basically, about their grades. One frequently asked question was, "How good does a project need to be in order to get full points?" Section 2 students, too, were concerned about their points, but they also asked more questions about how to improve projects and integrate technology into their teaching.

Other evidence supports Dr. Wang's observations. For instance, publishing Web pages was not required for this introductory course, but five Section 2 students loaded their Web pages on the Internet. One of the LTCA project groups in Section 2 continued to work with an in-service teacher to polish their Rainforest WebQuest, even though the semester had ended and grades were submitted.

In a study of participants' engagement in an online problem-solving environment, Wang et al. (2002) found that engagement is marked by exclamations, meaning negotiation, rational debate, and social talk in participants' interactions. A review of Section 2 students' conversations, as recorded in research notes and email messages, reveals such individual exclamation and group negotiation. The students' remarks indicate their curiosity, interest, confidence, and enthusiasm in the learning process. Additionally, several students sent unsolicited email messages to their instructor, reflecting on learning. In one such email, a student commented: "I truly cannot believe how much I learned in such a short time. . . . it was a great learning experience! You were so brave taking on the challenge of teaching a bunch of people like us with little background and turning us into a group that can go out there and put a page on the web." Table 3 summarizes the students' comments.

Thus, instructors of diverse classrooms should intentionally orient students toward the learning process itself. For instance, they should prompt students to reflect on the effective ways of learning, either through whole-class discussion or individual journaling.

Other Pedagogical Implications

Dr. Wang interacted with the Section 2 students at a more complex social level because of a higher level of acquaintance and more interaction. From their email and face-to-face conversations, Dr. Wang noted that the Section 2 students had definite ideas about what was key to successful teaching. These students supported the professor through comments about (a) the instructor's attitudes and efforts and (b) her characteristics (knowledgeable, enthusiastic, supportive, and patient).

Dr. Wang's major goals for teaching include instilling different modes of thinking, creating intellectual passions, and promoting broader understanding. The scenario described in the following paragraphs, which relates to intercultural and intergenerational communication, helped Dr. Wang expand her goals within the diverse Section 2 framework.

Mark, a student in Section 2, experienced some frustrations with Web page development. He emailed his frustration to Dr. Wang and asked her to change her instruction. An excerpt denotes his concern.

> I am writing you because I am not doing well in class. . . . I am failing right now, not grade-wise, but learning-wise and I don't mean this in any way personal. I just think that we are being given too much work to do with our very busy schedules to spend so much time on these webpages and having little if no success. So, how to solve the problem?
>
> One, the dates of assignments need to be extended; we are trying our best to meet them. Also, you really need to think of our learning as any students. We all have three levels of ability. They are independence, instruction, and frustration. Instruction is what we need, not frustration. Remember, most of us have NO prior knowledge of web page design, none. The only way we will depends on you helping us create it. Research and my own practice support concrete learning methods for establishing prior knowledge or schema. Teaching in small chunks at a time allows instructional success rather than frustration from too many instruc-

TABLE 3. Observations Reflecting Student Engagement

Category	Section 1	Section 2
Unsolicited reflection and comments on teaching and learning	Few unsolicited reflections or comments	Comments as individuals and in group negotiations
Orientation toward learning tasks	Task-oriented, fulfilling course requirements	Learning-oriented, uploading her home page, continuing to polish their group WebQuest
Reflection on learning	No written evidence	Unsolicited email messages

tions that are very unfamiliar. . . . You will use the same amount of time creating a whole class of understanding rather than spending your time answering individual questions. I promise.

On the receipt of this email, Dr. Wang was puzzled and offended by the message. She thought that she had taught the class how to develop Web pages exactly in the ways that Mark suggested. Later, Dr. Wang conversed with Mark and clarified the reasons for his frustration. Subsequently, she incorporated his suggestions into classroom instruction. Dr. Wang changed the pace of instruction, helped students build on prior knowledge, and established a whole-class understanding before moving on to the next topic.

Likewise, students from other countries preparing to be teachers in the United States shared their reservations about teacher-student interactions and Dr. Wang responded. In her notes, Dr. Wang recalled: "Nina mentioned that in Vietnam, students need to look down when they talk to a teacher. She added that now that she is becoming a teacher in the U.S., she might feel a cultural shock when meeting very challenging students." Dr. Wang responded to Nina that she felt the same way: "In China, teachers are considered authorities and deserve full-respect from students."

Another example concerning cultural and generational expectations occurred during a classroom discussion of Halloween. Several of the students in Section 2 were parents of young children and had requested that the class be canceled so that they could take their children "trick-or-treating." Dr. Wang recalled the incident in her notes.

> Several female students requested to cancel the class on Halloween because they need to take their kids to trick-and-treat. So I asked how many people have kids and many held up their hands, including some younger students. So I said, "Please bring your kids' pictures to class next week to prove that you have kids." One lady held up her shirt and showed her belly to me, "Well, you *could* look at my stretch marks!"
>
> I laughed aloud! I found this really amusing, because in China an educated woman will never show people her stretch marks from labor.

From these experiences, Dr. Wang drew three important conclusions. She observed that (a) her own cultural expectations caused her to be offended by Mark's critique of her teaching; (b) students, especially at the graduate level, have expertise, family demands, and expectations that should be considered in her teaching; and (c) age and culture differences can build classroom community if facilitated positively.

Dr. Wang's overarching goals now include not only listening to but also learning from her students in a transitive environment. She is also more aware of the impact that her own cultural expectations of students have on her reactions to critique and suggestions. In addition, Dr. Wang found that differences, both in age and culture, could enrich, rather than complicate, classroom community, especially if she, as the instructor, reflected an open and welcoming attitude to those differences. Dr. Wang's experience implies that faculty born in foreign countries may find it necessary to adopt a more democratic and issue-oriented stance in the classroom, while learning not to take negative remarks personally.

Conclusion

Diversity issues in college classrooms are beginning to be addressed because the growing diversity of the instructor and student populations have made these issues important. In this study, we describe and contrast the cultural and generational diversity in two sections of an educational technology course, noting differences in communication and learning outcomes. The analysis revealed that the wider range of diversity in one of the sections affected students' attitudes, motivations, dynamics of classroom interaction, and group collaboration.

Dr. Wang, as the junior, foreign-born instructor for both sections, noted the influence of her own cultural expectations on class interactions and student response. Being educated in American graduate schools, Dr. Wang dealt with the diversity issue for many years as a foreign student. In this chapter, we have addressed her strategies in facilitating diverse classrooms as an instructor. We have recommended strategies for instructors—in particular, foreign-born instructors—to facilitate communication, learning, and collaboration in diverse classrooms.

In Dr. Wang's course, cultural and generational differences were transcended by dedication to completion of tasks that were seen as worthwhile and applicable to future teaching. In summary, this study suggests that neither student diversity nor faculty diversity is a barrier to effective education; instead, diversity contributes to an environment conducive to an intellectually active learning community. Future research should explore these findings in more depth.

Appendix A
Incoming Student Survey
(items related to the study)

Which statement best describes you: A. I am not yet enrolled in a credential program. . . . B. I am enrolled in a credential program this semester. . . . C. I have my preliminary credential. . . . D. I have my clear credential and am here to update my skills.

Are you teaching or student teaching this semester?

Please rate your skills on the following items from 1 (low) to 4 (high):
• Basic computer operation skills
• File management
• Word processing
• Database management
• Spreadsheets
• Digital graphics
• Presentation software
• E-mail
• Internet
• Web authoring
• Ethical use of technology
• Classroom integration of technology

Appendix B
End-of-Semester Survey
(items related to the study)

Section 1: Please rate your skills on the following items from 1 (low) to 4 (high):
• Basic computer operation skills
• File management
• Word processing
• Database management
• Spreadsheets
• Digital graphics
• Presentation software
• E-mail
• Internet
• Web authoring
• Ethical use of technology
• Classroom integration of technology

Section 2: Please rate your perceptions on the following items from 1 (low) to
   4 (high)
• Instructor's knowledge/skills
• Relevance of the course to a real or anticipated teaching situation
• Variety of class activities conducted in the course
• Balance of individual work and teamwork
• Challenge of the course
• Point value of different activities or tasks
• Clarity/sufficiency of feedback received from the instructor

Appendix C
Semi-Structured Reflection

If you have a few minutes, would you please reflect on the following:
1. The intercultural issues you have observed during this semester.
      For example, do I teach the same way as teachers from your own culture?
      What are the cultural things you have learned from this class? etc.
2. The intergenerational issues you felt that you have with other students.
      I was born in the 70s in China, and grew up as the "young pioneer" gen-
      eration. How about you? How about the other students? Do you feel there
      is a generation gap between us?
3. How do you feel about your experience in your collaboration with others
   in the class, such as:
   • What are the projects you have collaborated on?
   • What brought you together to collaborate on your projects?
   • What are the ways you used to communicate and understand the projects
      and how to complete them?
   • Did you experience any mis-communication because of your age and
      cultural difference?
   • Any other thoughts you would like to share with me. Feel free to elab-
      orate.

Notes

   The authors acknowledge and thank Dr. Bernie Dodge for his coordina-
tion of the "Technologies for Teachers" course and for his leadership in the
LTCA projects. We also thank Dr. Marcie Bober for her generous sharing of the
LTCA survey data and analysis. Their endeavors have made this study possible.

   Research Paradigm. In qualitative research, researchers establish credibility
through prolonged engagement, persistent observation, and triangulation. All
three of these criteria are present within the methods of this study. As a participant-observer, Dr. Wang recorded written observations, participants' email
discussion and reflection, and artifacts participants developed in the course. All
of this was done over a sixteen-week period and at regular intervals. Addi-

tionally, the voluntary email interview questions provided a "member check" regarding the ongoing outcomes.

In the interpretive paradigm, the knower and known are inextricably intertwined. It is evident that Dr. Wang's perspective is influenced by her own background as a learner and an instructor. Dr. Wang's background was extensively addressed, so that the reader of this study might judge the effect. In fact, important findings in the study are linked to Dr. Wang's background. To broaden the research perspective, so that the researchers' "thinking would be informed by the data" (Bogdan & Biklen, 1998, p. 34), Dr. Wang requested that the coinvestigator (Dr. Folger) be primarily responsible for analyzing the narrative data. Ongoing analysis of the narrative data, Dr. Wang's observations, participant reflections, and course artifacts combined to increase the trustworthiness of the study. However, the nature of this study—action research within the interpretive paradigm—dictates how or whether to control for biases. We encourage future researchers to explore the effect of researcher bias when conducting classroom-based research.

Additional Resources

Publications

Alger, J. R. (1998, Spring). Leadership to recruit and promote minority faculty: Start by playing fair. *Diversity Digest*. Retrieved June 20, 2002 from <http://www.diversityweb.org/digest/sp98/faculty.html>.

    One of the most challenging issues facing diversity leaders is the task of recruiting and retaining a diverse faculty body. In this article, Jonathan Alger suggests some starting points for facing this challenge—for instance, ensuring that existing recruitment criteria are applied with a broad enough perspective so that each individual's true contributions to the learning environment at the university are fully and fairly taken into account.

Antonio, A. L. (1999, Winter). Faculty of color and scholarship transformed: New arguments for diversifying faculty. *Diversity Digest*. Retrieved June 20, 2002 from <http://www.diversityweb.org/digest/w99/diversifying .html>.

    This article made strong arguments for diversifying faculty. Using data from a nationally representative database developed from a 1995 faculty survey conducted at the University of California, Los Angeles, Antonio examined how faculty of color and white faculty differ in their perceptions and practice of scholarship. Data were collected regarding faculty work behaviors, uses of different types of pedagogy, personal goals, professional goals, and goals faculty hold for undergraduate education.

Barringer, F. (1993). *When English is a foreign language for college teachers* (2nd ed.). San Francisco: Jossey-Bass.

Eddy, W. (2000, Fall). Race, gender, and faculty work lives: Data from the University of Michigan. *Diversity Digest*. Retrieved June 2002 from <http://www.diversityweb.org/digest/f00/analysis.html>.

The University of Michigan conducted a research survey to assess what aspects of the faculty experience contributed to productivity and satisfaction. The research team sought to answer the question, How does the university help faculty succeed, and how might the university enhance professional development, satisfaction, and retention? The survey, mailed to faculty at the institution, included questions on climate, organizational structure, policies, resources, workload, productivity, family work-life issues, career satisfaction, and retention. The report found that both women faculty and faculty of color are less satisfied about their experiences of being faculty members. To see the entire study, go to <http://www .umich.edu /~cew/research.html>.

Gainen, J., & Robert, B. (Eds.). 1993. *Building a diverse faculty*. San Francisco: Jossey-Bass.

Humphreys, D. (1999, Winter). Moving beyond myths: New book examines faculty of color in the academy. *Diversity Digest*. Retrieved June 2002 from <http://www.diversityweb.org/digest/w99/myths.html>.

This article is a review of a book titled *Bittersweet Success: Faculty of Color in Academe*. The book's authors draw on scores of existing studies and their own qualitative and quantitative research to document the realities of the current job market and working conditions for faculty of color in higher education. The section "Facts about Faculty Diversity" provides convincing statistics on the need for improving faculty diversity.

Maimon, E. P., & Garcia, M. (1997, Fall). Transforming institutions: The Importance of faculty diversity. *Diversity Digest*. Retrieved June 2002 from <http://www.diversityweb.org/digest/f97/transforming.html>.

This article captures a dialogue between the two authors on the issues of diversity. Garcia, a diversity and multiculturalism scholar, believes that a diverse faculty provides students an opportunity to learn from many different perspectives and voices. In addition, diversification makes use of strengths from a variety of sources and enables different perspectives to enter into dialogue to find solutions.

Schoem, D., Frankel, L., Zuniga, X., & Lewis, E. A. (Eds.). (1993). *Multicultural teaching in the university*. Westport, CT: Praeger.

Smith, D. G. (1996). *Achieving faculty diversity: Debunking the myths*. Washington, DC: Association of American Colleges and Universities.

Organizations

Society for Information Technology and Teacher Education (SITE). The Society for Information Technology and Teacher Education (<http://aace.org/conf/site/default.htm>) is an international association of individual teacher educators and affiliated organizations of teacher educators in all disciplines who are interested in the creation and dissemination of knowledge about the use of information technology in teacher education and faculty/staff development. The society seeks to promote research, scholarship, collaboration, exchange, and support among its membership and to actively foster the development of new national organizations where a need emerges. SITE is the only organization that has as its sole focus the integration of instructional technologies into teacher education programs.

10
Understanding Science: Social Construction and Student Engagement

Randy Yerrick

What is this thing called science? It has long been believed by many outsiders to the scientific community, including many of our students, that science consists of fixed theories and facts and provides objective measures for observing and studying the world—with methods based on nonsubjective standards for research and practice. There are many reasons that individuals hold this view. Generally, laypeople rely on their science educations in school, and they are left to judge science in the world solely based on published articles and public announcements (King & Brownell, 1966; Mink, 1987). This pristine view has come under intense scrutiny by some in the past decades, however.

The purpose of this chapter is to use the work of experts to unpackage some of the beliefs that our students, and other laypeople, may hold about the sciences and to discuss ways in which our diverse students can be allowed into, and enjoy, the messy, socially constructed practices that are characteristic of the building of scientific knowledge.

Early Critiques of Science as Rational and Given

For many years, forward-looking scientists and others have challenged the view that science is rational, objective, and pristine and that scientific theories are somehow immutable (see, e.g., Barnes & Shapin, 1979; Chalmers, 1982; Kuhn, 1970; Mulkay, 1975). Early in the twentieth century, one of science's premier spokespeople, Werner Heisenberg (1933), noted that nothing could be observed without being changed by the simple act of observation. Others have completed studies of the nonobjective nature of science and the building of scientific theories. Barnes (1982) argues, "these studies point out that every theory has well recognized anomalies from the moment it is proposed [and] . . . scientists tend to celebrate experiments which have 'verified' theoretical predictions and not those that have falsified them" (p. 40).

Karl Popper (1963) noted that scientific theory does not arise solely from objective observation or logical reasoning. He viewed the development of theory as a process of attempting to falsify competing positions. Thomas Kuhn (1970), famous for his discussions of "paradigm shift," pointed out the need for the scientific community to make "rediscoveries," thus supporting Popper's thesis. He used as an example the fact that the scientific community had to "rediscover" oxygen on three different occasions prior to La Voisier's being credited with the achievement.

However, all of these scientists were ahead of their times. Certainly, their arguments were not translated into students' classrooms and textbooks—or into the discussions of science in the media.

Poststructural Interpretations of the Construction of Scientific Knowledge

Later, it became the task of other scientists, and sociologists of science, to continue to examine scientific practices as messy, human, and culture laden. In this section, I will discuss some of their findings.

Explorations into Scientific Laboratories and the Development of Theory

In recent accounts, the scientific laboratory and other data-gathering contexts have been viewed as very human arenas where theory is developed in a remarkably subjective manner and where all of the characteristics of other human institutions (competition, jealousy, etc.) flower (see Traweek 1988; Latour & Woolgar, 1986; Woolgar, 1988). Millar (1989, p. 1) points out:

> Social studies of science have produced an extensive body of work looking closely at scientific theory change, at the processes of development, negotiation, and acceptance of new knowledge. Sociologists, in particular, have rejected the older, idealized accounts and reconstructions of the scientific method and have undertaken detailed studies of historical and contemporary methods of science.

One approach to this research, in the laboratories and elsewhere, is through scientific discourses, the ways in which insiders discuss and present science as they develop and publish their work. Jay Lemke (1990), a former nuclear physicist turned sociolinguist, found the following to be the case.

> How does a scientific theory become established? Historically, a new theory always begins as somebody's way of talking about a problem. This person argues for the theory, or someone else does, to convince others. A faction appears that lobbies for the theory in many ways: by research papers, by experimental tests of predictions, by talks at scientific meetings, by writing books and textbooks, teaching students, and so on. In the end, a community of people, and the most influential, the most powerful people within that community, determine which of the theories gets published most, used most, taught most. (p. 125)

Traweek (1988) describes how a few scientists established and maintained their status within a group of high-energy particle physicists who thrived on winning. They planned strategies against their foes with reckless abandon, using acts of bravado and personal attacks against other scientists. Not surprisingly, the status of group members was not derived solely from intellectual achievements but was often based on the power of their discourses, as well as on their gender and ethnicity.

It is not unexpected, then, that Latour and Woolgar (1986) claim that scientific work is completed largely by building arguments to persuade or convince other scientists through competition—a process that forces data (and publications) to fit the particular theoretical outcomes and arguments desired. In other words, the development of theory through laboratories and elsewhere entails competition and power struggles. And the final products, such as publications, cover up these struggles—the chaotic, and very human, means by which theories are developed, challenged, and revised.

School Science Remains Virtually Unchanged

Despite these findings, school science in many contexts continues to consist of the transmission of knowledge to passive students, armed with considerable memorizing skills, of collected "facts," on which examinations are based. Though this approach misrepresents what occurs in scientific worlds, many instructors continue to separate the social contexts of science and the individuals who have made that science from the "facts" or "immutable theories" that appear in textbooks and are memorized by students for tests. Even when historical debates are presented to students, the colorful, impassioned, and power-driven controversies are usually overlooked.

Continuing in this vein, Duschl (1990) points out that scientific theory and "fact" have been presented in classrooms as "epistemologically flat." Students are not able to discern the human factors in theory development, and they are not introduced to the core underpinnings of evidence that lead to a particular theory. As undergraduates, at least, students are not considered sufficiently adept to test theories or to understand that competing explanations are available. Millar (1989, p. 8) argues:

> The outcome is a rhetoric of school science which is an uneasy amalgam, overemphasizing the ideas of science . . . and underemphasizing science as a body of consensually accepted knowledge. . . . The pedagogical danger is that teaching becomes an arid business of rote learning of standard facts, theories and methods. The epistemological danger is that this makes science look like infallible received knowledge. We need to find a way to avoid these dangers. (p. 8)

Millar (1989, p. 54) distills the lengthy discussions on the philosophy of science—bringing into focus core dilemmas implicit in teaching science in schools. Citing Barnes (1982) she identifies the central question that is raised by this stilted approach: "If teaching science is really the transmission of a consensually accepted knowledge, then what is its value in a student's general education?"

In addition to masking the very human, contested, and social nature of science, school curricula often fail to account for the students' daily experiences. Schwab (1902) points out that a necessary component for describing science in the classroom should be knowledge of the students' everyday worlds and the development of connections between these contexts and the science being presented. Though Schwab (1962), Bruner (1960), Dewey (1902), and others have argued over the years that learning should begin with the students' experience, very little has changed in most classroom curricula, particularly when students are novices.

Another, related problem with most curricula is that science is presented as a principally masculine endeavor, a mastery of "man" over nature. Kelly (1985) speaks of science as inherently masculine and patriarchal, representing a male-dominated society in which knowledge of science represents power. Students read about the work of Galileo and Sir Isaac Newton, who, because of their affluence and privilege (and because someone else was cooking the food and washing the clothes), were afforded the time, access, and opportunity to develop natural philosophy. There were fewer opportunities for female scientists then— and this remains true now, for schools often steer young women students away from the sciences and into the humanities or education.

It is sometimes argued that such representations of science simply reflect the natural differences and abilities of different genders. Traweek (1988), when studying high-energy physicists, described some of the arguments and assumptions held by these men: that women are unable to succeed in the rigorous and abstract world that these scientists inhabited.

It must be noted, however, that these opinions about the masculine place of science and science education have not always been held by all educators, or scientists, in North America. During the American colonial period, and later, men were prepared for "higher education" in the humanities and classics (Latin and philosophy). Women, on the other hand, were the scientists. Woody (1929), in his history of women's education, points out that natural philosophy, astronomy, chemistry, and botany were among the ten subjects most frequently taught in seminaries for women between 1722 and 1871. At the turn of the twentieth century, when Horace Mann's common-school movement was gaining strong support, science was thought to be more a practical subject than a rational and abstract one. In North Carolina schools, women were prepared to be "Southern belles," but their education included science and mathematics because these subjects would support their domestic skills of cooking and budgeting (Tolley, 1996).

Then the tide turned. Especially since the launching of Sputnik (1957), science has enjoyed masculine privilege, and the educational elite have been in charge. Scientific subjects have been a preserve of only the "best" (often white male) students. For disadvantaged secondary school learners in "lower-track" science classes, the education offered often limits their access to science majors in college (Oakes, 1985; Anyon, 1981). This raises issues of equity, of course, and results in the fact that even fewer nonwhite males than women are found in the science professions. Not surprisingly, disparities in science opportunities fall along economic, gender, and cultural lines (Oakes, 1990, 1985; Oakes & Guiton, 1995; Ogbu, 1978; Delpit, 1988).

In advanced high school and early college classes, the long lists of terminology to be memorized (as in biology, e.g.) and the extensive problem sets requiring difficult calculation and mathematical knowledge promote inequity by sorting out only those students who have mastered the core elements. These approaches also serve the purpose of convincing less-prepared students that science is something not everyone is able to master. These factors, combined with the previously discussed problem of disconnecting science from everyday experience, result in disillusionment and often failure on the part of many diverse students and women (Goodlad, 1984; Duschl, 1990; McNeil, 1986; Anyon, 1981). Some argue that science is taught this way because the scientific community wants to remain white, male, and exclusive, to limit access and stratify the workforce (Apple, 1979; Bowles & Gintis, 1976). Thus, the effects of promoting a constrained, abstract, fragmented, elitist, and misrepresentative version of school science in American culture have been major.

Where Can We Begin with New Curricula?

How can curricula at every level be revised to be more inclusive and more representative of the true nature of the sciences?

Recognize Similarities between Students and Scientists

Educators can begin by recognizing that the differences between scientists and students are one of degree and not of kind. How are the two groups alike?

- Both are actively making hypotheses about the world.
- Both bring prior knowledge and understanding to test their hypotheses, though scientists have been trained to present this knowledge in literature reviews and to examine it in light of its epistemological merits.
- Both examine their hypotheses; however, scientists have ready-made, discipline-specific theoretical and methodological frameworks with which they work.

What does this mean for the classroom? How can science faculty engage students in real scientific problems that relate to their life experiences? How can they actively solicit student hypotheses about everyday phenomena and engage them in posing and carrying out experimental designs to collect data that informs their hypotheses? How can students learn the processes of construing and refining knowledge—

thus learning how and why a scientific theory gains ground? In the section that follows, I will provide practical suggestions from my own experience and that of other experts in science education.

Develop Pedagogical Strategies

Strategy 1: Articulate Specific Content, Process, and Assessment Goals

Goals for the classroom are often developed over time from questions that instructors ask themselves. These include

- What are the major aspects of my discipline that excite and that I want to impart to my students?
- How do I impart these processes, values, and skills to students so that they take responsibility for their learning and use their prior knowledge?
- How can I incorporate the central tenets and processes of my research into the classroom?
- How do I know whether the students are involved? Whether they are engaged in real scientific work?
- How can I help the students to reflect on their work and the work of the sciences?
- And, perhaps most central, how can I assist my students to think like scientists using hypotheses and data that they understand?

Before we move on, it is important to review the "thinking issue" (see also Johns, this volume). I have attended many faculty workshops to improve university education. One of the common complaints I hear from faculty was summed up by a concerned scientist attending one of the institutes.

> Students these days simply don't know how to think. I'm lucky if they do the reading! They certainly don't take time to double-check their work or analyze it for its integrity. I give them a pop quiz now and then to be sure they did their assignments, but I don't dare ask them to think for themselves!

If thinking, not memorization, is really what faculty want from their students, then they need to make their expectations clear to students, choose appropriate problems, encourage hypothesizing, and give opportunities for practice and student reflection—and test students on this thinking as well.

Strategy 2: Encourage the Understanding of Science as Process and Debate

Duschl (1990) argues that one of the central responsibilities in teaching science is to focus on the importance of evaluating the substantive merits of scientific theories. He argues that not every theory is given equal merit and that "fringe theories" often push too hard on the conventional ideas of the sciences. Of course, some of these theories are tested and seen as hoaxes (e.g., Pons and Fleischman's cold fusion [Close, 1990] or Von Daniken's [1970] claim of extraterrestrial life visiting earth). However, other theories, many of which begin as someone's "off-the-wall" idea, become integrated into scientific constructs through the process of argument, testing, scrutiny, and refutation. Some are accepted because they are proposed by those in power (see the earlier quote of Lemke), but they are also interrogated and refuted by new groups who attain ascendancy. Delpit (1988) and others have argued that making the rules of power, participation, processes, and publication explicit to students assists them in understanding that science is evolving and only temporarily consensual.

One very effective procedure for developing this understanding in science classes involves integrating real-world experience and concepts presented in the classroom. After a lecture in which a concept is presented, the instructor can ask students to work together to pose hypotheses from real-world experiences relating to the concept. Then, in groups, they can work on how such a hypothesis could be tested, what data would have to be collected, and what methods should be used. Students should be given opportunities to test their hypotheses and to begin to construct theories about why they get certain results from the tests. The groups can then meet to debate which theory might be most tenable and why (Duschl, 1990).

However, students also need to explore the theories propounded by the scientific community. Thus, student groups can take a theory that is presented in their textbooks or lecture and interrogate it with questions such as the following (adapted from Duschl, 1990, p. 96).

- What are the background knowledge claims of this theory? (Then they can identify the core concepts.)
- On what empirical data is the theory based? (They can then also discuss what methodology was used to test the data.)
- How does this theory fit with other theories that are related to it? (This helps students to get a historical perspective on theory development.)

Studying the constant evolution of theory based on refutation, data, and other factors is central to students' understanding of what science is and why it's important for all citizens to understand its human, as well as data-driven, nature.

Strategy 3: Encourage Students to Integrate Their Beliefs and Life Experience into Hypothesis Testing

Duckworth (1987) argues that as faculty, we need to appreciate "the having of wonderful ideas" that students bring to the classroom. As mentioned earlier, it is their ideas and their questions that can be explored in a classroom on science. My students have brought to the classroom questions such as

- Why do lightbulbs burn out?
- How is music stored on audiotape?
- How did giraffes get long necks?
- Why do people come in different colors?
- What color was Jesus Christ?
- Why do the sun and moon look bigger on the horizon?
- Are the clouds we see day after day made of the same water?

From questions such as these, students can develop hypotheses, select appropriate methodologies, collect data, and, of course, construct theories. From this experience can come discussions of methodology, collective evidence, understanding what evidence counts, and identifying how evidence is used in scientific communities, and by the media, to answer questions.

What else can be done? (See table 1 for other activities.)

TABLE 1

Developing shared expertise	When assigning problem sets or essay responses, students can be given the responsibility of critiquing other students' responses and giving evaluative feedback.
Hypothesis generation	During and after lectures, students can be invited to use the concepts presented in class to make predictions about real-world events.
Experimental design	Once students have posed their hypotheses for explaining commonly observed phenomena, teachers can ask, "How could we test such an idea?" Teachers choose the best design and assign it to the class for homework to return with data.
Theory testing	Students can be asked to debate the competing theories given the available evidence or even to offer the criticism of contemporary fringe theories (Duschl, 1990).

Strategy 4: Encourage Problem Setting

Schon (1983) points out that in real scientific worlds, experts are not given problems to be solved. Rather, *problem setting* is the process that they practice as they observe and attempt to make sense of a situation. It is a process that involves framing the problem and managing the data to turn what appears to be random into a reasonable hypothesis. Lemke (1990, pp. 122–123) says that the way scientists learn to set problems is in "talking to other members of our community, in talking to ourselves, and writing about the issues."

When science is taught as problem setting, hypothesis testing, data gathering, and theory building—as the production of arguments from a set of available evidence, followed by the evaluation of that evidence and the theories that result—students begin to understand the messy, human nature of science and the reasons why consensus is temporary at best.

Strategy 5: Make Scientific Discourses More Accessible

There are other issues to deal with as well, such as the language and discourses of the sciences, which are very different from that of the everyday experience of most of our students. Educators have the problem of bridging the gap between the complex, ideological discourses of the sciences and the equally complex, but different, discourses of their students. We can make the gap between science and the students wider by avoiding the unpackaging of these discourses (Michaels & O'Connor, 1990, p. 24), for ignoring difference often exacerbates the separation between our diverse learners and the scientific worlds that they are attempting to understand. Researchers recommend that we find ways to involve students' cultures and languages in making the connections between their current discourse practices and the discourses of the sciences (Au, 1980; Brice-Heath, 1983; Delpit, 1988).

Conclusion

Encouraging students to use their everyday life experiences, and their own questions, to understand the nature of problem setting and the rest of the scientific process is empowering and motivating. It requires faculty to coach students through the process of evaluating theories (and arguments) on the basis of evidence. It requires faculty to play the multiple roles of observer, participant, and evaluator of knowledge claims. It requires them to insert new evidence to test the theories posited and to help students to see the flaws in their own thinking and problem-solving attempts (Yerrick, Doster, Parke, & Nugent, 2003).

Some of the best work in assisting students in this process has been done by McDermott, Shaffer, and Rosenquist (1996), who have spent two decades researching ways in which commonsense, everyday explanations can conflict with scientific constructions and designing events and scaffolded tasks that engage students in proposing models and testing them with real-world evidence. In their curricula, these practitioners scaffold specific experiences for group collaboration and individual exploration that make available evidence accessible for all group members to debate and use to construct a collective meaning.

As Duschl and others have argued, if students are left to fill in the gaps themselves for what science is and how knowledge is constructed, they can make frequent epistemological mistakes (see Duschl, 1990; Novak & Gowin, 1984; Osborne & Freyberg, 1985; Wittrock, 1986). So they must be guided by experienced scientists in their explorations and their critiques.

The history and philosophy of science tell us that science has come to be understood as a complex, social, and often messy human activity complete with all of the human attributes ascribed to other human endeavors, including power moves, bias, and subjectivity. However, science has also been utilized to promote stratification in society and to privilege only those individuals who come to excel in science in school. It has therefore become important to promote science as it really is practiced among scientists, drawing upon students' life experiences. Teaching science in this way engages and motivates students—much as scientists themselves are motivated.

Of course, accepting these pedagogical recommendations is not without cost. Science students are accustomed to considerable memorization and acceptance of "fact" and thus have difficulty making the transition to more active, inquiry-based learning. For teachers, the move from a traditional transmission model to an approach that is more constructivist is difficult, too, for it requires much more thought to create groups, pose problems, monitor student progress, and critique student-led investigations. All of this requires us to examine our beliefs about the discipline, about ourselves as instructors, and about how we can engage our students.

Additional Resources

Boyer, E. L. (1990). *Scholarship reconsidered: Priorities of the professoriate*. Princeton, NJ: Carnegie Foundation for the Advancement of Teaching.

In a book that caught the imagination of many higher education faculty, Boyer—then president of the Carnegie Foundation for the Advancement of Teaching—questioned the reward system that pushes faculty toward research and away from teaching. Boyer offers a new paradigm of balancing four general areas of scholarship: discovery, integration of knowledge, teaching, and service. While it remains unclear what Boyer meant by a scholarship of teaching, the text helped motivate an important discussion in higher education about how to both value and enhance faculty work in and on teaching.

Cambridge, B. (1999, December.) The scholarship of teaching and learning: Questions and answers from the field. *AAHE Bulletin, 52* (4), 7–10. Available at <http://www.aahebulletin.com/public/archive/dec99f2.asp?pf=1>.

This article offers brief responses to the following questions: "Does scholarly teaching differ from the scholarship of teaching?" "Who does the scholarship of teaching?" "Is this scholarship discipline specific or interdisciplinary?" "What role do students have in this work?" and "How do campuses encourage the scholarship of teaching?" Cambridge is optimistic about the future of the scholarship of teaching: "Although they may not have been acculturated through graduate school or their department's expectations to focus on questions of pedagogy or learning, [many faculty members] have through their teaching posed questions that call for systematic study, questions they really want to answer."

Glassick, C. E., Huber, M. T., & Maeroff, G. I. (1997.) *Scholarship assessed: Evaluation of the professoriate.* San Francisco: Jossey-Bass.

This book is a follow-up to the earlier Boyer volume. The authors examine the changing nature of scholarship in today's colleges and universities. They propose new standards for scholarship and faculty performance, with special emphasis on methods for assessing and documenting effective scholarship.

Huber, M. T. (1999.) Disciplinary styles in the scholarship of teaching: Reflections on the Carnegie Academy for the Scholarship of Teaching and Learning. Paper presented at the Seventh International Improving Student Learning Symposium, Improving Student Learning through the Disciplines, University of York, United Kingdom. Available at <www.carnegiefoundation.org/elibrary/docs/disciplinarystyles.htm>.

This is an important essay for its focus on disciplinary orientations. Huber observes, "Disciplinary styles empower the scholarship of teaching not only by giving scholars a ready-made way to imagine and present their work, but also by giving shape to the problems they choose and the methods they use." Huber also recognizes some limits of the disciplinary focus: "One's own disciplinary style may give direction to one's own work in this new area, but it can also limit one's appreciation of other people's work." And she looks ahead: "One of the big questions now is whether scholars of teaching and learning can fascinate their disciplinary colleagues as much as they fascinate those from other disciplines working in the same vein."

Schwab, J. J. (1978.) Eros and education. In I. Westbury & N. Wilkof (Eds.), *Science, curriculum, and liberal education* (pp. 105–132). Chicago: University of Chicago Press.

In this classic essay, Schwab discusses the purposes and associated challenges of using discussions as an instructional tool in pursuit of a liberal education. He argues that the teacher must simultaneously attend to the student's Eros, while also exposing the student to important content and to "ideas unfolding" (how knowledge is created in a field). Schwab shows the reader what happens when one of these aims is met to the exclusion of the others. The essay offers readers principles for considering their own facilitation of discussions.

Shulman, L. S. (2000.) From Minsk to Pinsk: Why a scholarship of teaching and learning? *Journal of Scholarship of Teaching and Learning, 1*(1), 48–52. Available at <http://titans.iusb.edu/josotl/VOL_1/NO_1/shulman_vol_1_no_1.htm>.

In this essay, Shulman argues for a more inclusive definition of scholarship in higher education. He argues that there are three different reasons for such a redefinition: professional obligations, practical responsibilities, and policy issues. We have, he argues, a professional obligation to be good—perhaps even scholarly—teachers. Pursuing a scholarship of teaching would also help our work: "Such work helps guide our efforts in the design and adaptation of teaching in the interests of student learning" (p. 3). Finally, as accountability and assessment continue to dominate policy discussions about education—both K–12 and higher education—working on a scholarship of teaching will contribute to those policy discussions. Shulman concludes, "A scholarship of teaching and learning supports our individual and professional roles, our practical responsibilities to our students and our institutions, and our social and political obligations to those that support and take responsibility for higher education. We should be making all three journeys . . ." (p. 6).

11
Teaching Mathematics in Our Multicultural World

Swapna Mukhopadhyay and Brian Greer

Mathematics: A Subject with Diversity?

Many people initially would be surprised at finding a chapter on mathematics in a book on teaching and diversity. Natural environments for multicultural education include history, social studies, literature, and the arts; could they also include mathematics? Aren't the rules for multiplying negative numbers, the theorem of Pythagoras, the solution of a quadratic equation, and so on the same the whole world over and fixed for all time? Hersh (1997, p. 9) observes: "Platonism . . . is the most pervasive philosophy of mathematics. . . . The standard version says mathematical entities exist outside space and time, outside thought and matter, in an abstract realm independent of any consciousness, individual or social." From this perspective, the teaching and learning of mathematics are the transmission of immutable truths, making issues of diversity irrelevant.

Problematizing Traditional Views of Mathematics

In recent years, there have been many developments that collectively problematize the preceding perceptions of mathematics and mathematics education, including the following:

- A major shift has occurred within the discipline of mathematics education, which can be summarized by the principle that mathematics is a human activity and, hence, is historically, culturally, and socially embedded. Moreover, a growing number of scholars within mathematics education and from other disciplines are now calling attention to the ethical implications and inherently political nature of mathematics education (e.g., Apple, 1995, 2001; D'Ambrosio, 1999; Skovsmose & Valero, 2001).

- A strong movement within the philosophy of mathematics has rejected Platonism (e.g., Ernest, 1991; Hersh, 1997; Tymoczko, 1986) and argued instead that mathematics is a human construction.
- There have been attacks on the Eurocentric account of the development of mathematics (Joseph, 1992), and mathematical activities found in all cultures have been identified (Bishop, 1988).
- There have been arguments that mathematics is more than academic mathematics—in particular, ethnomathematics, defined as "mathematics which is practiced among identifiable cultural groups, such as national-tribal societies, labor groups, children of a certain age bracket, professional classes, and so on" (D'Ambrosio, 1985, p. 45).

Thus, a very different view of mathematics as a human activity, grounded in practice, has been constructed from a variety of disciplines. This view implies diversity, in that different cultures and different groups within cultures, based on their environmental, social, and cognitive exigencies, have diverse ways of understanding the world through mathematical practices and reasoning. In this chapter, we argue that teaching informed by this perspective affords the possibility of students coming to see mathematics as intellectually ownable and relevant to the lives of all sorts of people, thus addressing diversity in the broadest sense. (See also Yerrick, this volume, for a parallel argument in the sciences.)

"Mathematics for All": The Unfortunate Trend toward Homogeneity in Mathematics Education

Modern mathematics is firmly established as a worldwide, unified discipline, close-knit through global communication and networks of scholars and institutions. Although, both historically and contemporarily, it represents the contributions of many cultures, in the words of D'Ambrosio (1999, p. 145), "mathematics as it is recognized today in academia developed parallel to Western thought (philosophical, religious, political, economical, artistic, and cultural)." Thus, the nature of mathematics as a discipline itself raises questions about cultural and intellectual diversity, part of the wider picture of the unquestioned assumptions of a dominant worldview (Dias, 2001). There is unresolved tension between those who fear the disappearance of cultural diversity as the result of globalization and those who see mathematics as a key component of technological progress that, it is hoped, will bring economic benefits to all (Atweh & Clarkson, 2001; Thomas, 2001).

Both reflecting and reinforcing the homogeneity of mathematics as a discipline, there are strong signs of the convergence of mathematics education in many parts of the world toward a uniform Western model. In response to his question "Is there a world-wide mathematics curriculum?" Usiskin (1999b, p. 226) answers in the negative, yet the relativity of this answer is clear in his statement that "at the broadest level, we are all teaching very much the same ideas, reflecting the commonalities of mathematics" (pp. 225–226). On the other hand, there are a few examples of countries that are attempting to develop mathematics curricula that are culturally and politically appropriate, a prime example being South Africa (Volmink, 1999; see also Skovsmose & Valero, 2001).

The Purposes of Mathematics Education Worldwide: Two Models

To substantiate the contention that there is widespread uniformity in mathematics education worldwide, we present two examples illustrating common answers to the question, What is mathematics education for? The first may be called mathematics education for the reproduction of mathematicians; the second, mathematics education for the training of a technologically and entrepreneurially skilled workforce. As an example of the first, Ebeid (1999) displays examination papers used in Egypt in which one of the questions is: "In an arithmetic sequence the 36th term is zero and the sum of the first n terms is double that of its first five terms. Find n, and hence deduce the sum of 49 terms of this arithmetic sequence starting from the 12th term" (p. 77). All of the other questions deal with similarly decontextualized exercises on various topics. There is not the slightest hint anywhere as to the cultural identity of the students sitting the examination.

As an example of the second model, consider the following statement from the People's Republic of China.

As the economy adapts to information-age needs, workers in every sector must learn to interpret computer-controlled processes.

Most jobs now require analytical rather than merely mechanical skills. So most students need more mathematical ability in school as preparation for their future jobs.

. . . people must deal daily with profit, stock, market forecast, risk evaluation etc. Therefore, mathematics relevant to these economic activities, such as ratio and proportion, operational research and optimization, systematic analysis and decision theory, etc., should be a part of school mathematics education. (Er-Sheng, 1999, p. 58)

The first perspective suggests a pyramid, at the top of which are a few individuals who become mathematicians or use technical mathematics in their work. The second presents mathematics as applicable, but only in the narrow context of serving to create a workforce to be competitive in the technological age. Neither acknowledges the inherently cultural embeddedness of mathematics or hints at the possible relevance of diversity. Indeed, Ebeid (1999, p. 71) explicitly says of mathematics, "For many educators and curricular makers, its content is sought as a culture-free set of intellectual tools needed for the advance of science and technology and in turn as a base for societal growth and development."

The papers of Ebeid and Er-Sheng are included in a section headed "Mathematics for All" in Usiskin, 1999a. What does this slogan mean? Clearly, there are many interpretations. In the examples just cited, it may be interpreted as trying to move more students further up the pyramid ("raising standards") or as trying to produce a higher number of technologically proficient and entrepreneurially minded workers. Often these aims go hand in hand, because it is assumed that the former will facilitate the latter.

NCTM Principles: Still an Assimilation Model

A more balanced vision is presented in *Principles and Standards for School Mathematics* (National Council for Teachers of Mathematics, 2000).

NCTM challenges the assumption that mathematics is only for the select few. On the contrary, everyone needs to understand mathematics. All students should have the opportunity and the support necessary to learn significant mathematics with depth and understanding. There is no conflict between equity and excellence. (p. 5)

Following the comment that "the need to understand and be able to use mathematics in everyday life and in the workplace has never been greater and will continue to increase," the reasons for learning mathematics are listed as "Mathematics for life; Mathematics as a part of cultural heritage; Mathematics for the workplace; Mathematics for scientific and technical communities" (p. 4).

From the perspective of this chapter, however, the NCTM document is disappointing in that, while stressing "the equity principle" (p. 12) and endorsing the rhetoric that "mathematics can and must be learned by all students" (p. 13), little of what it has to say about diversity is not couched in terms of assimilation within a common framework. It is depressing enough that the reality of mathematics education falls short of the idealized vision described by NCTM; it is much more depressing that many of those who control mathematics education do not even share that vision.

Theoretical (and educational) Alternatives

A key question (perhaps *the* key question) in mathematics education is, Why do so many people fear and dislike mathematics? Here is one answer, from a Bronx school (Wilgoren, 2001, p. A1).

> It is a morning ritual. . . . [The teacher] stalks across his classroom, scowls at his sixth-grade students and barks the same simple question: "What is this?" "This is math," they respond. "I don't have to like it to pass it. I don't have to enjoy it to learn it. I don't have to love it to understand it. But I must, and I will, master it."

Negative attitudes toward mathematics are common. Not only do students question the usefulness and relevance of school mathematics, but they also do not hesitate to express deep apathy toward the subject. Along with the questions, "Why do I have to learn this?" and "When will I need it?" it is not uncommon to hear phrases such as "Math is boring," "It is full of rules to be memorized," and "It makes no sense," followed by "Math is hard, I do not like it, I cannot do it, I am no good at it." Outside of school, we hear much the same statements; unfortunately, most people in our society do not view themselves as mathematically literate.

Mathematics for the Few: Disempowering Diverse Students

The problem is exacerbated in groups that typically underperform in mathematics as evaluated by test scores—in particular, Latinos (see, e.g., Ortiz-Franco & Flores, 2001; Townsend, 2001) and African

Americans (see Martin, 2001; Moody, 2001). According to Ortiz-Franco and Flores (2001, 251), while mathematics achievement levels of Latino students increased over the period 1972–1992, "the gains . . . were at the computational level and their performance in applications, reasoning, and problem solving needs to be improved." Given demographic trends, they point out, "The United States cannot afford to have a Latino population that is math illiterate." Townsend (2001) points to the impact of cultural differences, in particular suggesting that the emphasis on cooperation that is characteristic of Hispanic culture is incompatible with the individualism characteristic of mainstream White culture.

Moody (2001, p. 258) cites Ogbu's (1986) statement that "African Americans usually resist the dominant group's ideology by resisting school and the ideology of school because they view schooling as characteristic of the dominant group." Moody concludes that well-intended attempts at reform are "undermined by schooling practices that reduce African-American students' access to mathematical power" (p. 274).

Secada (1992, p. 654) suggests the following provocative "thought experiment."

> Assume that the existing curriculum is out of balance, misaligned, full of trivial facts, structured in ways that have little to do with how real people actually learn and perform mathematics, and out of touch with the mathematics people will need to live and function in our society. . . .
>
> Then consider the logical outcomes of such a state of affairs: disengagement from the tasks that make up school mathematics, low achievement, unwillingness to take additional courses, and dropping out of school. Furthermore, consider the populations that have been characterized in these ways . . . [the] poor and ethnic minorities.
>
> Consider, then, the possibility that their achievement patterns and the failure of so many interventions have been indicators of what the reform movement has finally realized. If so, then the label of incompetence generally applied to such students must be questioned and replaced. What should be puzzling is not their low achievement, but the social forces that coerced other students to forgive and to learn in spite of such a sorry state of affairs.

As we look at the current situation in mathematics education, we see very little cause for optimism. Despite all the efforts for reform, there seems no prospect of a population that will generally feel more positively toward mathematics or have mathematical competence beyond the most trivial. The aspiration for "mathematics for all," emasculated in a control system governed by test scores, is unlikely to succeed in any meaningful sense. Ironically, in relation to the supposed need for a technologically trained workforce, it may not matter. As Apple (1992, p. 421) pointed out, "the important thing is that technical/administrative knowledge is *available for use,* not necessarily that large numbers of people have it."

"Mathematics of All": The Case for Diversity

In contrast to the perception of mathematics as acultural, abstract, and homogeneous, we argue that mathematics is a cultural construction emerging from, and framing, people's lived experience and, consequently, that it is both as universal and as diverse as other forms of cultural construction.

In addressing the question that is the title of his book "What Is Mathematics, Really?" Hersh (1997) begins by stating that "from the viewpoint of philosophy, mathematics must be understood as a human activity, a social phenomenon, part of human culture, historically evolved, and intelligible only in a social context" (p. xi). We argue that this statement applies well beyond the academic mathematics with which Hersh is concerned.

A limitation of Hersh's work, as he admits, is that it reflects a Eurocentric view of mathematics. One aspect of our argument for the perspective of "mathematics of all" is acknowledging the achievements of non-Western cultures in academic mathematics, not just in contributing to the development of Western mathematics, but also in their own right. In documenting these achievements, Joseph (1992) undermines standard Eurocentric accounts of the development of mathematics that, he argues, reflect the ideology of European superiority and ignore or devalue the contributions of colonized peoples (D'Ambrosio, 1999). A parallel can be found in presentations of world history that reduce it to the development of Western civilization (see Nash, Crabtree, & Dunn, 1997). Joseph (1992, p. 12) recommends that a more balanced view should highlight

- the global nature of mathematical pursuits of one kind or another;
- the possibility of independent mathematical development within each cultural tradition; and
- the crucial importance of diverse transmissions of mathematics

across cultures, culminating in the creation of the unified discipline of modern mathematics.

In relation to the first of these points, Bishop (1988), describing mathematics as "a pan-cultural phenomenon" (p. 187), contended that "there are . . . six fundamental activities which . . . are both universal, in that they appear to be carried out by every cultural group ever studied, and also necessary and sufficient for the development of mathematical knowledge":

- Counting. The use of a systematic way to compare and order discrete phenomena. It may involve tallying, or using objects or string to record, or special number words or names;
- Locating. Exploring one's spatial environment, and conceptualizing and symbolizing that environment with models, diagrams, drawings, words, or other means;
- Measuring. Quantifying qualities for the purposes of comparison and ordering, using objects or tokens as measuring devices with associated units or "measure-words";
- Designing. Creating a shape or design for an object or for any part of one's spatial environment. It may involve making the object, as a "mental template," or symbolizing it in some conventional way;
- Playing. Devising, and engaging in, games and pastimes, with more or less formalized rules that all players must abide by; and
- Explaining. Finding ways to account for the existence of phenomena be they religious, animistic or scientific. (p. 182)

"Mathematics of All": The Ethnomathematical Perspective

This broad conception of mathematics as human activity is captured by the term *ethnomathematics,* coined by D'Ambrosio (1985). Much of the work using this label has been concerned with identifying activities in exotic cultures that could be interpreted as mathematical. However, D'Ambrosio (1985) defined the term more widely, to mean "the mathematics which is practiced among identifiable cultural groups, such as national-tribal societies, labor groups, children of a certain age bracket, professional classes, and so on." D'Ambrosio continued:

Its identity depends largely on focuses of interest, on motivation, and on certain codes and jargons which do not belong to the realm of academic mathematics.

. . . Of course, this concept asks for a broader interpretation of what mathematics is . . . a very broad range of human activities which, throughout history, have been expropriated by the scholarly establishment, formalized and codified and incorporated into what we call "academic mathematics," but which remain alive in culturally identified groups and constitute routines in their practices. (p. 45)

Thus, ethnomathematics represents, in a particularly powerful way, the principle of "mathematics of all," since it acknowledges activities that are central to the lives of "ordinary" people as being mathematical.

As Usiskin (1999b) pointed out, one interpretation of "mathematics for all" is associated with curricula that stress applications and data analysis. This interpretation, in contrast to others considered earlier, potentiates diversity at the level of both societies and individuals, since applications may involve modeling of controversial social, economic, and political issues that can be selected for their relevance to students. For example, Skovsmose and Valero (2002) discuss examples whereby mathematics can be used to analyze social and political issues in Denmark and Colombia (see also Frankenstein, 1989).

To summarize, the slogan "mathematics of all" is intended to convey the message that mathematics is created and practiced by all peoples and all people. In the next section, Swapna Mukhopadhyay describes activities that have been developed and used to help future teachers toward this realization and the implications that it has for the teaching of mathematics.

Principles into Practice: Students as Constructors of Knowledge

In this section, I (Swapna Mukhopadhyay) describe how my teaching follows the mathematics of all philosophy, and I provide illustrative examples. My work is strongly influenced by principles of multicultural education, such as those set out by Banks (1995), who has provided a framework of five dimensions that address cultural diversity in classrooms: (1) content integration, (2) the knowledge construction process, (3) prejudice reduction, (4) an equity pedagogy, and (5) an empowering school culture and social structure.

As a teacher of mathematics to future and practicing teachers, and previously to adults learning "basic" mathematics in a community college setting, I have always been very conscious of a sharp contrast between two polarized aspects of self-concept in many of my students—on the one hand, a strong practical intelligence in everyday life; on the other, the expressed belief "I cannot do mathematics." Thus, one of my aims is to make students aware of the contradiction inherent in this contrast, through changing their perception of mathematics as unconnected with people's lived experiences. My aim is to help students appreciate that people operating effectively in the world outside school, including themselves, are often engaged in mathematical activity—not just when they are doing obviously mathematical processes such as calculation or measurement, but in interpreting information, making decisions, gauging probabilities, planning, playing games, creating artwork, and so on.

Further, since my approach to the teaching of mathematics is based on projects and problem solving, the students are given opportunities to conduct investigations within sociocultural contexts. Such activities help them to realize that they can extend their mathematical activity beyond their immediate concerns by using mathematics as a powerful tool for the analysis of issues important in their lives or in society and that they can thus find access to powerful mathematical ideas (Skovsmose & Valero, 2002). The process of empowerment has been described in terms of five perspectives on knowing by Belenky, Clinchy, Goldberger, and Tarule (1986). Although they were characterizing women's ways of knowing, arguably their analysis applies to all. The five epistemological perspectives that they identified are

- silence, a position in which we experience ourselves as mindless and voiceless and subject to the whims of external authority;
- received knowledge, a perspective from which we conceive of ourselves as capable of receiving, even reproducing, knowledge from the all-knowing external authorities but not capable of creating knowledge on our own;
- subjective knowledge, a perspective from which truth and knowledge are conceived of as personal, and subjectively known or intuited;
- procedural knowledge, a position in which we are invested in learning and applying objective procedures for obtaining and communicating knowledge; and
- constructed knowledge, a position in which we view all knowledge as contextual, experience ourselves as creators of knowledge, and value both subjective and objective strategies of knowing. (p. 15)

I attempt, therefore, to move the students to the epistemological perspective in which they regard themselves as constructors of knowledge. The wider context is defined in the second of the dimensions defined by Banks (1991, p. 6): "The knowledge construction process relates to the extent to which teachers help students to understand, investigate, and determine how the implicit cultural assumptions, frames of references, perspectives, and biases within a discipline influence the ways in which knowledge is constructed within it."

Example 1: Geometry of Cultural Artifacts

To many people, geometry is associated with Euclidean theorems and the writing of double-column proofs. Such mathematical instruction has potential validity in terms of leading students to appreciate mathematics as intellectual achievement and as training in argumentation and proof; however, the experimental evidence is that very few American students demonstrate the conceptual understanding that these laudable aims would imply (see, e.g., Clements & Battista, 1992). Yet geometry, perhaps the strongest of all branches of mathematics, is apparent in the world around us and offers myriad opportunities for intellectually engaging students through stimulating investigations. In both the natural world and the constructed world, geometry is pervasive.

Geometry is also ubiquitously present in out-of-school contexts. Fasheh (1991, p. 38), for example, describes his "illiterate" mother's strong sense of intuitive geometry in dressmaking. With a few measurements and no patterns, she routinely converted "rectangles of fabric" into "perfectly fitted clothing for people" (see also Harris, 1987). There are innumerable examples that illustrate the incidence of geometrical thinking in out-of-school contexts in every culture (e.g., Gerdes, 1999; Washburn & Crowe, 1988; Zaslavsky, 1973). Attracted by the aesthetics of patterns and forms, we respond to artifacts such as baskets, pottery, and textiles from different cultures but are often unaware of the mathematical thinking that goes into creating these patterns. Designing occurs in all cultures (Bishop, 1988; Washburn & Crowe, 1988, is an excellent resource for an investigation on symmetric patterns from various cultures).

Since repeating patterns are the basic ingredients for studying transformation geometry, our in-class investigations begin with observing and classifying patterns from a variety of artifacts. Using simple material tools such as grid papers, mirrors, and tracing papers to study reflection, rotation, translation, and glide in a hands-on manner, the elements of various patterns from photographs of artifacts are carefully studied. The patterns on different artifacts are then reconstructed in accordance with the process presumably adopted by the artisans. To augment the learning process of design making and the definitions of transformation geometry, each student is encouraged to make a simple motif by cutting a stamp on an eraser, which then serves as the unit in creating different strip patterns.

For further analysis of cultural artifacts, we visit local museums that provide the opportunity of looking at actual objects. Given that a museum visit is typically not associated with learning mathematics, transporting the mathematical discussions into a nonfamiliar setting provides a chance to push the boundaries as to how the students view mathematics in general and geometry in particular. There is usually an overwhelming awe in responding to the mathematical thinking of many non-Western cultures, as evidenced by their geometrical designs. Follow-up research focuses on locating artifacts from different cultures, analyzing the patterns, and investigating the social and cultural background of the artisans. Since most of the patterned artifacts are cultural products of now socially and economically marginalized people, the students get a chance to share their different points of view on the situatedness of cognitively complex processes of pattern making as a part of the everyday thinking of people who are often unschooled and barely "literate." The students' product, unlike a test taken for a math class, is a set of posters that are displayed along the corridors of the building where the classes are held. This display creates an opportunity to share with other members of the college the evidence from different cultures that mathematics is a human creation.

Many students start asking atypical questions about the status imparted to knowledge, the meaning of knowing and not knowing, and how one sees other people's knowledge. Thus, the activity is aligned with Banks's idea of "the transformation approach," where the emphasis on diversity is in terms of changes that "enable students to view concepts, issues, events, and themes from the perspectives of diverse ethnic and cultural groups" (Banks, 2001, p. 229). The students also confront their initial belief that mathematics is inherently dull and disconnected from life. Seeing that mathematics exists in the form of aesthetically pleasing creations, beyond the realm of standard textbooks and test questions, produces a paradigmatic shift in many. Through this exercise, mathematics is connected not only to artistic cultural representations but also actively to issues of inequalities and power that marginalize the lives of many in our diverse world.

Many other activities that I use in class relate to other forms of mathematical activity that fall into the categories defined by Bishop (1988). These include counting (e.g., various counting systems, the quipu recording device of the Incas), locating (maps, navigation), and play (games such as mancala and puzzles such as magic squares).

Example 2: Analysis of Barbie as a Cultural Phenomenon

In an exercise intended to develop in my students a disposition toward critical thinking that does not require complex mathematics, I use Barbie dolls. In focusing on what is perhaps the ultimate icon of American popular culture, and hence familiar to almost all of the students, I make the point that culture is not something that only exotic others have. According to the manufacturer Mattel, typically an American girl gets her first Barbie at about age 3 and is given six more Barbies by the time she is age 12. The statistics on sales of Barbie are staggering (Mukhopadhyay, 1998, p. 154)—on average, two Barbies are sold every second. The doll is manufactured in factories in China, Malaysia, and Indonesia, and Mattel has a worldwide market in more than 150 nations throughout the world, with sales reaching $1.9 billion in 1997 (Mattel, 1999).

As a hands-on activity, this investigation begins with the distribution of Barbie dolls and tape measures to groups of students and with the question "What would Barbie look like if she was as big as an average adult?" The task of constructing the "real-life" Barbie begins with measuring different body parts and converting those measures. The mathematics required by this task is not perceived as daunting in terms of particular formulas to remember and apply; rather, the relevant mediating concepts, such as scaling factor, emerge naturally from the logic of the situation and through negotiation within the group. Apart from the mathematical skills of proportional reasoning, the starting point of this exercise also evokes another judgment, namely, finding the representative, or "average," person for the group. Though the students are competent with the computation of averages, the concept of choosing an "average" person is much more complex, particularly bearing in mind the variation in race and gender within the groups.

In the course of constructing a life-size Barbie, the students recognize how strikingly distorted Barbie's shape is. Comments such as "her neck is too long," "her waist is too narrow," and "her pelvic area is too small to bear a child" are common. Invariably, a consensus is reached that Barbie's shape is unnatural. Consequently, the students, both men and women, acquire a heightened appreciation for the legitimacy of different body types.

Being aware of the international market, Mattel has produced Barbie in several "ethnic" variations (and Becky, a Barbie friend and look-alike in a pink wheelchair, was recently marketed). Ethnic differentiation is seen in the styles of the dolls' costumes and the colors of their skin and hair. However, working with Barbies of different apparent ethnicity, the students are stunned to find that irrespective of the pigment of their plastic skins, all Barbies, whether Native American, German, or Polynesian, are identically proportioned. In fact, they share the same mold in the factories in Asia where they are made. The subsequent discussions, passionate and involved, lead to debunking the myth of Barbie as a model for "every girl," and issues about body image and body type in relation to self-worth and cultural identity are examined.

Our investigations on Barbie do not stop at this juncture. The process of manufacturing Barbie for the world market is the next part of the agenda. Mattel produces Barbie on non-U.S. soil: the cheap labor of Southeast Asia is another target of Mattel. Who makes Barbie dolls for our children and our valued collections? What operating conditions are available to the overseas workers? How do their wages and benefits and the terms and conditions of their labor compare to those of other factory workers? These questions are just a few to kindle social and political consciousness (see also Frankenstein, 1989; Skovsmose & Valero, 2001).

Example 3: The Tax and Discount Problem

If you have not encountered the following question before, you are invited to answer it before proceeding further.

> If you buy something with a certain percentage of tax and a percentage discount, will you pay less if the store adds the tax first and then takes off the discount, or if they take the discount off first and then add the tax?

We have used this problem with several classes, by having students (a) give their first intuitive answers, (b) work in groups to discuss the problem, and (c) interview five people about the problem. Most people (both among the students and among their interviewees) answer intuitively on the basis of one of the following arguments: (a) it is better to add the tax first, because then you get a discount on a larger amount or (b) it is better to take the discount off first, because then you pay tax on a smaller amount. In fact, the order does not matter.

When students work in groups, or when interviewees work on the problem, the typical response is to take round numbers by way of example (e.g., 8 percent tax and 20 percent discount on an item priced at $1,000), carry out the calculations (by working out tax and adding it, then working out discount and subtracting it, and vice versa), and find that the answer is the same each way. Contrary to the mathematician's standards for proof, this is almost invariably accepted as convincing evidence that it will always work out the same. Even among those who may be presumed to have learned the algebra required, an algebraic solution of the problem has almost never been observed.

From the point of view of the present chapter, what is interesting about this example is that it demonstrates how adults who may be considered to be functioning effectively are nonetheless disempowered in a number of ways. For example, they have access to a powerful tool, a calculator, but very few, even among those whose work involves such calculations, are aware that an efficient way to use a calculator to work out the price of an item plus tax or with a discount is the multiplicative method (e.g., for 8 percent tax, multiply by 1.08). It seems strange that this useful knowledge is not more widely distributed.

A large majority is surprised by the outcome when they check by calculation. Almost none have thought about the problem, even though they have been in the situation often. Most agree that this sort of problem should be taught in school mathematics. A further subtle point is that none of the respondents inferred that the order could not make a difference, since they assumed that if it did, that fact would surely be part of common knowledge.

This example illustrates many aspects about the lack of a disposition in most people to recognize familiar situations of their lives as open to mathematical analysis and the lack of an expectation that they could use mathematics to evaluate those situations. Most people unthinkingly accept what the cash registers do and the practice of the stores ("this is how they do it"), abdicating any responsibility to understand.

Mathematics of All, for All: An Inclusive View of Diversity

The position advocated in this chapter is that "mathematics for all," to the extent that it is achievable, depends on promoting "mathematics of all." By the latter, we mean, on the one hand, recognizing the diversity of human activity that is mathematical and, on the other, promoting the idea of every individual being a person who can meaningfully use mathematics.

The first activity described in the previous section addresses the first of the dimensions of multicultural education listed by Banks (1991, p. 6): "Content integration deals with the extent to which teachers use examples and content from a variety of cultures and groups to illustrate key concepts, principles, generalizations, and theories in their subject area or discipline." The examples Mukhopadhyay uses in this activity are from a wide variety of cultures, and Mukhopadhyay also encourages the students to find examples from their own family and community backgrounds. Often, the effect is to raise the consciousness of students about their cultural identity (and this applies just as much to those of European ancestry).

The other two activities described make the point forcefully that culture is not just a matter of ancestral heritage but is also in the contemporary life shared by everyone living in the United States. Mukhopadhyay constantly alerts students to the ubiquity of mathematics in our work, play, social interactions, and physical environment, so that they begin to see it everywhere. For example, a group of students jokingly told Mukhopadhyay once that they could not escape from mathematics—waiting at a bakery, they found themselves analyzing the patterns on the wall.

In conjunction with this change in perception of mathematics, Mukhopadhyay works to promote a change in the students' self-concept as a mathematical learner, thinker, and user. Many students enter the course expressing beliefs such as the following: "For as long as I can remember, math has been difficult. . . . We were forced to memorize formulas and I never really caught on to them." Achieving a change in self-concept and escaping from the alienation from mathematics that comes from perception of it as coming from, or being imposed by, "others" comprise an essential first step for teachers toward becoming independent mathematical thinkers and not, at best, competent followers of procedures and, at worst, mathophobes. Unless they can achieve that for themselves, what hope is there that they will help their students achieve it?

The activity with Barbie dolls differs radically from the normal diet of textbooks, which are mostly short and isolated exercises for the practice of routine computations or procedures, decontextualized or artificially contextualized. The mathematical procedures of measurement, scaling, proportional reasoning, and so on emerge in the course of collectively making sense of the situation. Negotiating the meaning of "the average person" entails understanding of the concept of average, rather than the routine calculation of the arithmetic mean of a set of numbers that is typically the intellectually limited fare offered to students.

Further, the mathematical analysis is given meaning in the context of important and controversial social issues. In this activity, therefore, Mukhopadhyay is modeling for students the processes of using mathematics as a tool for critical analysis that is relevant to their personal experience. In particular, by making students aware of the implications of Mattel's attempts to globalize Barbie through manufacturing dolls of different pigments but with the same body shape and of their use of cheap Asian labor, Mukhopadhyay addresses the third level of integration of multicultural content identified by Banks, namely, the transformation approach: "The structure of the curriculum is changed to enable students to view concepts, issues, events, and themes from the perspectives of diverse ethnic and cultural groups" (Banks, 2001, p. 229). Moreover, this activity lays the groundwork for the fourth level, the social action approach: "Students make decisions on important social issues and take actions to help solve them" (Banks, 2001, p. 13).

The problem concerning tax and discount works remarkably well as a consciousness raiser. Particularly when they interview others, students realize that this is a situation very familiar to almost everyone but that nobody seems to have wondered about it, let alone worked out the mathematical implications. Yet, when prompted to do so, it is not difficult for most people to do, at least by checking an example using a calculator. The activity serves to illustrate for students how most people abdicate responsibility for understanding and are content to rely on machines. This passivity is part of the general attitude that Mukhopadhyay works hard to change, people's lack of expectation that they might be able to apply a mathematical technique that is not particularly advanced and that they have almost certainly "learned" in school in a real situation—as opposed to a routine textbook exercise. While this attitude remains predominant, the call for "mathematics for all" remains hollow.

What has been presented here is "work in progress." It does not succeed with all students, many of whom resist it as contrary to their conception of mathematics. It is difficult to achieve such a radical shift in students' beliefs about mathematics and mathematics education in such a short time, against the background of their previous experience as learners of mathematics. It has been encouraging, however, that on several occasions, former students have come back two or three years later to tell Mukhopadhyay that they are beginning to understand what this teacher was trying to do.

Mathematics education is a negative experience for too many people. It does not have to be that way.

Additional Resources

Resources in the Environment

Besides publications (including Web sites), a representative sample of which is given later in this section, our approach implies that there are resources in the students' social and physical environment that can be accessed and exploited to promote understanding of the relevance of mathematics in their lives.

Most immediately, within students' families and communities there are family and community members with collective cultural memories, a variety of work expertise, and social organizations that may be involved in community action. The physical environment in which students live affords many opportunities for mathematics analysis—for example, in terms of architecture, topography, and demographics—open to analysis both geometrically and in terms of investigations of social issues.

An obvious way to convince students of the applicability of mathematics as a tool is through topical issues reported in the news media. Newspapers and other publications are full of data and other mathematical material used to present analysis of current events, which a teacher can opportunistically exploit. For example, *USA Today* carries a simple graphic each day presenting data relating to some social phenomenon. An essential component of teaching from such sources is the need to develop an appropriately critical stance toward data (Best, 2001).

As is illustrated in this chapter, depending on what is locally available, museums can be a further invaluable resource through displaying and analyzing artifacts from many cultures and many centuries.

Publications

Ahmed, A., Williams, H., & Kraemer, J. M. (Eds.). (2000). *Cultural diversity in mathematics (education): CIEAEM 51*. Chichester, England: Horwood.

This book contains the proceedings, comprising sixty-one papers, of the 1999 meeting of the Commission International pour l'Etude ed l'Amelioration de l'Enseignement des Mathematiques, an international organization based in Europe. The conference was organized into five subthemes: "Looking Back, Moving Forward"; "Effective Co-operation between Mathematicians, Mathematics Educators, and Users of Mathematics"; "Coping with Diversity of Student/Pupil Interests, Abilities, Aptitude, and Background"; "Mathematics Cultures across Different Sectors of Education"; "Beliefs and Practices in Mathematics and Mathematics Education."

Best, J. (2001). *Damned lies and statistics: Untangling numbers from the media, politicians, and activists*. Berkeley: University of California Press.

In this book, the author analyzes in depth examples of misuse and misinterpretation of statistical data. The concluding paragraph (p. 171) reads as follows:

> Statistics are not magical. Nor are they always true—or always false. Nor need they be incomprehensible. Adopting a Critical approach offers an effective way of responding to the numbers we are sure to encounter. Being Critical requires more thought, but failing to adopt a Critical mind-set makes us powerless to evaluate what others tell us. When we fail to think critically, the statistics we hear might just as well be magical.

Boaler, J. (Ed.). (2000). *Multiple perspectives on mathematics teaching and learning.* Westport, CT: Ablex.

This collection of ten chapters from leaders in the field of mathematics is illustrative of the shift in the field toward a broader sociocultural and political perspective. Issues addressed include teaching practices, equity, language, assessment, group work, and the broader political context of mathematics education reform from multiple perspectives—sociological, anthropological, psychological, cultural, and political.

Davis, P. J., & Hersh, R. (1986). *Descartes' dream: The world according to mathematics.* Brighton, England: Harvester.

In this book, two mathematicians argue that through the contemporary ubiquity of applications of mathematical modeling to social phenomena, mathematical thinking imposes its own, often distorting, reality on aspects of human behavior that are not amenable to such modeling. In the preface (p. xv), they state, "The social and physical worlds are being mathematized at an increasing rate," and draw a moral: "We'd better watch it, because too much of it may not be good for us."

English, L. D. (Ed.). (2002). *Handbook of international research in mathematics education.* Mahwah, NJ: Lawrence Erlbaum.

Several chapters in this handbook relate directly to themes addressed in our chapter, in particular: "Democratic Access to Mathematics through Democratic Education: An Introduction" (Carol Malloy), "Access and Opportunity: The Political and Social Context of Mathematics Education" (William Tate & Celia Rousseau), "Mathematics Education in Out-of-School Contexts: A Cultural Psychology Perspective" (Guida de Abreu), "Democratic Access to Powerful Mathematical Ideas" (Ole Skovsmose & Paola Valero).

Nasir, N. S., & Cobb, P. (Eds.). (2002). Diversity, equity, and mathematical learning [Special issue]. *Mathematical Thinking and Learning, 4,* 2 & 3.

The articles for this special issue resulted from two meetings at which the issues of diversity and equity, within the specific context of the mathematics classroom, were discussed. The primary emphasis was on developing adequate conceptual understanding of the underlying phenomena as a necessary prerequisite to proposing solutions. In undertaking this task, the inherently political nature of the enterprise is acknowledged. In focusing on inequitable social structures, relationships of power, identity, and language are analyzed. In particular, a reconceptualization of diversity is offered that characterizes it as a relation between the community of practice of the mathematics classroom and the other communities of practice in which the students participate.

Powell, A. B., & Frankenstein, M. (Eds.). (1997). *Ethnomathematics: Challenging Eurocentrism in mathematics.* Albany: State University of New York Press.

This is an edited volume of eighteen chapters by international scholars on critical examination of the Eurocentrism that pervades in mathematics education. It is divided into subsections such as "Ethnomathematical

Knowledge," "Uncovering Distorted and Hidden History of Mathematical Knowledge," "Considering Interactions between Culture and Mathematical Knowledge," "Reconsidering What Counts as Mathematical Knowledge," "Ethnomathematical Praxis in the Curriculum," and "Ethnomathematical Research." Each section, introduced by the editors, validates Paulo Freire's ideology of education for all.

Web Sites

<http://www.rpi.edu/~eglash/eglash.dir/afractal.htm>. Ron Eglash of Science and Technology Studies at Rensselaer Polytechnic in Troy, New York, maintains a detailed Web site in which he elaborates on mathematical topics, such as fractals, that have wide applications in nature, in high-tech computerized designs, and also in visual representations generated in African cultures. In his recent work, Eglash "investigates fractals in African architecture, traditional hairstyling, textiles, sculpture, painting, carving, metalwork, religion, games, quantitative techniques, and symbolic systems." He also "examines the political and social implications of the existence of African fractal geometry."

<http://www.rpi.edu/~eglash/eglash.dir/nacyb.htm>. Under the title "Native American Cybernetics: Indigenous Knowledge Resources in Information Technology," Ron Eglash explores "Native American cybernetics" in terms of indigenous knowledge of the Native Americans and how a virtual bead loom and SimShoBan (simulation of Shoshoni social ecology) can help us understand the complexities of the "flow of information across mental and material, natural and human, and mundane and spiritual domains."

<http://www.rpi.edu/~eglash/isgem.htm>. Web site of the International Study Group on Ethnomathematics.

<http://www.rethinkingschools.org>. Rethinking Schools is a grassroots organization of teachers and others interested in public education. Its publication of the same name "is a non-profit, independent newspaper advocating the reform of elementary and secondary public schools," with an emphasis on "urban schools and issues of equity and social justice."

OUTSIDE THE CLASSROOM: INVOLVING STUDENTS IN THE CAMPUS AND COMMUNITY

12

Community-Based Service Learning: Actively Engaging the Other

Pat Washington

Community-based service learning (CBSL) is a joint academic and community endeavor that encourages meaningful service for the student, the academic institution, and the community by integrating community service, academic study, and student reflection on the CBSL experience in ways that enhance civic, academic, social, and moral learning (Washington, 2000b).

In a longitudinal study of 22,236 undergraduates conducted by Astin, Vogelgesang, Ikeda, and Yee (2000), the authors conclude that participation in service learning positively impacts grades, writing skills, and critical-thinking skills. Similarly, Eyler and Giles's (1999) study of 1,500 students from twenty different U.S. institutions reveals that students who participated in CBSL reported greater motivation to learn, deeper understanding of the subject matter, greater appreciation for the complexity of social issues, and an increased ability to apply what they learned in the classroom to real-life situations. Based on both quantitative longitudinal research and qualitative research, these two works support the findings of earlier, less comprehensive studies suggesting a positive correlation between student participation in service learning and enhanced academic performance (Astin & Sax, 1998; Batchelder & Root, 1994; Boss, 1994; Bringle & Hatcher, 1996; Cohen & Kinsey, 1994; Conrad & Hedin, 1982; Hammond, 1994; Markus, Howard & King, 1993). They also provide data to support many preexisting arguments that participation in service learning promotes racial understanding, reduces negative stereotypes, and increases appreciation for diversity (Astin, Sax, & Avalos, 1996; Battistoni, 1995; Burns, Storey, &

Certo, 1999; Cone & Harris, 1996; Delong & Groomes, 1996; Hamm, Dowell, & Houck, 1998; Marullo, 1998).

This chapter explores ways in which CBSL may be used to enhance in-class explorations of diversity. It stems from both secondary and original research[1] regarding the efficacy of CBSL in challenging entrenched cultural values and beliefs about the homeless, welfare recipients, lesbians and gays, feminist organizations, and other socially and politically marginalized groups—groups that, for the purposes of this chapter, constitute "the other." In addition to providing data suggesting that appropriately designed and monitored CBSL partnerships can reduce "us-them" frameworks, challenge stereotypical views and beliefs, and enhance understanding of collective responsibility for social problems, this chapter offers practical suggestions that faculty can use either to design new CBSL courses or to incorporate CBSL components into existing course content.

The chapter begins with a definition and discussion of major components and characteristics of CBSL, as well as a discussion of specific factors instructors need to consider when incorporating CBSL into their courses. After reviewing relevant literature regarding the usefulness of CBSL in promoting respect for differences, I will illustrate the discussion of CBSL and diversity with specific reference to CBSL options developed for the "Sex, Power, and Politics" course I have taught for the past four years. The chapter will conclude with a brief overview of some recent course-community partnerships, as well as student comments suggesting that their work with these partners resulted in increased social awareness and greater respect for diversity.

What Is Community-Based Service Learning?

Bringle and Hatcher (1996, p. 222) describe the essential components of CBSL when they define it as "a course-based, credit-bearing educational experience" in which students

- participate in an organized service activity that meets identified community needs and
- reflect on the service activity in such a way as to gain further understanding of course content, a broader appreciation of the discipline, and an enhanced sense of civic responsibility.

This definition clearly anchors CBSL to the academic curriculum: it is a structured "credit-bearing educational experience" aligned with a specific course in a specific academic discipline. Further, the definition speaks to a reciprocal arrangement between the academy, which offers skills and theoretical knowledge (in the form of students who "participate in an organized service activity"), and the community, which offers experiential learning in real-life settings with experienced community partners. Finally, the definition of CBSL highlights the necessity of student reflection—the process whereby service-learning experiences are brought to bear on academic course content and vice versa. As Bringle and Hatcher (1999, p. 180) explain, this third component is integral to ensuring that CBSL results in active learning: "community service does not necessarily, in and of itself, produce learning. Reflection activities provide the bridge between the community service activities and the educational content of the course."

Community as Concept

While Bringle and Hatcher's (1996) definition of CBSL captures the essential characteristics of CBSL in broad strokes, there are numerous other factors that faculty need to consider when incorporating CBSL into their own teaching. For instance, since the experiential component of CBSL is meant to take place in the community, how should "community" be defined? While acknowledging the lack of consensus around what constitutes "the community" in CBSL, Zlotskowski (1999, p. 98) argues, "For the most part, the community referred to primarily consists of (1) off-campus populations underserved by our market economy and (2) organizations whose primary purpose is the common good." For Cone and Harris (1996, p. 34), "community" is the unfamiliar: "it is important to make the experience a 'discontinuous' one, distinct from students' everyday experiences, so that students are challenged to broaden their perspectives on the world." Stewart (1990, p. 37) similarly refers to CBSL as a "new experience . . . in an unknown context."

Such definitions of "community" have a significant bearing on our discussion of the ways in which CBSL may be used to enhance in-class explorations of diversity by providing opportunities for students to "broaden their perspectives" through active engagement with people whose lives and circumstances are different from theirs. One of the most powerful illustrations of the potential CBSL has to expand our concept of "community" and to create opportunities for active engagement of the "other" is an Iona College course on immigration law ("Iona in Mission"). The course, taught by Dr. J. L. Yranski Nsuti, provides students the opportunity to put a human face on issues underlying U.S. immigration law by arranging homestays in squatters' villages throughout Nogales, Mexico. As Dr. Nsuti's syllabus notes, visits to *maquiladoras* and health clinics, as well as U.S. Customs and Border Patrol, serve as opportunities to "observe the conditions which explain the push/pull factors for immigration to the United States from Mexico." Upon returning from Mexico, students continue their service-learning commitment by doing fieldwork with a nonprofit organization that is concerned with immigration issues.[2]

Service-Learning Activities

Another consideration for faculty wishing to incorporate CBSL into their courses is how to determine what constitutes an appropriate service-learning activity. Gent and Gurecka (1998, p. 262) provide a very useful analysis of service activities by distinguishing between direct service activities, which "involve personal contact with some individuals in need" (e.g., serving food at a homeless shelter or providing tax counseling to the elderly); indirect service activities, which "involve channeling resources to solve a problem" (e.g., undertaking a clothing drive or holding a fund-raiser); and civic action, wherein "students participate in citizenship by performing a community project in which the community in general benefits" (e.g., park cleanup or tree planting). Which type of activity is most useful or appropriate for a course that incorporates CBSL is likely to be driven by the expertise of student participants, as well as the requirements of a particular discipline.[3]

Given the wide range of activities that fall under the service-learning rubric, all three CBSL partners (instructor, student, and community) must make concerted efforts to ensure the success and quality of the service-learning experience. Gent and Gurecka (1998) argue that for true service learning to occur, several essential elements must be present.

First, harkening back to Bringle and Hatcher's (1996) definition of CBSL, service-learning activities must be directly connected to academic course content and learning objectives; otherwise, the activities are not properly "service learning" but community service, or voluntarism.

Second, students need service-learning activities that are relevant, exciting, and interesting. This second element is closely tied to the first, as well as to the concept of reciprocity and shared partnership (between student, instructor, and community). Zlotkowski (1999, p. 105) addresses this when he cautions:

> [C]ommunity service activities must always be grounded in a deliberate, carefully articulated understanding of how such activities advance the specific learning goals of the course in which they

are embedded. . . . [When the distinction between service learning and voluntarism is not clearly understood by all parties, the value of] community service assignments can easily come to naught: instead of creating the donor database that a computer science instructor envisioned, students are busy stacking boxes or standing at a copy machine. Such mis-assignments represent more than a frustration of educational design; they also represent a loss of opportunity for the community partner because the potential contribution of the college student is unrealized.[4]

Third, and finally, Gent and Gurecka (1998, p. 263) argue that if true service learning is to occur, service activities must address "a real, recognized need." This element again harkens back to Bringle and Hatcher's (1996) definition of CBSL, namely that the student must be engaged in an "organized service activity that meets identified community needs" (p. 222). Absent this "real need" (which must be identified by the community to be served, rather than projected onto the community by the service provider), the service activity degenerates into "busywork" that benefits no one and undermines the academic integrity of CBSL (Enos & Troppe, 1996; Howard, 1998).

Other Faculty Choices

Various other theorists and practitioners suggest additional factors to consider regarding the implementation of CBSL, including choices about making service learning optional or mandatory, making it central or ancillary to the course, and/or determining the number of hours students will spend in the community (Chapin, 1999; Enos & Troppe, 1996; Howard, 1993a; Zlotkowski, 1999). Additionally, there are many excellent discussions regarding designing effective tools for enhancing student reflection (Bringle & Hatcher, 1999; Cone & Harris, 1996; Cooper, 1998; Kottkamp, 1990; Zlotkowski, 1999). Many of these points will be discussed more fully in the following section regarding the utility of CBSL in fostering diversity.

Diversity and CBSL

CBSL has a number of philosophical, experiential, and pedagogical features that make it a potentially effective tool for teaching about diversity. Use of the word *potentially* here is deliberate, as much rides on individual interpretation of service-learning philosophy, as well as the design and application of experiential and pedagogical activities. Of these variables (philosophical orientation, service-learning experience, pedagogical activities), the instructor's philosophic perspective or "screen" (Boyle-Baise, 1999, p. 310) is likely to have the greatest influence on student learning outcomes relative to appreciation of diversity; therefore, it will be addressed first here. The following analyses are not meant to be comprehensive but are intended, instead, to outline or highlight the context for viewing CBSL as a vehicle for teaching about diversity and to provide general guidance for faculty wishing to incorporate service learning into their courses for this purpose.

Establishing a Framework Promoting Social Awareness and Respect

Initiating a Caring Relationship

A number of CBSL theorists and practitioners have addressed the necessity of clarifying the operative philosophical frame(s) for service learning. Kahne and Westheimer (1996), voicing concern that recent national service-learning policy initiatives have resulted in "more attention . . . [being] focused on moving forward than on asking where we are headed" (p. 592), discuss the vastly different philosophical perspectives that undergird service-learning programs.[5] These opposing ideological perspectives, which (at the risk of oversimplifying Kahne and Westheimer's arguments) may be distilled into the dichotomies of "change" versus "charity" or "caring" versus "giving," result in very different student learning outcomes.

The ultimate goal of the "charity" and/or "giving" model appears to be helping students understand "the value of altruism," the value of self-sacrifice, and the importance of having "compassion for the less fortunate" (Kahne & Westheimer, 1996, p. 594). Within this framework, the "community" becomes a "client" for whom something is done, rather than a "resource" (p. 595) for deeper learning, and the primary benefit reaped by the student is "the joy of reaching out to others" (p. 593). In contrast, the ultimate goal of the "change" or "caring" model is both individual and social transformation. Citing Noddings (1984), Kahne and Westheimer (1996, p. 594) explain:

> In caring relationships . . . we try to consider the life and disposition of those for whom we are caring. We attempt to "apprehend the reality of the other" and then to "struggle for progress together." In so doing, we create opportunities for changing our understanding of the other and the context within which he or she lives.

These aspects of a "caring relationship"—the "attempt to 'apprehend the reality of the other'" and to understand "the context within which he or she lives"—are the essence of what it means to value diversity.

Understanding Context

Understanding "the context" in which CBSL constituent populations live is an especially important feature of the "change" and/or "caring" model—one that distinctly separates it from "charity" or "giving." Specifically, understanding social context is essential for addressing problems that are embedded in systemic or structural injustices, rather than in individual failings. Kahne and Westheimer (1996, p. 596) argue:

> [E]ducators may miss important opportunities if they disconnect the act of service from a critical examination of the setting in which it occurs. . . . While requiring students 'to serve America' (the rhetoric of . . . federal legislation) might produce George Bush's 'thousand points of light,' it might also promote a thousand points of the status quo. . . . Citizenship in a democratic community requires more than kindness and decency; it requires engagement in complex social and institutional endeavors. . . . Citizenship requires that individuals work to create, evaluate, criticize, and change public institutions and programs.

Transformation through Equal Benefits

Depending on one's orientation toward service learning, then, CBSL can be used as a tool to either transform or maintain the status quo (Boyle-Baise, 1999; Cone & Harris, 1996; Gent & Gurecka, 1998). According to Weah, Simmons, and Hall (2000), swaying the balance toward transformation requires understanding that "service" and "learning" are equally important outcomes of service learning. Without this understanding of reciprocity—that the student is "both the server and the recipient of service" (Weah et al., p. 674)—the service rendered is largely misguided charity, or worse, an act of "exploitation" or "oppression" that runs counter to efforts to teach about diversity (Maybach, 1996, quoted by Weah et al. 2000).[6]

Designing Experiential Activities to Promote Respect and Awareness

Many of the theorists and practitioners who value the transformative dimension of CBSL—specifically, the utility of service learning in reducing negative stereotypes, promoting understanding across differences, and inspiring social awareness—share Cone and Harris's (1996) perspective (discussed earlier in this chapter) that the most effective service-learning experience is "a 'discontinuous' one, distinct from students' everyday experiences, so that students are challenged to broaden their perspectives on the world" (p. 34).[7] For instance, Kahne and Westheimer (1996, p. 595) point out that "the experiential and interpersonal components of service-learning activities can achieve the first crucial step toward diminishing the sense of 'otherness' that often separates students—particularly privileged students—from those in need." Describing CBSL as "an encounter that involves crossing cultural borders," Boyle-Baise (1999, p. 315) observes similarly, "community service learning can unsettle one's assumptions of familiarity, prompt self-reassessment, and engender respect for different 'others.'"

Speaking from the perspective of international service learning, Grusky (2000, p. 858) also remarks on the likely—if not inevitable—"discontinuity" between the world(s) of the student service provider and the world(s) of the constituency (or constituencies) being served: "Service learning, whether it takes place across borders or across neighborhoods, most often brings together oppressed, marginalized, or underprivileged groups of people with more privileged and economically wealthy young students." Like Cone and Harris (1996; cf. also Kahne & Westheimer, 1996), Grusky (2000, p. 859) argues that such "discontinuous" experiences "generate profound questions on the part of the students involved," provide for "an abundance of teachable moments," and prepare students "to become highly motivated seekers of answers." Consistent with Kahne and Westheimer's (1996) distinction between the philosophy of "change" or "caring" and the philosophy of "charity" or "giving," Grusky (2000, p. 867) concludes that service learning is "not so much a 'life-enriching' but rather a 'complacency-shattering' or 'soul-searching' experience." This view accords with Dewey's (1916) contention that "thinking begins in what may . . . be called a forked-road situation, a situation that is ambiguous, that presents a dilemma, that proposes alternatives" (p. 14).

Instituting the Process

A final, essential component for teaching about diversity through CBSL is thoughtful preservice training and subsequent, appropriate monitoring and mediation of students' learning and reflection processes. Ideally, participation in CBSL will increase student self-awareness and lead to values clarification, as well as enhanced understanding of collective responsibility for social problems. The CBSL experience will also, ideally, dispel students' stereotypical assumptions about disenfranchised and marginalized groups, reduce victim blaming, and increase understanding of the complex nature of social problems.

However, mere exposure to the oppressive social, educational, and political conditions that confront disenfranchised groups does not automatically result in greater sensitivity and concern for these groups (Bringle & Hatcher, 1999). College students are racially, socially, politically, economically, and educationally diverse. They come to the classroom with varying degrees of knowledge and sensitivity regarding members of other groups (Boyle-Baise, 1999; Grusky, 2000; Kahne & Westheimer, 1996; Marullo, 1998).

Thoughtful Preservice Training

Cone and Harris (1996, p. 39) note:

> [S]tudents engaged in service-learning . . . bring with them beliefs, attitudes, and values which frequently are at odds with the communities in which they work. The discontinuity between student and community, while provoking active learning, also represents a danger in which their 'learning' may simply be built upon their prior attitudes and values. . . . Students who enter into communities and react in racist or patronizing ways may be doing far more harm than the ills they are supposedly addressing.[8]

Therefore, it is important to provide preservice activities for students regarding the communities they plan to partner with, as well as the service-learning expectations and "conceptual tools" (Cone & Harris, 1996) they will need in order to fulfill those expectations (see also Boyle-Baise, 1999; Eyler & Giles, 1999; Grusky, 2000).[9] Preservice activities must be followed by ongoing reflection activities that allow students to critically analyze their experiences and construct meaning from them.

Activities for Reflection

Nearly all CBSL theorists and practitioners view the process of student reflection on the service-learning experience as an essential—perhaps the single most important—element of CBSL, and there is considerable written guidance on developing effective reflection activities (Bringle & Hatcher, 1999; Cone & Harris, 1996; Cooper, 1998; Kottkamp, 1990; Zlotkowski, 1999). However, a number of theorists also observe that—as is the case with simply exposing students to difference—

merely incorporating reflection activities into a CBSL course component does not guarantee critical analysis of service-learning experiences or effect desired service-learning outcomes (in this case, reduction of negative stereotypes and increased appreciation for diversity). For instance, Kahne and Westheimer (1996, p. 597) note, "having students share their thoughts and experiences with one another can be valuable, but reflective activities (commonly in the form of journal entries and discussions) may simply reinforce previously held beliefs and simplistic, if generous, conclusions." Kottkamp (1990, p. 200) poses a similar argument.

> We cannot reflect for anyone else. We cannot force anyone else to change behavior through reflection. Thus, although reflection is a powerful means for improving the practice of those who desire to do so, it is not a panacea. We cannot use it to change the recalcitrant, the malicious, the unmotivated, or those who have given up all hope.

Nonetheless, as Kottkamp also argues, another person can facilitate the reflective process by "setting conditions or structure and providing the data necessary for [reflection] . . . to occur" (p. 200).[10] While acknowledging the fine line between intervening and interfering in students' reflection processes, Cone and Harris (1996) and Cooper (1998) provide examples of facilitated reflection. Cone and Harris (1996), for instance, have used appropriately trained student assistants to "extend the discourse, clarify ill-conceived arguments, and direct students to additional sources of information through the use of 'Socratic' questions, which challenge student statements" (p. 41). The importance of rooting students' experiential learning in the academic curriculum becomes very clear at this point, as the process of reflection does not occur in a vacuum (rendering all inferences "equally valid") but instead relies on course content and theoretical underpinnings as reference and/or departure points (Battistoni, 1995; Bringle & Hatcher, 1999; Cone & Harris, 1996; Zlotkowski, 1999).

A Pedagogical Example from My Class: "Sex, Power, and Politics"

The following description of how I use CBSL to teach about diversity in my "Sex, Power, and Politics" course is organized in accordance with Zlotkowski's (1999) recommendations for CBSL course design.

Zlotkowski (1999, p. 104) argues that faculty wishing to incorporate CBSL into their courses must carefully consider

- the rationale behind and purpose of the community service activity to be introduced;
- the kind of community service most appropriate to the goals of the course, the level of student expertise available, and the needs of the community partner; and
- the course format most appropriate for the learning and the community service goals.

The Rationale for and Purpose of the CBSL Component in This Course

My "Sex, Power, and Politics" course examines social, economic, and political factors influencing the status of women in the United States and abroad. Topics include, but are not limited to, institutionalized systems of power and domination, media representation of women as political objects or agents, gender and sexuality socialization as they relate to political status, and women's individual and collective struggles for positive social change. I teach this course from a feminist perspective grounded in the critical analysis of the "intersectionality" (Crenshaw, 1997) of gender, race, sexual orientation, and class oppression (Washington, 2000a).

Students who enroll in my "Sex, Power, and Politics" course are predominantly White,[11] female, and—ostensibly—heterosexual, although there are usually some students of color (mostly Chicana/o or Black and, less frequently, Asian), several men, and one or two "out" lesbian, gay, or bisexual students. Most enroll in the class with the expectation that they will be guided through an exclusive exploration of the gendered oppression of women and the obstacles that "generic" (read "normative," or "White, heterosexual, middle-class, able-bodied") women must overcome to prevail against sexism. They often enter the classroom resistant to studying "Woman" in her multiple social locations and express dismay—and sometimes anger—at efforts to demonstrate that various social markers (not just sex) determine one's location along the power-privilege continuum.

Like numerous CBSL practitioners before me (see, e.g., Battistoni, 1995; Marullo, 1998), I have discovered that establishing the theoretical framework and providing appropriate course materials (while necessary) are insufficient to overcome resistance and/or dispel misconceptions about who "legitimately" constitutes an oppressed group "deserving" of social justice. Therefore, the rationale and purpose behind incorporating a CBSL component into my "Sex, Power, and Politics" course is to challenge entrenched cultural values and beliefs and reduce student resistance to the theory of intersectionality by providing opportunities to actively engage "the other."

The Course Format

The objectives of my "Sex, Power, and Politics" course are

- to explore the various forms of domination and control that constrain women's formal and informal political participation in the United States and abroad;
- to understand historical and contemporary tensions between, and coalitions among, various strands of U.S. women's (and other social) movements;
- to examine some political issues addressed by contemporary feminists, especially as they intersect, or conflict, with (inter)national policies and practices;
- to explore how institutionalized U.S. and international political attitudes and practices perpetuate systems of gender-based inequity in the United States and abroad; and
- to understand the role of individuals and groups in maintaining or dismantling systems of oppression.

Students enrolled in my "Sex, Power, and Politics" course receive course credit along several dimensions: oral class participation, completing email assignments, written course examinations, and a group research project or community service option that is aligned with course objectives. My reasons for making the CBSL component optional include "the importance of being sensitive to students' personal circumstances and the dangers of sending unwilling, even resentful students into the community" (Zlotkowski, 1999, p. 106). Additionally, as a yet untenured junior faculty member at an institution where service learning has only recently made inroads, I find it more expedient to allow students to choose whether or not they wish to participate in service-learning activities.[12]

For students who choose service learning in lieu of a group research project, the CBSL option evolves as follows:

- Community service options from which students may select are predetermined prior to the start of the semester.
- Representatives from the preselected organizations make class

presentations during the first two to three weeks of the semester.

- Each student and his or her selected community partner draw up an agreement, in consultation with me, committing the student to working at the service-learning activity approximately three hours a week for ten weeks.
- The community partner provides interim reports (ranging from phone calls or emails to typewritten reports of one to two pages) on student progress, so that I may assess the quality and level of involvement.
- At the end of the semester, students submit final reports (reflection papers) critically analyzing the relationship between the community service performed and the course's objectives.

Because several students ultimately select the same community partner, the service-learning option may evolve into a group project, with students commuting to the selected organization together, meeting in groups with the community partner(s), completing projects in teams, discussing their service-learning experiences in class as a "unit," and conferring with each other regarding the reflection process.

Central to the classroom treatment of CBSL are the focused lectures provided by the community partners who visit the class during the first two to three weeks of the semester. Community partners lecture on the work their organizations do in the surrounding community and provide detailed descriptions of what students will be doing to fulfill CBSL requirements through their organizations. I immediately follow up with additional lecture material (largely drawn from information covered in our course materials and from additional research) that illuminates how each agency's community work coincides with our course objectives, course readings, and other related materials (such as upcoming documentary material).

Regardless of whether or not students select a community service option (and regardless of which agencies the students who opt for community service work with), they are required to integrate key issues raised in community service providers' lectures with other course materials throughout the semester. This ensures that all students treat the presentation from each of the community partners (and myself) as an integral part of the classroom learning experience.

Class time is made available throughout the semester for students to discuss the ways in which their actual CBSL experiences support or contradict other course materials. In addition, students have focused written assignments throughout the semester that are conducive to helping them discover for themselves other connections between what they are doing in the community and what is happening in the classroom. We also address tensions and concerns that emerge from being involved with a community service agency. Periodically throughout the semester, I engage in various forms of evaluation, including participant observation, to ensure that students are on task, that concerns and problems are addressed efficiently, and that the amount of time students are engaged in the service-learning project is appropriate. In addition, I confer periodically with the community partners to ensure that the benefits derived from working with my students outweigh their expenditure of time and energy in monitoring student involvement.

CBSL projects are selected and closely monitored for their relationship to course materials and learning objectives. Students are typically given a "menu" of three or four CBSL projects per semester, which allows them to correlate their specific skills and/or interests with particular service-learning activities. Past projects have ranged from developing and conducting surveys on residents' responses to hate literature in their communities, creating skits and games to teach children tolerance, building a Web site to facilitate referrals to human services agencies, helping children who are affected by domestic violence to use arts and crafts as a creative outlet for their emotions, and teaching art and creative writing to the homeless.

Providing quality CBSL opportunities requires building relationships (and trust) on both sides. Having incorporated CBSL components into my courses for the past eight semesters, I have a core group of community partners that I know will provide students with quality experiences and who are willing to work with me to ensure that students are following through on their commitments. These are partners that I can freely check in with regarding student confusion or discontent about projects and who will freely check in with me if they feel students are not holding up their end of the service-learning agreement.

Of course, not all community partnerships are successful. There have been agencies and individuals that I have stopped working with because they did not provide the quality of experience that I wanted my students to have. In one of the most disappointing instances, a candidate for local office simply doled out work assignments to students rather than engaging them in the political process. Furthermore, while the candidate supposedly promised students that they would get to meet and interact with certain political power brokers at an upcoming campaign fund-raiser, the students were "disinvited" from the event, allegedly because the host did not want "a bunch of college kids" in his home.

Just as some individuals and agencies do not make good community partners because they fail to provide "connected" learning experiences, some students who select quality service-learning opportunities end up either rejecting these opportunities or, seemingly, gaining nothing from them. One obvious mismatch occurred when an extremely conservative White female who firmly believed the myth about women on welfare (lazy, Black, bear children to increase welfare payments, etc.) worked with single female welfare recipients. This student ultimately had to be removed from the project because of her obvious disdain for and disrespect toward the women with whom she was working. Despite this and the preceding example, I am normally very satisfied with the partnerships (and service-learning activities) arranged between community partners and students, and I find inappropriate behavior on either side to be extremely rare.

Community Partners and Student Experiences

Students enrolled in my "Sex, Power, and Politics" course over the past four years have had opportunities to work with a broad array of community partners, including (but not limited to) the YWCA Battered Women's Shelter; the Supportive Parents Information Network founded by ACLU lawyer Joni Halpern; Harvest for the Hungry, a multiservice agency for the homeless founded by the grassroots activist, and formerly homeless person, Mary Mahy; Peace and Freedom Party candidate Janice Jordan; the San Diego State University's Women's Resource Center; and the San Diego Lesbian and Gay Pride organization. Each of these partners brought something to the table that accomplished one or more course objectives while simultaneously meeting the mutually identified needs of their organizations.

San Diego Lesbian and Gay Pride

The mission of San Diego Lesbian and Gay Pride (SDLGP) is to provide resources for affirming and celebrating lesbian, gay, bisexual, and transgender communities while building bridges of understanding and respect between these communities and the larger society. Partnering with this organization provided students the opportunity to accomplish several objectives of the "Sex, Power, and Politics" course, including exploring a form of domination and control (i.e., heterosexism), exploring how institutionalized political attitudes and practices perpetuate systems of gender-based inequity, and understanding the role of individuals and groups in dismantling systems of oppression. The majority of students who elected to work with SDLGP self-identified as heterosexual, and, as expected, they revealed in their reflection papers a shift in beliefs and attitudes toward lesbians and gay men.

Reminiscent of Kahne and Westheimer's (1996) contention that the "interpersonal components of service-learning activities can achieve the first crucial step toward diminishing the sense of 'otherness' that often separates students . . . from those in need" (p. 295), one student wrote, "SDLGP helped me break down some of the stereotypes that I didn't even realize I had. It taught me that gays and lesbians are as 'normal' as I am, and that they face many of the same prejudices that I have to deal with as a Latina." Another student who elected to work with SDLGP submitted a photographic essay as her reflection paper. Taken at SDLGP's major annual Pride event, the student's photographs included "dykes on bikes"; a "transfamily" (i.e., transgender) float, a six-member family unit that ranged in age from a grandmother to an infant in a stroller; and an Asian male in a T-shirt bearing the logo "Honorary Lesbian." The student used these and other photographs to illustrate her point that Pride is an example of what one of our assigned readings (Benmayor & Torruellas, 1997) describes as "cultural citizenship"—"the process whereby a subordinated group of people arrive at a common identity" (p. 189). Applying terminology employed by Benmayor and Torruellas to what she saw at the Pride event, the student argued that "'perceived collective identities' affirmed 'cultural citizenship' by extending our perceptions of the concept of 'family' beyond the restrictive limitations of the dominant society and its 'legal canon.'" This is an excellent example of how an experiential activity combines with classroom learning to produce a higher level of understanding than would be possible with either just experience or just classroom learning alone.

Harvest for the Hungry

A similarly "higher level of understanding" was recorded by a student who elected to work with Harvest for the Hungry, the multiservice grassroots agency founded by formerly homeless Mary Mahy. The student acknowledged in her reflection paper that before taking "Sex, Power, and Politics," she had "treated homeless people like they didn't exist. . . . [and] thought that if [she] ignored them openly enough and long enough, they would just go away." However, her service-learning experience (alternately serving food and sitting and talking with homeless people who came to a shelter for meals) profoundly changed her thinking about the poor.

> Seeing the families that came to meals regularly and speaking with them taught me that they were parents who cared, but needed some help. The welfare system labels the father as incompetent for

not being able to support his family, and society feels that the mother shouldn't have brought the kids into the world if she couldn't take care of them. The reality is that they are people—they are not just providers and caretakers. And sometimes people come upon hard times. They need help. They do not need to be disregarded and cast away.

Supportive Parents Information Network

One of my long-term CBSL partners is Joni Halpern, founder of Supportive Parents Information Network (SPIN). Every semester since fall 1998, Joni has visited my "Sex, Power, and Politics" classes to talk about the impact of welfare reform on families in San Diego. Over the past three years, students have been offered a range of service-learning options with SPIN, including helping to arrange a two-day conference for parents on welfare regarding their rights to education and gainful employment under the Cal-Works Program, developing a SPIN Web site with links to community service providers, creating an organizational newsletter, and helping SPIN members lobby local and federal officials regarding welfare issues. During the past academic year, the SPIN community service option included creating a physical space for SPIN, establishing a database of SPIN members, updating the newsletter, and christening the newly established office by arranging an open house for SPIN members and community officials.

Students who partnered with SPIN have drawn multiple connections between their service-learning experiences and the course's content and objectives. For instance, one student stated that her experience with SPIN accomplished the general course objective that we "examine some political issues addressed by contemporary feminists, especially as they intersect or conflict with national policies and practices." With specific reference to course content, this student stated that her experience with SPIN "drove home" Elizabeth Martinez's reference to welfare reform as "a terrorist war on immigrants" (1998), especially since "San Diego is a border town and there are a number of documented immigrants who live here." Another student observed similarly that "[w]elfare reform should be of primary concern for contemporary feminists . . . [because] the majority of women on welfare are employed in low-paying jobs that offer no health-care benefits." Noting the disconnect between the lived experience of welfare recipients and the assumptions made by those who "made the rules" regarding government assistance, the student stated further that "working with the SPIN office . . . helped me understand . . . how much we need to pay attention to the decisions made by policy-makers."

Peace and Freedom (political campaign)

A final example of the natural fit that can occur between academic course content and service-learning activities is the partnership developed with Peace and Freedom Party candidate Janice Jordan. During the 1999–2000 academic year, Jordan ran for the San Diego City Council and for San Diego mayor, respectively. In addition to attending official campaign events where she was featured as a candidate for city council or mayor, students who elected to work with Jordan were expected to orient themselves to the perspectives of the Peace and Freedom Party of California in general and to Jordan's stand on local issues in particular. These issues included, but were not limited to, the environment, law enforcement, housing, development, same-sex marriage, the prison industry, Indian gaming, worker's rights, public transportation, and animal rights.

One of the most compelling aspects of the community service option provided by Jordan was that it involved student participation beyond the election period and provided opportunities to work with a "multi-issues" feminist whose activism is grounded in understanding the "intersectionality" of sex, race, class, disability, sexual orientation, citizenship status, and more. Students working with Jordan became well versed in her party's platform, which reinforced a central tenet of my course: "The struggle against sexism . . . must be pursued actively at the same time as the struggle to eliminate oppression and discrimination based on class, race or nationality, age, or physical disability."

Because Jordan's campaign embraced a broad range of social justice issues and students gravitated to those aspects of her campaign that most resonated with them, reflection papers were highly varied. While one student was clearly drawn to environmental issues and public education for today's youth, another focused on efforts to raise public awareness regarding nuclear waste, unemployment, and homelessness in San Diego. A third student raised a different range of issues as she delved into Jordan's misrepresentation by the media, attacks on racism within the criminal justice system, and emphasis on the rights of Native Americans.

Service learning with the Jordan campaign resulted in other important learning outcomes, with several students indicating that they would continue to be politically active past the CBSL experience. Speaking as someone with no prior formal political experience, one student indicated that her experiences with the Jordan campaigns "gave her a reality check" and enabled her to make decisions about how she wanted to be involved in the government. Another student, who continued to work with Jordan and the organizations Jordan introduced to her (and who still does as of this writing), wrote in her reflection paper: "I now take part in as many activities as my time will allow, and then some. And, in my effort, I see a little progress now and then. That makes it all worthwhile. We all need to take part in directing where the world around us [is headed]."

Conclusion

While community-based service learning is an effective tool for enhancing student learning in any setting, it is particularly useful for challenging entrenched cultural values and beliefs about the homeless, welfare recipients, lesbians and gays, feminist organizations, and other socially and politically marginalized groups. Well-designed and structured service-learning projects with community organizations whose missions are aligned with course objectives allow students to integrate theory with application, often with the result that students unlearn stereotypes and misinformation, gain new levels of social consciousness, and even develop a burgeoning sense of civic responsibility.

Notes

1. I have written three related articles using classroom-based research: see Washington 2000a, 2000b, 2002.

2. A copy of Dr. Nsuti's syllabus may be found under "Syllabi by Discipline" on the Campus Compact Web site at <http://www.compact.org>.

3. Cf. Zlotkowski, 1999, p. 105: "Courses in research methodology, capstone seminars requiring the production of original work, and courses sufficiently advanced to permit policy analysis and recommendations are at least as suitable for service-learning initiatives as are courses that lend themselves to direct kinds of assistance."

4. Cone and Harris (1996, p. 39) also speak to the need for careful planning of experiential activities in order to reduce frustration and prevent "limited access to new information about the community in which . . . [the student] is working." Speaking about the potential for student exploitation, they suggest "weekly journals or reflective questions [that] offer . . . [students] a chance to air their frustrations, and, as a consequence, a chance for educators to help establish conditions in which they are more likely to learn."

5. Boyle-Baise (1999) also examines various philosophical frameworks for service-learning programs, including "conservative views," the "liberal perspective," "communitarian views," "radical democratic views," and "postmodern views." She concludes, "multicultural education seems to be a communitarian, radical democratic, and postmodern project" (p. 315).

6. Grusky (2000) also addresses the danger of exploitation, when she self-ironically explores the "fundamental contradiction . . . [in] the concept of international service learning" (p. 866). Cf. Guo, 1989, p. 108:

> Only in countries such as the United States and among the upper and middle classes in these countries could one even conceive of the concept of international service learning—which was once described as "allowing relatively well-off people in this world to travel long distances to experience other people's misery for a life-enriching experience."

7. Significantly, Eyler and Giles's (1999) study of 1,500 university students revealed that 57 percent of CBSL participants believed that service learning had given them their "first opportunity . . . to work alongside someone quite different from themselves" (p. 26).

8. Cone and Harris's observation is at least partially rooted in John Dewey's *Democracy and Education* (1916). Bringle and Hatcher (1999, p. 180) note:

> Dewey acknowledges that experience by itself does not necessarily result in learning; experiences can be either "miseducative" or "educative." Experience becomes educative when critical reflective thought creates new meaning and leads to growth and the ability to take informed actions. In contrast, experiences are miseducative when they fail to stimulate critical thought and they more deeply entrench existing schemata.

9. While advocating preservice training, Cone and Harris (1996, p. 37) provide the following important caveat: "What educators tell students to expect in communities will clearly shape what they observe. Educators need to be aware that in providing training on issues such as child abuse, gangs and delinquency, and other problem-focused views of community, students will be more likely to 'see' such things, even if these problems are rare or difficult to observe."

10. For instance, Bringle and Hatcher (1999, p. 182) suggest the following "conditions" or "structure" for effective reflection.

> [R]eflection activities should (a) clearly link the service experience to the course content and learning objectives; (b) be structured in terms of description, expectations, and the criteria for assessing the activity; (c) occur regularly during the semester so that students can practice reflection and develop the capacity to engage in deeper and broader reflection; (d) provide feedback from the instructor about at least some of the reflection activities so that students learn how to improve their critical analysis and develop from reflective practice; and (e) include the opportunity for students to explore, clarify, and alter their values.

11. Despite the fact that communities of color have long-standing and extensive histories of community service, and despite the fact that such service has long been a core value of communities of color (Weah, Simmons, & Hall, 2000), research on academic CBSL indicates that students of color are less likely to participate in CBSL than are their White counterparts and that men, in general, are less likely to participate than are White women and, to a lesser extent, women of color (Stanton, Giles, & Cruz, 1999). My neglect of this discussion, as well as my neglect, overall, of the impact CBSL has on diverse students or of factors instructors should consider when using CBSL in a diverse classroom, is in no way meant to suggest that this discussion is unimportant or to imply that CBSL is ineffective in diverse classrooms. Rather, the focus of my discussion has been determined largely from my experience as a Black female assistant professor teaching from a critical race-feminist perspective in a predominantly White institution.

12. Significantly, out of 120 students enrolled in the "Sex, Power, and Politics" classes I taught during the 1999–2000 academic year, almost two-thirds ($N = 76$) selected a CBSL option in lieu of a group research project. I establish the framework for the course within the first weeks of the semester through lectures and assigned readings from Cohen, Jones, and Tronto's *Women Transforming Politics: An Alternative Reader* (1997). This text, which incorporates essays from women across all race-ethnic lines (writing about topics as varied as domestic workers, disability rights, and lesbian activism), does an excellent job of representing "intersectionality," as well as redefining politics as a range of both formal and informal actions situated along the continuum of power and resistance. I also provide a more "traditional" look at "sex, power, and politics" by assigning readings from Norris's *Women, Media, and Politics* (1997), which examines the gendered roles and representations of women journalists, politicians, and activists. Additional texts include Cohen's *The Boundaries of Blackness: AIDS and the Breakdown of Black Politics* (1999) and Martinez's *De Colores Means All of Us: Latina Views for a Multi-Colored Century* (1998). Cohen's text examines the processes whereby certain "consensus" issues (e.g., Black male incarceration rates, Black male death rates, Black male unemployment) are labeled worthy of the Black community's attention, whereas equally important "crosscutting" issues (e.g., Black female incarceration rates, teenage pregnancy, lesbian and gay rights, and HIV/AIDS prevention) are ignored. Martinez's text is another model of "intersectionality" in that it explores the author's thirty years of activism in the movements for civil rights, women's liberation, Latino/a empowerment, economic justice, and the Latino/a youth movement.

Additional Resources

American Association for Higher Education. (n.d.). *AAHE's service-learning in the disciplines* (Monograph series). Washington, DC: AAHE Publications.

This series, covering a broad range of academic disciplines, offers a wide range of theoretical and practical approaches to developing service-learning strategies both inside and outside the classroom. Each volume is written by professionals in the field, combining specific expertise with suggestions for disciplinary practices.

Bringle, R. G., & Hatcher, J. A. (1996). Implementing service learning in higher education. *Journal of Higher Education, 67,* 221–239.

Bringle and Hatcher outline different ways for universities to implement service-learning principles through connecting their institutions to the surrounding community. Covered are usable programs for the institution as a whole, as well as for faculty members, students, and the community.

Canada, M., & Speck, B. W. (2001). *Developing and implementing service-learning programs* (New Directions for Higher Education No. 114). San Francisco: Jossey-Bass.

This issue in a series focuses on ways to align classroom work and activities with service to organizations in the community. The authors compare programs already in place at a variety of academic institutions, emphasizing the need for finding specific and appropriate organizations for students to work with.

Eyler, J., & Giles, D. E., Jr. (1999). *Where's the learning in service-learning?* San Francisco: Jossey-Bass.

Arguing against critics who suggest that service learning offers little in the way of academic rigor, this volume uses both recent national research results and individual student responses to suggest that service learning offers more than simply a connection between students and their communities. Eyler and Giles contend that service learning complements the goals of higher education, providing methods for combining the theoretical and practical in instruction.

Howard, J. (Ed.). (1993). *Praxis: Vol. 1. A faculty casebook on community service. Vol. 2. Service learning resources for university students, staff, and faculty.* Ann Arbor, MI: Office of Community Service Learning.

These two volumes, produced by the Michigan *Journal of Community Service Learning,* devote equal time to faculty testimony and advice (*Praxis* 1) and student and staff responses (*Praxis* 2). The faculty volume is devoted to experiences in service-learning programs in 14 disciplines already in place at the University of Michigan. The second volume, written primarily by students and service-learning specialists, offers a variety of suggestions for initiating and sustaining programs elsewhere.

Jacoby, B., & associates. (1996) *Service-learning in higher education: Concepts and practices.* San Francisco: Jossey-Bass.

Drawing from a wide range of educational institutions, this volume deals with both the conceptual issues in service learning and useful curricular and instructional approaches.

Kendall, J. (Ed.) (1990). *Combining service and learning: A resource book for community and public service* (Vols. 1 and 2). Raleigh, NC: National Society for Internships and Experiential Education.

Volume 1 in this series addresses the theoretical issues facing service-learning programs: intellectual, moral, and ethical questions; theories of social responsibility and cross-cultural awareness; and strategies for gaining institutional support for programs. Volume 2 addresses practical issues: curriculum development, recruitment, and supervision/evaluation.

Michigan Journal of Community Service Learning, 3. (1996). Available at <http://www.umich.edu/~mjcsl/>.

This issue includes articles and information from leaders in the field of service-learning education. The Web site offers abstracts of past issues as well as ordering information for subscriptions and back issues.

Stanton, T. K., Giles, D. E., Jr., & Cruz, N. I. (1999). *Service learning: A movement's pioneers reflect on its origins, practice, and future.* San Francisco: Jossey-Bass.

A collection of stories from three of the founders of service-learning education, this volume offers a close look at how the movement developed, how it has grown in recent years, and where it might be headed. Of central concern is preserving the role of the community activist as the idea of service learning becomes more prevalent.

Zlotkowski, E. (Ed.). (1998). *Successful service-learning programs: New models of excellence in higher education.* Boston: Anker.

By comparing ten different types of service-learning programs, Zlotkowski provides comprehensive guidelines for creating and strengthening programs in various types of institutions. He emphasizes the potential flexibility of theoretical tools to respond to different needs and goals.

13

Cross-Cultural Experiential Learning

Russell L. Young

In our increasingly diverse American society, the potential for cross-cultural interaction is enormous. Stereotypes, prejudice, and language differences are just a few of the obstacles to effective communication. Effective cross-cultural interactions have been a high priority to people of many fields for years. The high stakes of cross-cultural understanding can make the difference in making or losing millions for multinational corporations, in war or peace between conflicting countries, or in effectively treating millions of people against disease.

Agencies and organizations have declared the need for cross-cultural training in policy and action. For example, the Foreign Service Act of 1946 established the Foreign Service Institute to help train Foreign Service officers (Brislin & Pedersen, 1976). The American Psychological Association established the Office of Cultural and Ethnic Affairs in 1978 and the Board of Ethnic Minority Affairs in 1980 (Atkinson, Morten, & Sue, 1989). The Society for Intercultural Education, Training, and Research (SIETAR) has grown from a small newsletter for Peace Corps trainers and educators involved in international exchange to an association with chapters all over the world.

During the 1970s, a number of educational organizations, such as the American Association of Colleges for Teacher Education (AACTE), the National Council of Teachers of English (NCTE), and the National Council for Social Studies (NCSS), issued position statements and publications that encouraged schools to integrate the curriculum with content and understanding about ethnic groups. The inclusion of multicultural education in teacher education has been a requirement of the National Council for Accreditation of Teacher

Education (NCATE) since 1978. NCATE accredited institutions prepare over 70 percent of the new teachers annually (National Council for Accreditation of Teacher Education, 1977; Gollnick, 1995).

Learning about other cultures through experiential activities has been used in many learning contexts. Experiential learning has been used to understand other cultures in such diverse fields as social work (Davidson, 1997), counseling (Merta, Stringham, & Ponterotto, 1988), language courses (Sadow, 1987), and communications (Ostermeier, 1992). Teacher educators have also found success in incorporating experiential learning in teacher training programs (Mahan, Fortney, & Garcia, 1983; Ochoa, 1986; Young, 1993).

The purpose of this chapter is to describe the process and assess four experiential learning activities in an introductory multicultural education course. Implications for other cross-cultural college courses will be discussed.

Definitions and Considerations

Cross-cultural Experiential Learning Defined

Cross-cultural experiential learning (CCEL) brings concrete experiences into the student learning model; it assists students in applying classroom concepts and content to the real world, thereby completing the learning process (Katula & Threnhauser, 1999). It is similar to community-based service learning (see Washington & Weber, this volume), though it requires a onetime only activity, a brevity essential for the busy lives of many working students.

Wilson (1982) differentiates CCEL from simple cross-cultural experiences in that the former is reflected on so that one can evaluate the experience. The learning becomes very real for the learner because he/she is active and interacting with others rather than passive and often isolated in the learning experience. Wilson points to the need for CCEL in teaching because (1) teaching itself is a cross-cultural encounter, (2) cross-cultural experiences aid in self-development, (3) cross-culturally effective persons have characteristics desirable for effective teachers, and (4) cross-cultural learning leads to more global perspectives.

Considerations

Cross-cultural experiential learning can be adapted to many classrooms across disciplines. Following is some advice to best facilitate CCEL in the college classroom.

1. Allow for a variety of assignment possibilities for the students, thus increasing the chances for student motivation and interest. Mandatory experiences can have several repercussions. For example, a student may feel very uncomfortable going to a religious activity. Forcing one to do so would cause resentment. Having experiences that can only be sampled on certain days might interfere with family or religious activities. The range of experiences may be thought out by the instructor depending on the course. For example, a course on interethnic relations may require that students have assignments with a person or context outside of their ethnic realms. A cross-cultural communication class may want students to interact with people who speak different languages.

2. Integrate the experience with classroom goals, concepts, and content. For example, students in engineering may be involved in an assignment to interview engineers from a culture other than their own. Students in business might observe the ways in which businesses run by people from a variety of cultures are operated.

3. As assignments are being completed, allow for experience sharing during class.

4. Encourage students to reflect by juxtaposing their assigned experience with their own life experience.

5. Detail for students how they will be assessed for their response to the experience.

Pedagogical Implications

The Context and Students in the Course

In this chapter, I will use as an example an undergraduate class called "Introduction to Multicultural Education," a three-unit prerequisite for students in the teacher credential program. The course typically enrolls twenty to thirty students in each class, from a variety of ethnic groups. During the academic year 1999–2000, a total of 116 students were enrolled in the course. In this group, 71 (61.21 percent) identified themselves as White, 3 (2.59 percent) as African American, 24 (20.69 percent) as Latino, 15 (12.93 percent) as Asian or Pacific Islander, and 3 (2.59 percent) as other. Ninety-two (79.31 percent) were female, while 24 (20.69 percent) were male. The objectives for the course related to the CCEL were to (1) increase one's awareness of the role culture plays in the educational process, (2) increase one's awareness of self as a cultural being, (3) increase one's knowledge of strategies needed to educate a culturally diverse classroom, and (4) increase one's knowledge of major cultural groups in the area.

In each class, students were asked to select their CCEL from one of the following options, requiring about three hours of out-of-class time: a cultural plunge, work in a social service agency, a language interview, or a cultural interview. Each of these options is described in detail shortly.

Four Steps of CCEL

Wolsk (1974) suggests that there are four steps in CCEL. The first is the students' out-of-class experience. The second is the development of observational and descriptive skills to analyze the experience, bringing subtle elements to the conscious level. The third is the use of these skills to analyze and make decisions. The fourth is reflection on the experience, drawing from steps 2 and 3. Finally, students are involved in follow-up activities that link the experience with the theory, content, and concepts studied in the classroom. These experiences complement the course, yet they encourage students to reflect on their own life experiences and their personal responses to the assignments.

The first step is the experience itself. Students can choose an experience that is "culturally" different from their own. Culture is loosely defined as a different race, ethnicity, sexual orientation, language, generation in the United States, economic class, and disability. It is important to go into a "new" experience without much preparation, to lessen the preconceived expectations one might get from someone else. The assignment should be interesting personally to the students. So having several options to complete the assignment can maximize student motivation.

The second step is to develop observation and descriptive skills. This step is important because it helps bring to consciousness many experiences that may not be noticed. Within each cultural assignment is a written assignment. Students are required to describe the place visited or the person interviewed. The purpose of having this as part of the written requirement is to bring to the conscious level experiences that one might not normally be aware of. For example, a person going to a place of worship might describe the church, the way people are dressed, and modes of transportation used. A person often interviews someone he or she knows and discovers information about the interviewee's background that he or she did not know despite having a long relationship.

The third step is to develop analysis and decision-making skills. The instructor can help guide each student's analysis with questions the student needs to answer on the subsequent write-up. Students can be encouraged to integrate course readings with their interpretation of the experience. Guiding questions should be tailored to the experience and course objectives. For example, a person conducting a language interview would be asked to find out how the interviewee learned English, the role of school in learning English, how the native language is maintained, and views on bilingual education. The person would then write on how he or she would use the knowledge in his or her own future teaching.

Students should also tie in the experience with the overall goal of the course. In the case of the multicultural education course, each write-up should address what one learned from the assignment to help them in their future teaching. In a cross-cultural counseling class, the instructor may ask the student to analyze counseling issues presented when having clientele from the encountered culture. In a communication course, the student assignment may entail a contrast/comparison in communication styles between oneself and people of the encountered cultural group. A child development class might compare upbringing styles in different cultures. In this case, depending on the option chosen, students might address such issues as how the interviewed person learned or maintained language skills, how culture impacted his or her life, how the interviewed person's experience in school compares with their own, and stereotypes encountered.

The fourth step is to do follow-up activities that link the experience with the ongoing curriculum. Other assignments include a class presentation and academic paper. One could do all three assignments on the same cultural group. One could also hear a presentation on the same group from a fellow classmate. Other follow-up activities include readings and guest speakers. This step is important so that the cultural experience does not seem like an isolated experience disconnected from readings, guest speakers, or other assignments.

Experiential Activities

Cultural Plunge

Twenty-eight of the students enrolled in "Introduction to Multicultural Education" chose to engage in the cultural plunge. The cultural plunge is an assignment in which the student goes into a setting very different from his or her own culture. Plunges have been quite diverse and have included attending Black churches, gay bars, Buddhist temples, Native American powwows, and Mexican weddings. Plunges that were passive, such as going to a museum or an arts and crafts show, were unacceptable. Plunges also had to be done during the semester, thus eliminating experiences reconstructed from memory. Students were instructed to actively engage in the plunge and talk to people. In order to develop observation and analytic skills, they had to summarize and reflect on their plunge by writing a three-page paper describing (1) the event, (2) their perception and attitudes of the cultural group before and after the plunge, (3) what they would like to teach their future students based on the experience, and (4) teaching strategies to be used to teach their future students.

Community Service Agency

The second option was to spend time in a community service agency. Eighteen students went to a community service agency. They were to talk to the people that ran the agency as well as to people who utilized the service. Each student was then to write a three-page paper describing (1) the agency and the people it serves, (2) changes in the student's perception of the cultural group after the observation, and (3) how the student would incorporate the information to make him or her a more effective teacher for this population. Community agencies that are often visited include homeless shelters, agencies that serve people with AIDS, and juvenile detention centers.

Language Interview

The third option was to interview a person who was not a native English speaker but who had attended U.S. public schools. Twenty-one students conducted a language interview. The interview and subsequent three-page report was to (1) give a short biography of the person, (2) discuss the extent to which bilingualism and other factors (including school) influenced current language abilities, and (3) analyze factors that helped or hindered this person's education and discuss implications for future teaching of English language learners.

Cultural Interview

The fourth option was to conduct a cultural interview with a person who grew up in a country other than the United States or in a rich multicultural setting in the United States. Forty-eight students conducted a cultural interview. The three-page report was to include (1) a short biography of the person, (2) a description of the person's self-perception as a cultural person (ethnic labels, degree of assimilation, cultural knowledge), of prejudice the person has encountered, and of stereotypes people hold of his or her ethnic group, and (3) a discussion of ways to reduce prejudice and facilitate a smooth cultural transition to the U.S. classroom, based on the interview.

Debriefing with the Students

After the assignments are done, it is important to have a sharing time for students. Students enjoy being able to share their experiences in small-group discussions. In small groups, students often can get even greater clarification of the experiences. For example, a student who conducted a language interview with a Spanish-speaking interviewee may get an additional perspective from a bilingual Spanish-speaking classmate. The role of the instructor is to facilitate such discussion in a respectful atmosphere. The cultural assignments are just a continuation of what will hopefully be a lifelong process of becoming an effective multicultural teacher.

Although time may have varied for each assignment, students typically spent about three hours on the experience itself. On the day the cultural assignments were due, students were allowed to discuss in small and large groups their own findings. By doing this, students were able to hear about the learning that took place with other classmates. Students then engaged in a "blind trust walk" to demonstrate a simple experiential learning activity where one depends on senses other than one's sight. Students paired up with each other. One was to walk with closed eyes while the other guided. To make the experience more vivid, they were instructed not to talk, to avoid preconceived notions. Afterward, the instructor guided the students in connecting the experience with the four steps of experiential learning. They may "observe" for the first time many sounds and feelings through the act of "describing" their experiences. These sounds and feelings are experienced everyday, but probably not at the conscious level because of one's dependence on vision. Students would comment on the change going from concrete to grass, on how it felt to be "looked" at, and on feelings of trust or distrust. Students were able to analyze the situation by connecting the learning to the school environment when asked what adaptations were needed for visually impaired students. Last, the blind trust walk was tied into the course by connecting it with the components and benefits of experiential learning. This experience was then linked to the four options.

To further link their cross-cultural learning experiences with the course, students were exposed to guest speakers during the term. Students also wrote research papers on cultural groups and presented lesson plans to fellow students that were related to their cultural awareness assignment.

The Students' Evaluation of the Experiences

Survey

All students were given a survey to complete after turning in their cultural awareness assignments. Items on the survey were based on writings by Bennett, whose 1999 book is a widely used text on multicultural education that discusses the areas to which teachers and students need to be sensitized in order to effectively work in a culturally diverse classroom. Bennett writes that there are six curriculum goals in multicultural education. These goals include (1) to develop multiple historical perspectives; (2) to develop cultural consciousness; (3) to develop intercultural competence; (4) to combat racism, sexism, prejudice, and all forms of discrimination; (5) to raise awareness of the state of the planet and global dynamics; and (6) to develop social action skills.

Students were given twelve statements that they were to rate on a five-point Likert scale ranging from "strongly disagree" (1) to "strongly agree" (5). The statements were to assess the impact that the cultural assignment had on students' understanding of themselves and others.

Quantitative Data

Results indicate that all four cultural assignments were effective according to students' responses to the twelve survey statements. Table 1 shows that the mean response was higher than the neutral 3.0 on all of the responses for all four cultural assignments. The cultural assignments seemed particularly effective in promoting empathy toward people of other cultures (statement 5) and interest in the cultural group (statement 6), as indicated with a 4.0 response or higher for all four cultural assignments. The overall effectiveness of the assignment seemed validated with the students' high mean responses to statements 7 ("I would recommend others to have the same experience as I") and 8 ("I believe that cultural assignment is an important aspect to better understand multicultural education").

Results found the cultural plunge to be significantly more effective than the language interview and the cultural interview in decreasing one's fear of interacting with members of the cultural group. Likewise, the community service was more effective in reducing interaction fear than was the language interview. Through statement 9, the language and cultural interviews were found to be more effective than the cul-

TABLE 1. ANOVA of Degree of Agreement of Effectiveness of Four Cultural Assignments

| | Type of Assignment | | | | |
	Cultural Plunge (M, SD)	Language Interview (M, SD)	Community Service (M, SD)	Cultural Interview (M, SD)	F
1. I felt that several of my stereotypes of the cultural group were broken	(3.7, .94)	(3.6, .68)	(3.9, .68)	(3.7, .95)	.36
2. My fear of interacting with members of the group lessened	(4.2, .77)	(3.5, .81)	(4.0, .59)	(3.6, .84)	4.7★
3. I understand better what it feels like to be in the minority	(4.0, .88)	(3.9, .94)	(3.9, .80)	(4.0, .60)	.05
4. I have a better understanding of myself as a cultural being	(4.2, .66)	(4.0, .90)	(3.8, .65)	(4.1, .66)	1.29
5. I feel I have more empathy towards people of other cultures now	(4.0, 1.04)	(4.1, .77)	(4.4, .70)	(4.3, .62)	1.28
6. I would like to know more about the cultural group	(4.2, .86)	(4.1, .70)	(4.1, .73)	(4.3, .64)	.52
7. I would recommend others to have the same experience as I	(4.4, .69)	(4.3, .85)	(4.5, .71)	(4.4, .64)	.33
8. I believe that cultural assignment is an important aspect to better understand multicultural education	(4.4, .92)	(4.7, .56)	(4.4, .61)	(4.5, .55)	1.13
9. I feel more committed to combat prejudice than before	(3.6, 1.03)	(4.3, .97)	(4.1, .54)	(4.31, .72)	4.13★
10. I think that my ability to communicate with people of this cultural group was enhanced	(4.0, 1.07)	(3.8, .72)	(3.9, .68)	(4.1, .73)	.81
11. I have a better understanding of the history of the cultural group	(3.6, 1.23)	(3.7, .92)	(3.6, .78)	(4.1, .66)	2.79★
12. I have a better awareness of the state of the planet and global dynamics	(3.4, 1.06)	(3.2, .89)	(3.5, .71)	(3.9, .73)	4.76★

★$p < .05$.

tural plunge in instilling a sense of commitment to combat prejudice. Through statement 11, the cultural interview was found to be more effective than the cultural plunge in understanding the history of the cultural group. Through statement 12, the cultural interview was found to be more effective than the cultural plunge in increasing awareness of the state of the planet and global dynamics.

Qualitative Data

The actual graded cultural assignments provided rich qualitative data on the experiences of the students. The assignments validated the process as well as the survey results. Processwise, students seemed to increase their descriptive and observational skills. Cultural assignments where the students "immersed" themselves into a new environment (plunge and community agency) seemed to reduce fear of interaction with others more than did the interviews. In contrast, the students who conducted interviews were better able to relate in-depth to another person and commented on their commitment to multicultural goals. In general, all of the assignments helped instill a sense of equity and justice. Following are examples from selected cultural assignments.

Observation and descriptive skills increased as evidenced by student comments on the experiences. It is through this "cultural contrast" that one becomes aware of one's own culture, perhaps for the first time.

> A student who interviewed a Taiwanese person: "In Taiwan, it is considered rude, disrespectful, and a sign of challenging for a student to look their teacher directly in the eyes. . . . this body language is often misunderstood by an American teacher thinking that the Asian student is not paying attention."

> A non-Jew attending Rosh Hashanah: "After the service, however, I was much more comfortable with this foreign language. I was able to recognize certain words and even participate in some of the prayers and songs during the service."

> A student who interviewed a Mexican immigrant: "The rule for adding 'ed' to words did not apply for all the words in English; for example she wanted to write the word 'run' in the past tense as 'runed.'"

Students' analysis skills were increased. Integration of course readings helped link theory to observed experiences.

A student who interviewed a Korean American: "Byoung feels he has greatly assimilated into the American culture, feeling a part of the culture (identificational assimilation), but he feels he still retains the Korean culture within. This could very possibly be due to the fact that he and his family were voluntary minorities, and therefore less resentful and more accepting of the new culture."

The quantitative results indicated that the community service agencies and cultural plunges were especially effective in decreasing one's fear of other cultural groups. Student papers supported this result.

A student visiting the homeless at a community agency: "I have always thought that homeless people do not care enough about their well being to do something to change their situation. To me a homeless person is portrayed or looks like a bum. . . . I have changed some of my views and assumptions about the homeless. The people I saw that day weren't a bunch of bums or losers, but people hard on their luck and very unfortunate."

A student going to an African American friend's family lunch: "I was nervous at first, not knowing how I should act or what I should say. This feeling immediately left me when we got inside the house. . . . after having lunch with his family, my overall view about African Americans changed. Not only has my views about that ethnicity changed but also I have changed it for all ethnicities. I now know that I cannot make general statements about a group of people. I now take with me the belief that everyone, when approached in the right situation, can be as loving as my family."

A student visiting a family-owned house in Mexico: "When I first started going to Mexico with my family I was scared of the people there, not necessarily because I thought they would hurt me but because they were different and I couldn't communicate with them or understand them. . . . when I went to Mexico for my cultural plunge I thought about how I used to feel about and see these people and I realize how wrong I was. Now when I look at and interact with the people of Mexico (and other cultures) I see how alike we are."

Those conducting the cultural interviews felt more of a sense of commitment to combat prejudice, of understanding another's history, and of global awareness than did those on a cultural plunge.

A student who interviewed a Mexican coworker: "Although the struggle Raul has encountered, he has grown to be a strong person. I have more of a respect for him knowing what he went through for his family. Everyday he devotes his day to working, in order to help support his family back in Mexico."

A student who interviewed a cousin from Vietnam: "I noticed Niem spoke with a little accent: something I really did not notice before. . . . Talking to Niem made me take a good look at myself, how I thought of myself as a cultural being, and the troubles I went through as a child growing up. . . . the troubles I had were minimal compared to Niem's."

Overall, all four assignments proved to be effective in instilling values needed to work with a diverse population. A sense of commitment to justice and equity was supported.

A student visiting a women's assistance center: "I put this into action in my own classrooms this month. We started a Thanksgiving food drive in order to replenish the dwindling food supply. I believe that if you give children the opportunity to help others, they will."

A student attending a Mexican *Quinceanera* celebration for a girl's fifteenth birthday: "[O]pen-mindedness to different cultures also shows the students that diversity is a factual part of life. As a teacher, I will have to apply teaching tactics, which are conducive to each culture."

A student attending an African American church: "It saddened me deeply when I realized that all my life I have had African-American friends, but we never talked about it [ethnicity]. It is always uncomfortable to talk about what my ancestors were a part of, as well as how my friends felt about their parents' struggles. This lack of communication is what we are missing in our school system. I believe we can accomplish our goals of world unity only through communication and exposure: exposure to all the issues that face all ethnicities. By doing this, even as young as third grade, maybe we can make sense of this rapidly changing world that we live in not only for ourselves, but our children as well."

A student attending an inner-city after-school program: "As a teacher I will have to work hard for these bilingual children to realize that they are also part of the American culture."

Discussion

The cultural plunge, the cultural interview, the language interview, and community service are techniques that are not only effective but relatively easy to implement. The short amount of student commitment required (approximately three hours) makes all of the assignments easy to implement. This decreases the amount of logistical support from that an instructor would need to provide for semester-long experiential activities. Also, student choice helps assure that students will do an activity with personal relevance and interest.

All four assignments were proven to be highly effective in promoting multicultural goals, from increased commitment to reduce prejudice to a better understanding of the history of the various ethnic groups.

Of interest are the different effects the assignments had on students' attitudes. This may be due to the type of interaction each student had to do in their cultural assignment. Students going on a cultural plunge often mentioned anxiety before onset. For example, Whites going to a Black church would fear there would be hostility toward them. Students attending a Hare Krishna temple would fear devotees would "brainwash" them. Students were to go to a strange setting and interact with people they would not normally interact with. The anxiety of being a "fish out of water" forced many to confront deep-rooted fears of members of the cultural group. However, the large majority had very positive experiences that helped alleviate stereotypes and anxieties. The process may explain why the cultural plunge had a bigger impact than the other assignments in lessening the fear of interacting with members of the group. The community service visit also helped to lessen fear toward those the students visited.

The cultural and language interviews tended to be with people familiar with the students. In fact, at times, students used the assignment as an opportunity to interview family members on issues that they had never discussed before. Several found the in-depth interviews to be personally fulfilling. The one-on-one nature of the interviews may help explain some of the results. By having an in-depth interview, many students may have bonded with the interviewees in a way not possible through the cultural plunge or community service. This may explain why students conducting the cultural interviews felt more committed to combat prejudice than did those that had a cultural plunge. Likewise, more than students who had a cultural plunge, those who conducted cultural interviews felt they had a better understanding of the history of the cultural groups as well as a better awareness of the state of the planet and global awareness.

Regardless of the type of course one teaches or the form of the assignments, one must realize that multiculturalism is really a process, not a goal. One assignment, or even one course, cannot ever completely train one to be effective in every cross-cultural interaction in the future. Rather, it would hopefully spark one's interest and inspire one to see multiculturalism as an asset to the world and to one's immediate career.

Additional Resources

Publications

Brislin, R., & Pedersen, P. (1976). *Cross-cultural orientation programs*. New York: Gardner Press.

> This book prepares the reader in five areas of competency. First, there is a review of the basic issues in cross-cultural orientation and adjustment. Second, there is a review of the most widely used training models to prepare and orient persons for cross-cultural involvement. Third, there is a description of the large audiences that benefit from increased cross-cultural orientation. Fourth, there is a discussion of how the reader might evaluate programs of cross-cultural orientation. Last, there is a series of practical suggestions on how the reader might design and implement a program of cross-cultural orientation appropriate to his or her particular needs.

Crews, Robin. (2002). *Higher education service-learning sourcebook*. Westport, CT: Oryx Press.

> This resource book includes journals, Web sites, programs around the nation, organizations, awards, internships, grants, and conferences concerning higher education service learning.

Eyler, J., & Giles, D., Jr. (1999). *Where's the learning in service-learning?* San Francisco: Jossey-Bass.

> Academic service learning continues to grow rapidly. Practitioners at colleges press for more empirical research about learning outcomes. This book helps define learning expectations, presents data about learning, and links program characteristics with learning outcomes.

Introduction to service-learning tool kit: readings and resources for faculty.

> This comprehensive set of articles on service learning for the college faculty includes readings on theory, pedagogy, community partnerships, student development, assessment, redesigning curriculum, use of reflection, and model programs. It is available from Campus Compact, whose mailing address and Web address are as follows: Box 1975, Brown University, Providence, RI 02912; <http://www.compact.org>.

Jackson, L., & Cafarella, R. (Eds.). (1994). *Experiential learning: A new approach*

(New Directions for Adults and Continuing Education No. 62). San Francisco: Jossey-Bass.

This useful edited volume has chapters on experiential learning theory and practice for adult learners. Chapter topics include foundations of experiential learning, techniques to engage learners in experiential learning activities, assessment, portfolio construction, and characteristics of adult learners.

Albert, G. (Ed.). (1994). *Service-learning reader: Reflections and perspectives on service*. Raleigh, NC: National Society of Experiential Education.

This interdisciplinary anthology for students, interns, and volunteers includes chapters on orientation skills and getting started; interaction, reflection, and dialogue; roots of service; community; ethics, decision making, and social justice; and global awareness. Featured authors include Paulo Freire; Tim Stanton; Nel Noddings; Robert Coles; Martin Luther King, Jr.; Ram Dass; Alexis de Tocqueville; Deepak Chopra; Jesse Jackson; and Robert Bellah. This book can be used in classrooms or as a training resource. It is available from the National Society for Experiential Education (see "Organizations").

York, Darlene. (1994). *Cross-cultural training programs*. Westport, CT: Bergin and Garvey.

This book explores the relations of ethnic groups in the United States, cultural shock, cross-cultural training programs, organizations that have used cross-cultural training, and implications of findings.

Organizations

Council for Adult and Experiential Learning (CAEL). This nonprofit organization is committed to providing better access to education for adults, through partnerships with business, government, labor, and higher education. The mailing address and Web address for CAEL are as follows: 55 East Monroe Street, Suite 1930, Chicago, IL 60603; <http://www.cael.org>.

National Society for Experiential Education (NSEE). NSEE is a nonprofit membership association of educators, businesses, and community leaders. Founded in 1971, NSEE also serves as a national resource center for the development and improvement of experiential education programs nationwide. The mailing address and Web address for NSEE are as follows: 9001 Braddock Road, Suite 380, Springfield, VA 22151; <http://www .nsee.org>.

14

Community Action: Students as Agents of Change

Shirley N. Weber

The *Brown v. Board of Education* desegregation decision of 1954 and the civil rights, black power, and women's protest movements of the mid-1960s brought to predominantly White university campuses an influx of students of color unlike any seen in the history of this country. Students were being recruited not only from different ethnic groups but also from across socioeconomic lines. The face of this new university challenged the institutions to examine their long-held traditions and practices. No longer could the academy assume that its student body came from similar academic and social backgrounds with equally similar reasons for attending the university. Additionally, students who had been isolated in homogenous communities learned very quickly that many of the things they had thought were universally understood and accepted were not. Thus, conflicts were born.

As a student of this era, I learned quickly, to my surprise, that my reason for being at the University of California, Los Angeles (UCLA), was very different from the reasons of many of my classmates. I was on a mission to improve my social status and uplift my community. It seemed to me as if no one else except other African Americans, Hispanics, and a few poor Whites shared my mission. The other 590 (out of 600) students in my dormitory appeared to be on an excursion of self-discovery and expansion. Consequently, they enjoyed dialogue for dialogue's sake. They felt the key to their future lay in finding the right Greek organization and meeting the right Greek-connected people. I kept asking, "How would this help me?" and, "What does this mean for African Americans?" To my peers, I did not seem to enjoy education. To me, education did not seem to want me. Thus, my first two years of college seemed meaningless. Many of my friends of color dropped out,

247

not for academic reasons, but because nothing appeared to make sense. Most of us did not come to terms with the fact that we were culturally different, with unique family backgrounds and educational legacies. We could not articulate our needs, because we knew none of the academic terms like *culturally relevant teaching strategies* or *learning styles*. This lack of self-knowledge caused me, as well as many of my peers of color, to feel alone and excluded from campus life. For the first time, we who had been leaders in our respective communities were misfits in the academic community. We were accustomed to being involved and making a difference; now, we were miles away from home base and community. Finding an anchor would be no easy task.

Those of us who remained at UCLA shared with each other the names of "relevant" professors and "relevant" classes. Through this process, I found courses during my junior and senior years that added focus and purpose to my studies. Years later, these courses became the foundation for the development of my current course in Africana studies titled "Communications and Community Action."

Civic and Curricular Responsibilities of Ethnic and Women's Studies Departments

Various ethnic studies departments that spread across the nation in predominantly white universities were by-products of the activism and personal and cultural estrangement of the 1960s. Africana studies departments, followed by other studies departments, became a logical extension of the call for relevant education made by students and faculty who shared my experiences. These departments were called on not only to teach the Black, women's, or Chicano "experience" but also to revolutionize the academy. In their initial phases, these departments employed persons who were activists first and scholars second. In some instances, departments rejected the notion of tenure and other institutional trappings in order to keep the faculty relevant to the masses. This structure quickly fueled its own demise. As the academy demanded higher standards of its faculty, the interest and commitment to community endeavors waned. Also, because activism was not always linked to the curriculum or research of the faculty, its role in the evaluation, promotion, and tenure was always in question. The conflict between scholars and activists divided departments. In the process, activists were becoming extinct.

Despite the move away from total activist structures, Africana studies departments and similar units remained philosophically committed to relevant education. This commitment can be found in the preambles, philosophy statements, goals, and objectives of department mission statements, as well as in program proposals and the publications of the National Council for Black Studies. This organization subscribes to the philosophy that education should engender "academic excellence and social responsibility" (National Council for Black Studies, n.d.). Likewise, the philosophy statement of the Africana Studies Department of San Diego State University states that the department "seeks to develop students who are competent and *committed* scholars [my emphasis]" (San Diego State University, 1994).

In addition to the stated philosophical commitment, the San Diego State University Africana Studies Department realized in a very tangible sense that students who gravitated to it were seeking meaning in the academic experience. This was evident in nonmajors taking several courses in ethnic studies and in the students organizing to make a difference. Few freshmen are Africana studies majors or minors. Generally, they declare their intent to major or minor in their junior or senior year after much exposure to the discipline. Students in our classes form groups that create community-based activities. For example, one group of students formed a leadership group offering high school students workshops and summer experiences to promote academic excellence and leadership skills. Another group, called Sisters Incorporating Sisterhood (SIS), has been formed to mentor African American elementary students. Recently, a group of students started a Saturday school to tutor elementary school students. In each case, the students involved in community outreach efforts remained enrolled at the university and saw a reason for excelling in their classes. Each organization provided emotional and academic support for its members, which in turn increased their involvement and retention at the university.

Therefore, in trying to fulfill its mission, our Africana Studies Department wants to provide an invaluable service for the community, help students understand the connection between knowledge and social change, and increase student success and retention. In its early development, the department analyzed several models. The first model involved special studies in which a student identified a specific area of interest, mapped out a plan of action and research, and proceeded to fulfill the prescribed academic plan. However, the value of such experiences was sporadic and unpredictable because they were not always regulated and consistent enough for the department to be able to assess where the courses fit in the overall undergraduate education of the major or minor. The department then turned to other models, consistent with departments on campus and in other universities—but also consistent with its community-related goals.

Building a Community Action Course: Two Models

In this section, I will discuss one upper-division course in our Africana Studies Department and the course's origins. Africana Studies 360, "Communications and Community Action," was modeled after two undergraduate courses at UCLA. One course was in the Speech Communications Department and required students to evaluate an organization utilizing the principles of effective communications and group dynamics. In that course, students were required to identify an organization engaged in decision making and to evaluate the role of communications in accomplishing the organization's goals. Often, this involved attending board and membership meetings. Students were outside observers who provided the organization with an alternative assessment of the effectiveness in communicating its mission to its constituents. They were not involved in influencing the process; they only observed.

The second course model, also taken from UCLA, was a twelve-unit experience that placed students in a community organization or movement for an entire semester. When I enrolled, I worked with Jesse Jackson and Operation Bread Basket. Students were given little academic support; what happened in the community during the semester was not discussed in an academic context. It was left to the students to make sense of what was happening around them. The experience of working in a community agency was rich; however, it was difficult to make a connection between our experiences and the classroom. In their agencies, students were seen as temporary volunteers who provided an important labor force for the organization. Seldom were they included in evaluations of what was going on or invited to structure the agenda of the organization. In Operation Breadbasket, for example, my primary task was picketing and canvassing neighborhoods and educating parents on consumerism. The program was handed to me in final form, without consultation, and I implemented it.

Almost forty years later, I teach Africana Studies 360, "Communications and Community Action," a blend of the two courses already described. The principles of community activism, social policy, and communication are taught through direct involvement in a community organization. For one semester, the entire class is involved with an organization located in the African American community. This differs from earlier efforts by the Africana Studies Department and from the current models of service learning, because involvement is not *integrated into* the course, it *is* the course. Classroom lectures, discussions, films, and so on augment the involvement experience. In this course, the community organization provides the class with a living laboratory in which students can learn community issues and concerns while attempting to address those issues and initiate viable change.

Community Action Course Content, Demands, and Objectives

The objectives of the communications course are

- to provide an authentic connection between real-life activity and academic knowledge;
- to provide valuable human resources to struggling organizations and programs;
- to help students appreciate the difficult work of community agencies;
- to help students see how they factor into the life and development of their community; and
- to introduce students who might be unfamiliar with the city to the larger outside community.

Over the past twenty years, the course has evolved into a valuable resource for the African American community. It has become so valuable that organizations call early asking to be "adopted" by the class. Many nonprofits see the class as a way to launch new projects as well as to sustain continuing community outreach. Over time, students in the course have helped

- develop an African-centered Saturday school;
- organize community forums;
- collect data for the Driving While Black/Brown (DWB) campaign;
- design a new logo and brochure material for a parent advocacy group;
- create a gang diversion program in southeast San Diego; and
- organize Black male programs at two local high schools.

The class has experienced positive results; however, it has also experienced disappointing setbacks. Nonetheless, projects that could not be brought to completion still provided an invaluable learning experience for the students. In many cases, those unsuccessful efforts proved to be better learning experiences than the more successful ones.

There are problems with developing a course that is different from others on campus, of course. Too often, students come to the class believing that it will be an "easy" course because of its structure. They soon learn that it is not easy; in fact, it demands a lot of time, creativity, sensitivity, and independent initiative. It is the type of course in which students can easily get lost; therefore, it requires much signposting from the instructor, along with false deadlines to keep the projects moving forward and the students meeting expectations.

Some History

In the initial offering of Africana Studies 360, students were given lists of agencies and were required to select their agency within a two- to three-week period. The list had been preapproved, which meant that the instructor had talked with the agency and that the leaders had given their permission to be included in the class options. Students were given contact names and encouraged to visit a few of the agencies prior to making a selection. They were also given a set of questions to ask in order to know as much as possible about the agency and its needs. If a student had another choice than one listed on the class options, he or she could submit that choice and a rationale to the instructor for approval. Most of the time, the alternate selection was approved.

This method of self-selection clearly had its advantages. First, the student likely felt more committed to the project, because he or she had selected it from the list or through his or her community contacts. Also, with this approach, if things were going poorly with an agency, the student would frequently work harder to bring the project back in line. Additionally, a student could align his or her interests with a particular project. For example, a journalism student chose to volunteer at the local African American newspaper and cover stories on an educational movement occurring in the community. This project was so closely designed for the student that it became instrumental in determining his future employment. Under this self-selection model, a class of twenty students meant twenty separate projects and more community agencies receiving help. The variety of the projects also made for interesting class dialogue. Students were intrigued when they learned that many agencies experience the same problems of poor community support, limited resources, and poor leadership, while facing the reality of overwhelming community needs.

Despite the advantages of this multiagency approach, the negative factors surrounding this self-selection method often outweighed the benefits. Self-selection assumes that students have enough knowledge of the San Diego community to make informed choices. Because most students in the Africana studies course come from areas outside the county, it was hard for them to make a choice. Too often, the instructor was asked to pick an agency because the deadline for selection had passed. The real weakness, however, came in the area of focus and supervision. It was impossible for the instructor to know whether or not the students were having a quality experience, because there were so many agencies that it was almost impossible to keep track of what was happening. In many cases, students were merely used as clerical assistants and were not allowed to do much other than answer the phone. Too many students learned very little from working as receptionists or at equivalent jobs in an organization.

Furthermore, the students felt uncomfortable asking for more involvement and participation if they were the "only" students in the agency. Many organizations did not know how to include students, so the best they could do was to relegate them to clerical tasks. However, in extremely small organizations, where the staff consisted of three to five persons, students got lots of experience but poor supervision and direction because the need for workers was so great. Last, students did not have anyone with whom they could collaborate and discuss in detail what was happening, to determine if they were on the right track.

For students who were self-directed and motivated, the self-selection format worked well. For students who were not as independent, the format was difficult and revealed more about them and their ability to move into organizations than about the organization itself.

So, changes in the class had to be enacted. As an interim approach, agencies that had agreed to accommodate three to four students were offered to the class. In this case, the list consisted of only four to six agencies. This structure addressed the problems that had occurred by having a single student in an organization. It also responded to the question of supervision, by lowering the number of projects to a manageable size for the instructor. However, the other issues remained a concern for several of the organizations and students.

About ten years ago, the San Diego Urban League approached the department for student volunteers from the class. When I asked how many students they could use, the education director's reply was, "How many do you have?" When I said, "Between sixteen and twenty," her answer was, "All of them." Thus began the one-agency model employed today.

Current Course Structure

Providing Background for the Students

From these experiences, our department learned several things about structuring a course of this nature. First, a carefully crafted curriculum is central. Without it, students lack the critical eyes and ears necessary to be actively involved, and they become ordinary volunteers rather than leaders and change agents. The first three weeks of the course are spent providing students with a foundation. Students are given lots of material to absorb about the general concepts of effective communication and public relations. Then, they are introduced to the concepts of community, and materials on the city's Black community are read. Local speakers who have knowledge of the history of the community and how it operates as a unique entity are invited to talk to the class. These speakers need not be elected officials but may be persons who have started community agencies or social groups and who are familiar with community groups and how they operate. Just from working and living in the community, these individuals bring a wealth of information about how to approach change, when to seek change, and why change might take longer in certain communities. This vital information is not found in textbooks.

It is advantageous for the instructor to locate the most current information, because the issues students are dealing with are contemporary, not theoretical. Every year, the National Urban League publishes *The State of Black America*. When available, this is an invaluable resource. Contained in the book is the most up-to-date research by African American scholars on issues facing the Black community. Unfortunately, the publication is released at different times during the spring and is not always available at the beginning of the semester. However, even a year-old report provides valuable information that can be used in conjunction with other materials.

If there are local research agencies that produce reports, they should also be made available to the students. In San Diego, for example, reports from local groups such as San Diego's Regional Planning Agency (SANDAG) and the San Diego Policy Initiative are required class reading, because while it is important to know what Billingsley (1988) and others have to say about the Black family, it is equally important to know whether national norms can be applied locally. Similarly, reports from local school districts are critical to making decisions about the educational needs of students. Most often, a local environment has different nuances, and mistakes can be made when a sweeping national view is used as the only lens to approach the areas of concern.

Students also discuss theories of social change. Over the years, various theories have been selected. One currently in use is the "ten steps for change" found in Hampden-Turner's *From Poverty to Dignity* (1974). The discussion of such theories allows students to understand where they are in the change process. Because the course is dynamic, as change is, students are encouraged to research the area and even to develop their own theories of change.

Agency Contact and Integration

During the three-week orientation period, the class is taken to the agency and introduced to all the key personnel. The specific projects available are discussed, and students are able to match their particular interests, majors, and skills to the various programs. For example, students in journalism and public relations become involved in marketing a new program. In one case, a student majoring in graphic design developed a new logo and fund-raising material for the agency. This logo, which was developed over five years ago, is still used today.

The course is organized so that there is contact by the student with the agency every week. Class meetings are reduced in accordance with the time required for volunteering. A minimum of three hours per week of volunteer time is required. Class meetings consist of lectures, films, and discussions concerning the evolving issues in the community. For instance, if there have been major changes occurring at the state or county level with regard to funding of after-school programs and if the project currently underway at the agency is an educational one, then the class focuses on the policy issues in an effort to understand the impact of those issues on the goals and objectives for the organization. It is important to keep the curriculum current so that the students do not just intellectualize change but also feel the dynamics of change in the life of a community. In the process, students become extremely sensitive to governmental changes (elections, funding cycles, etc.) and therefore are compelled to stay current on news items. They voluntarily read the local papers, watch the news, and attend news conferences and community forums.

Course Outcomes

One of the primary outcomes of the course is to implement programs and plans in the African American community. This outcome is reflected in the actual work in the agency, in the completion of projects, and in a written analysis of the agency's efforts at change. Depending on the agency, students present written or, occasionally, oral reports on their work. The papers and presentations address the current obstacles to change and the agency's efforts to overcome those obstacles. Generally, students prepare two papers for the course. One paper is for the instructor and leans heavily on the theoretical discussions in class. As the basis for their analysis and recommendations, students use the theoretical frameworks they have been given in class concerning social policy and change. The second document is a composite paper written by the entire class. This paper provides the organization with a comprehensive view of the project(s), as well as of accomplishments and obstacles, in an effort to maximize the organization's efforts. The assumption here is that the average director does not have time to read twenty papers that may overlap in their comments about the current activities of the agency. Additionally, the use of one comprehensive report helps to keep mention of the individual problems that students might have had with persons in the agency to a minimum unless those problems are widespread and affect the operation of all the projects.

Comments and Advice for Faculty

Clearly, such a course requires a tremendous amount of preparation in order to be effective. Student project selection is the most difficult aspect. For the class to be successful, the projects need to be carefully considered, and the project director in the agency must understand that students need to learn and are not just about free labor.

The agency selected does not necessarily have to be the most established organization in town. In fact, established organizations with large budgets are sometimes the most difficult for students to enter into and find a meaningful experience in, unless the organization is venturing into a new area and is receptive to change. The most important element of an organization is the leadership. The person(s) in charge should have a clear idea of the organization's current mission, where it is going, and how the new venture complements its current programs. Additionally, the leadership must acknowledge the need for change. Without the support of the leadership, students are defenseless in organizations whose staff might be threatened by alternative thinking.

Agencies must also have a variety of defined needs. Bringing ten to twenty students into an organization could be overwhelming if it has not assessed its needs. Having a broad need for volunteers is inadequate; the needs must be placed into categories so students can select specific projects. In addition, the organization must be able to handle volunteers. Community organizations often continue to struggle because, despite the fact that their need for workers is great, they are not organized enough to adequately utilize students. Someone on the staff has to be responsible for the supervision of volunteers. For instance, if a project demands contacting individuals in the community, someone has to make a contact list available. Without that level of support, student volunteer time is often wasted.

Before an agency is selected, the instructor must spend time with the director, listening to his or her concerns and ideas. Listening to an agency's leadership will provide the instructor with enough information to determine if the current infrastructure can accommodate the class. Then, clear guidelines need to be developed concerning the projects being proposed and the contact persons for the class. The agency must be willing to provide a thorough overview and orientation for the class within the first two weeks of the semester. They also must be willing to keep accurate records of student participation.

Once an agency is selected, student self-selection is important. Unfortunately, not every student who signs up for the class may be ready for this type of experience. Students who are independent workers and who can ask questions and see ambiguities will benefit from the course. From the beginning, students must realize that the course is in the community. Those who believe they can take the course and minimally participate in the project are deceiving themselves. It is not an easy course that frees students from traditional requirements; it requires imagination, creativity, analytical thinking, and interpersonal skills. Getting the job done is a critical part of this course, and nothing else can be substituted.

Problems Encountered

Given the numerous variables involved in offering such a course, there is always room for things to go wrong. Projects fall apart. Leadership changes in midsemester. Agencies promise and commit to things they cannot deliver. Even with the best planning, certain variables cannot always be anticipated. However, if students are actively involved in community work, they can face these kinds of obstacles. In these situations, the main concern becomes how well students handle the obstacles and what they learn in order to be able to avoid them in the future.

During one semester, an agency was selected that was in dire need of volunteers. This had all the makings of a successful relationship. The agency had clearly stated goals, a willingness to include others, a mission that was central to the community's growth in the area of education, respectability as a nonprofit agency, and good local public transportation. As the term progressed, student projects that did not require the support of staff went well. However, the support staff was extremely weak and incompetent. Students whose task was to provide evaluation and statistical analysis of the program's effectiveness for the past ten years were stifled because no one could remember to bring the files and materials for them to analyze. Students prepared questionnaires and tested them for validity, but they lacked access to past client data that included addresses and phone numbers so the surveying could be done. Activities that required the staff fell apart despite the director's promises to cooperate. The organization had gone from a two-person operation to a ten-person operation, yet the director felt the need to micromanage everything. He had not adjusted to a larger structure, and pieces of the project fell apart. In that case, students learned an invaluable lesson about structure and delegation of authority. They learned quickly why this organization could not grow to meet the growing needs of its community. The good heart and intentions of the director were not sufficient enough to overcome the obvious management problems, and given the personal attachment the current director had to this project, he would not let it go. Students who could not complete their project learned as much as, if not more than, those who did.

Project Models: The Good and the Bad

Two specific projects of particular interest involved the class and became models for future work. Agency A is a large social service agency with lots of grant funding. It was seeking to expand its educational programs but had limited funding for such efforts. Agency B is a nationally known nonprofit agency with high visibility and poor local funding. In both cases, the programs were diverse enough to allow for great variety among the students and allowed them to utilize their major interests and skills effectively and efficiently.

Agency A

Agency A was able to articulate clearly what its needs were. It needed an Afrocentric curriculum to be written for a Saturday school, an African American male mentor project at the local high school, a parent mobilization/education drive, and a conference for high school students. The agency hosted the class at its headquarters and had all of the division heads present to discuss the aspects of the programs for which they were responsible. Each director prepared a packet of material for the students to read so they could thoroughly understand the agency and projects. At that meeting, the students selected their projects and began discussions with their specific project directors concerning issues and a time line. All of the directors expressed enthusiasm about having extra hands, legs, and eyes to make the projects work.

The students in the course had academic majors from a wide range of departments. Each student selected a project that complemented his or her academic interest and expertise. Those interested in education wanted to write the curriculum for and experiment with developing a Saturday school. Political science and sociology majors found that the project of parent education and mobilization fit into their training and future goals. Several young men from various majors wanted to work with the high school to develop an African American male club to promote academic excellence. Students with an interest in business and marketing chose to work with the high school conference because it provided them with an opportunity to use their accounting and management skills. The results from these projects were excellent. All of the projects had good results because the structure of the organization supported student input. Additionally, the leadership of the organization communicated its support from the top to the bottom, and therefore students felt needed from the very beginning.

The results of the project lasted a long time. The agency ran its Saturday school for several years. The parent advocacy group is still active in the southeast community. The African American male club eventually became an integral part of the high school and was taken over by a counselor and funded out of the school's budget. The format of the conference designed by the students was implemented for four or five years, until the education director resigned from the agency. The twenty students in the class learned valuable lessons about community action. Each student commented on how much time it took to make small steps of progress. They eventually became very appreciative of those small steps and respected those who worked hard to make things happen in the community. At the end of the spring semester, the director was so impressed with the students and their diligence that she hired some of them to work part-time during the summer on a grant that the students had been instrumental in acquiring.

Agency B

Agency B, like Agency A, is a well-respected organization in the African American community both locally and nationally. The difference is that Agency B is run almost totally by volunteers. Its paid staff is only part-time and has limited skills. This agency has some of the most prestigious volunteers on its board and as chairs of various committees. It is, however, in serious need of committed volunteers. This organization, like others, hosted the class during a monthly board meeting. The students attended the meeting and afterward met with all committee chairs concerning the programs and the need for support. The organization had been faltering because there was no support to run current programs or to organize the ambitious programs it was proposing.

The focus of the organization is civil and human rights. The leaders laid out three programs of need for the orientation. The first was involvement and liaison work with several organizations concerning the harassment of African American drivers (the Driving While Black/Brown [DWB] campaign). The second was the establishment of an intake and referral system for handling complaints of discrimination. The final project was to promote African American city contracting and equal opportunity and was to be implemented in conjunction with a city commission. Each of these projects had a chairperson who was willing to share information and work with the students to get the information, make recommendations for program development, and develop the program model.

The night of the orientation meeting, students selected their project while the chairs were present and met with the chairs to discuss a work plan. Each student found the chair to be open and receptive to his or her input. The students left enthused and energetic. The students were impressed with the caliber and stature of the members of the organization's board and committee chairs. Some of the most prestigious African Americans in San Diego were represented from all walks of life, including lawyers, doctors, judges, teachers, and businesspersons— a real "dream team."

Then, the dream became a nightmare. The staff of the agency had a change in personnel, and when students appeared to work, the door of the agency was locked. This lasted for over a week. Eventually, after several attempts, the class was able to get a commitment that the staff would be in the office. This event had an adverse effect on the students' morale. This agency included individuals who were verbally supportive, but when it came to physical support, there was none. The "prestigious" chairs were so busy with their own professional lives that they could not organize themselves to take advantage of the volunteer support.

Chairs of committees in this organization had complained in the past that they believed they could accomplish great things if only they had staff support. However, when the staff support was available, the chairs could not provide the direction necessary to make things happen. Therefore, the students had to quickly reorganize themselves and become "chairs." They could not wait for direction but had to take the initiative and then inform the official chairs what was going on. This role reversal caused adjustment problems for some students, and those students kept complaining about what was not happening. They could not adapt and make things happen. They had memorized models of community action, and they knew where they fit on the charts; however, when the script flipped on them, they were left scratching their heads and making excuses. The innovative students, who were determined to make things happen, did.

At the end of the semester, students submitted an individual paper to me and a composite paper to the agency. It was a difficult composite paper to write because there was much disagreement. Long discussions in class about what went wrong and what went right took place. Students who were able to handle the change in roles had a great experience, but others did not. In fact, the reactions were so different that the discussions reminded me of the story of blind men feeling an elephant—each had a different explanation of what they felt. The agency, however, was so impressed with two students that they were celebrated at the end-of-the-year board meeting. Clearly, these two had a wonderful experience in being flexible and staying focused. It was, however, an invaluable experience for all the students.

Conclusion and Advice for Approach Replication

This course is unique in its ability to impact a community agency and the lives of students simultaneously, but it could be adapted to other contexts. For many students, this experience serves as their introduction to the African American community as an adult. Many have been members of the community as children who participated in various programs. This class gives them an opportunity to be leaders, program developers, and agents of change. As a result of the course, students find focus and purpose in their studies. They see how theories they studied were developed first in real-life situations and are not mere inventions of some bored academician. Additionally, students develop an appreciation for community workers. From their experiences, they learn that the progress they enjoy is a result of unsung heroes working very hard. Finally, many become lifelong volunteers. Students who participate in class projects often continue to volunteer at their specific agency or start organizations for change on their own. The course can be very rewarding if time is taken to adequately prepare community groups, students, and the curriculum.

Those who seek to replicate the course must engage in the following steps.

- Decide what academic area of focus you are interested in for the curriculum emphasis. In the case of this class, communications

and public relations were the focus, with a community development foundation.

- Let students know the type of course you are offering. Do not let
  them believe that it is easy and requires little work. Do not compromise in order the meet the minimum number of students
  required to keep a class at your institution. Emphasize the need
  for progress and a final report.
- Send notices to organizations detailing your idea and inviting
  them to submit requests for volunteers. For the first time, be
  extremely selective and strict about what you want. Too much
  compromising in the selection of the agency will compromise
  the quality of the project. In other words, demand much of the
  agency concerning its support of students and its time in working with students. Do not settle for less.
- Develop a system in conjunction with the agency to monitor the
  hours students work on the project, whether at the agency office
  or in the community.
- Make the class experience count. Focus on theory and practice.
  Challenge the theories and encourage students to develop their
  own theories of social policy and change. Make sure time is
  spent in each class discussing obstacles and how to overcome
  them. Let the students brainstorm for solutions.
- Always express gratitude to agencies that include you in their
  work. Make sure they receive a report and that it includes encouraging and positive comments as well as critical ones.

The work done to bridge the academy with the community does
not always produce immediate results. Often, the impact is seen years
later, in the lives of students who include community service as an integral part of their lives. I am confident that my professors have no idea
that the courses I took at UCLA that incorporated community involvement changed my life—forever.

Additional Resources

Books

Blackwell, J. E. (1997). *The Black community: Diversity and unity.* Upper Saddle
River, NJ: Addison-Wesley/Pearson.
    This text provides insights into the development of African American
communities beginning in the post–Civil War era. It addresses issues confronted by those communities as they attempted to organize and meet their
economic and cultural needs. The lessons learned can be of considerable
value to individuals working with diverse communities today.

Hampden-Turner, C. W. (1974). *From poverty to dignity.* New York: Anchor Books. Hampden-Turner suggests a framework for working in a community and for evaluating this work. His "ten principles" assist students unfamiliar with community building to understand the stages of community development and to assess the success, or failure, of their efforts.

McGoldrick, K. M., & Ziegert, A. (2002). *Putting the invisible hand to work: Concepts and models for service learning in economics.* Ann Arbor: University of Michigan Press.

This anthology provides an overview of the theoretical and practical aspects of service learning, with a focus on the teaching of economics. However, most of the issues raised can be generalized to other disciplines at the postsecondary level. This is a good volume for those who want to integrate service learning into their undergraduate curricula.

Rhoads, R. A., & Howard, J. P. F. (Eds.). (1998). *Academic service learning: A pedagogy of action and reflection* (New Directions for Teaching and Learning No. 73). San Francisco: Jossey-Bass.

Distributed by the National Service Learning Clearinghouse (see "Web Site") and edited by two Michigan professors actively involved in service learning on their campuses, this volume focuses on the reflection component of service learning. Also included are chapters on the importance of service learning for a democratic education, essential multicultural aspects of service learning, and the integration of service learning into faculty development.

Articles

Ciaccoi, J. (1999, January). The community as a lab for service learning. *Education Digest, 65,* 63–66.

In this article, the author discusses the importance of student growth and maturity in a service-learning curriculum. He argues that student participation builds self-esteem as well as understanding of the communities in which they live.

Gelman, S. B. (2000). Challenges in assessing service learning. [Special issue]. *Michigan Journal of Community Service Learning,* 84–90.

Assessment is a key term in obtaining funding or arguing for the continuation of a program. In this article, Gelman outlines successful approaches for assessment of service-learning programs.

Hondagneu-Sotelo, P. (1994). Community service learning: Promises and problems. *Teaching Sociology, 22,* 248–254.

Though there is much to be said for service learning, there are also obstacles and drawbacks. This author discusses some of the challenges and problems faced in implementing service learning in the sociology curriculum. Suggestions are offered to address these in an undergraduate curriculum.

Myers-Lipton, S. (1998). Effect of a comprehensive service learning program in college students' civic responsibility. *Teaching Sociology 26,* 243–258.

The article reports on research with two groups of students to determine the impact of service learning on civic responsibility. The results indicate that the group involved in service learning showed larger increases in civic responsibility compared to the control group.

Varlotta, L. (2000). Service as text: Making the metaphor meaningful. *Michigan Journal of Community Service Learning, 7,* 76–84.

This author examines service learning as a classroom text, a "reading" that is studied by those enrolled. She makes suggestions for how this text metaphor can become meaningful to students and the curriculum in an undergraduate classroom.

Wade, R. C., & Saxe, D. W. (1996). Community service learning in social studies: Historical roots, empirical evidence, and critical issues. *Theory and Research in Social Education, 24,* 331–360.

This is a comprehensive discussion of the value and impact of integrating service in the K–12 curriculum. Much of what is said can be applied to a postsecondary situation as well.

Web Sites

<www.servicelearning.org>. National Service Learning Clearing House provides up-to-date information and research on service learning. Information on articles, new books, and conferences is accessible through this site, and there are excellent links with other sites.

Bibliography

Ada, A. F. (1995). Foreword. In J. Frederickson (Ed.), *Reclaiming our voices: Bilingual education, critical pedagogy, and praxis* (pp. 5–11). Ontario, CA: California Association for Bilingual Education.

Ahmed, A., Williams, H., & Kraemer, J. M. (Eds.). (2000). *Cultural diversity in mathematics (education): CIEAEM 51*. Chichester, England: Horwood.

Albert, G. (Ed.). (1994). *Service-learning reader: Reflections and perspectives on service*. Raleigh, NC: National Society of Experiential Education.

Alger, J. R. (1998, Spring). Leadership to recruit and promote minority faculty: Start by playing fair. *Diversity Digest*. Retrieved June 20, 2002 from <http://www.diversityweb.org/digest/sp98/faculty.html>

Allen, D., Goldstein, G., Heyman, R., & Rondinelli, T. (1998). Teaching memory strategies to persons with multiple sclerosis. *Journal of Rehabilitation Research and Development, 35,* 404–410.

Allen, M., Berube, E., McMillin, J. D., Noel, R. C., & Rienzi, B. M. (Program Assessment Consultation Team [PACT]). (2000). *PACT Outcomes Assessment Handbook*. Bakersfield: California State University, Bakersfield.

The Alliance for Technology Access. (2000). *Computer and Web resources for people with disabilities* (3rd ed.). Alameda, CA: Hunter House.

Allport, G. W. (1954). *The nature of prejudice*. Reading, MA: Addison-Wesley.

American Association for Higher Education. (n.d.). *AAHE's service-learning in the disciplines* (Monograph series). Washington, DC: AAHE Publications.

American Psychiatric Association (1994). *Diagnostic and statistical manual of mental disorders* (4th ed.). Washington, DC: Author.

Americans with Disabilities Act of 1990, 42 U.S.C. § 12101 *et seq.* (1990).

Anderson-Inman, L., Knox-Quinn, C., & Szymanski, M. (1999). Computer-supported studying: Stories of successful transition to postsecondary education. *Career Development for Exceptional Individuals, 22,* 185–212.

Angelo, Thomas A., & Cross, K. P. (1993). *Classroom assessment techniques: A handbook for college teachers* (2nd ed.). San Francisco: Jossey-Bass.

Antonio, A. L. (1999, Winter). Faculty of color and scholarship transformed: New arguments for diversifying faculty. *Diversity Digest*. Retrieved June 20, 2002 from <http://www.diversityweb.org/digest/w99/diversifying.html>

Anyon, J. (1981). Social class and school knowledge. *Curriculum Inquiry, 11,* 3–41.

Apple, M. W. (1979). The hidden curriculum and the nature of conflict. In *Ideology and curriculum* (pp. 82–104). London: Routledge and Kegan Paul.

Apple, M. W. (1992). Do the standards go far enough? Power, policy, and practice in mathematics education. *Journal for Research in Mathematics Education, 23,* 412–431.

Apple, M. W. (1995). Taking power seriously: New directions in equity in mathematics education and beyond. In W. G. Secada, E. Fennema, & L. B. Adajian (Eds.), *New directions for equity in mathematics education* (pp. 329–348). New York: Cambridge University Press.

Apple, M. W. (2001). Mathematics reform through conservative modernization? Standards, markets, and inequality in education. In J. Boaler (Ed.), *Multiple perspectives on mathematics teaching and learning* (pp. 243–259). Westport, CT: Ablex.

Aragon, S. R. (2000). Beyond access: Methods and models for increasing retention and learning among minority students. *New Directions for Community Colleges,* no. 112. San Francisco: Jossey-Bass/Wiley.

Association for Children with Learning Disabilities. (1986, September–October). *ACLD description: Specific learning disabilities. ACLD Newsbriefs,* 15–16.

Astin, A. (1993a). Diversity and multiculturalism on the campus: How are students affected? *Change, 25*(2), 44–49.

Astin, A. (1993b). *What matters in college: Four critical years revisited.* San Francisco: Jossey-Bass.

Astin, A. (1999). Involvement in learning revisited: Lessons we have learned. *Journal of College Student Development, 40,* 587–598.

Astin, A., & Sax, L. (1998). How undergraduates are affected by service participation. *Journal of College Student Development, 39,* 251–262.

Astin, A., Sax. L., & Avalos, J. (1996). *Long-term effects of volunteerism during the undergraduate years.* Los Angeles: UCLA Higher Education Research Institute.

Astin, A., Vogelgesang, L. J., Ikeda, E. K., & Yee, J. A. (2000). *How service learning affects students.* Los Angeles: UCLA Higher Education Research Institute.

Atkinson, D. (1997). A critical approach to critical thinking in TESOL. *TESOL Quarterly, 31,* 71–94.

Atkinson, D., Morten, G., & Sue, D. W. (1989). *Counseling American minorities: A cross-cultural perspective* (3rd ed.). Dubuque, IA: Wm. C. Brown.

Atweh, B., & Clarkson, P. (2001). Internationalization and globalization of mathematics education: Toward an agenda for research/action. In B. Atweh, H. Forgasz, & B. Nebres (Eds.), *Sociocultural research on mathematics education* (pp. 77–94). Mahwah, NJ: Lawrence Erlbaum.

Au, K. H. (1980). Participation structures in a reading lesson with Hawaiian children. *Anthropology and Education Quarterly, 11,* 91–115.

Au, K. H., & Jordan, C. (1981). Teaching reading to Hawaiian children: Finding a culturally appropriate solution. In H. Trueba, G. P. Guthrie, & K. H. Au (Eds.), *Culture and the bilingual classroom* (pp. 139–152). Rowley, MA: Newbury House.

Badrona, E., & Leon, D. (1996). *Tools of the mind: The Vygotskian approach to early childhood education.* Englewood Cliffs, NJ: Prentice-Hall.

Balliet, B. J., & Heffernan, K. (Eds.). (2000). *The practice of change: Concepts and models for service-learning in women's studies.* Washington, DC: American Association for Higher Education.

Banks, J. A. (1991). The dimensions of multicultural education. *Multicultural Leader, 4,* 5–6.

Banks, J. A. (1995). Multicultural education: Historical development, dimensions, and practice. In J. A. Banks & C. A. M. Banks (Eds.), *Handbook of research on multicultural education* (pp. 3–24). New York: Macmillan.

Banks, J. A. (1997a). Multicultural education: Characteristics and goals. In J. A. Banks & C. A. M. Banks (Eds.), *Multicultural education: Issues and perspectives* (3rd ed., pp. 3–31). Boston: Allyn and Bacon.

Banks, J. A. (1997b). *Teaching strategies for the ethnic studies* (6th ed.). Boston: Allyn and Bacon.

Banks, J. A. (2001). Approaches to multicultural curriculum reform. In J. A. Banks & C. A. M. Banks (Eds.), *Multicultural education: Issues and perspectives* (4th ed., pp. 225–246). New York: John Wiley.

Banta, T. (Ed.). (1993). *Making a difference: Outcomes of a decade of assessment in higher education.* San Francisco: Jossey-Bass.

Barnes, B. (1982). *T. S. Kuhn and social science.* London: Macmillan.

Barnes, B., & Edge, D. (Eds.). (1982). *Science in context: Readings in the sociology of science.* Milton Keynes, Buckinghamshire, UK: Open University Press.

Barnes, B., & Shapin, S. (Eds.). (1979). *Natural order: Historical studies of scientific culture.* London: Sage.

Barringer, F. (1993). *When English is a foreign language for college teachers* (2nd ed.). San Francisco: Jossey-Bass.

Batchelder, T. H., & Root, S. (1994). Effects of undergraduate programs to integrate academic learning and service: Cognitive, pro-social cognitive, and identity outcomes. *Journal of Adolescence, 17,* 341–356.

Battistoni, R. (1995). Service learning, diversity, and the liberal arts curriculum. *Liberal Education, 81,* 30–35.

Baugh, J. (2002). African American language and literacy. In M. J. Schleppegrell & M. C. Colombi (Eds.), *Developing advanced literacy in first and second languages: Meaning with power* (pp. 177–186). Mahwah, NJ: Lawrence Erlbaum.

Belenky, M. F., Clinchy, B. M., Goldberger, N. R., & Tarule, J. M. (1986). *Women's ways of knowing: The development of self, voice, and mind.* New York: Basic Books.

Bell, D. (1987). The world and the United States in 2013. *Daedalus, 116,* 1–31.

Bell, Y. R., & Clark, T. R. (1998). Culturally relevant reading material as related to comprehension and recall in African American children. *Journal of Black Psychology, 2,* 455–475.

Benmayor, R., & Torruellas, R. (1997). Education, cultural rights, and citizenship. In C. Cohen, K. Jones, & J. Tronto (Eds.), *Women transforming politics: An alternative reader* (pp. 187–204). New York: New York University Press.

Bennett, C. (1999). *Comprehensive multicultural education: Theory and practice.* Boston: Allyn and Bacon.

Best, J. (2001). *Damned lies and statistics: Untangling numbers from the media, politicians, and activists.* Berkeley: University of California Press.

Billingsley, A. (1988). *Black Families in White America.* New York: Simon and Schuster.

Bishop, A. J. (1988). Mathematics education in its cultural context. *Educational Studies in Mathematics, 19,* 179–191.

Bishop, M., Tschopp., M., & Mulvihill, M. (2000). Multiple sclerosis and epilepsy: Vocational aspects and best rehabilitation practices. *Journal of Rehabilitation, 66*(2), 50–55.

Blackwell, J. E. (1997). *The Black community: Diversity and unity.* Upper Saddle River, NJ: Addison-Wesley/Pearson.

Boaler, J. (Ed.). (2000). *Multiple perspectives on mathematics teaching and learning.* Westport, CT: Ablex.

Bogdan, R. C., & Biklen, S. K. (1998). *Qualitative research in education: An introduction to theory and methods* (3rd ed.). Needham Heights, MA: Allyn and Bacon.

Boss, J. A. (1994). The effect of community service work on the moral development of college students. *Journal of Moral Education, 23*(2), 183–198.

Bowles, S., & Gintis, H. (1976). *Schooling in capitalist America: Educational reform and the contradictions of economic life.* New York: Basic Books.

Boyer, E. L. (1990). *Scholarship reconsidered: Priorities of the professoriate.* Princeton, NJ: Carnegie Foundation for the Advancement of Teaching.

Boyle-Baise, M. (1999). As good as it gets?: The impact of philosophical orientations on community-based service learning for multicultural education. *The Educational Forum, 63,* 310–21.

Branch, A. J. (1999). *Teachers' conceptions of their role in the facilitation of students' ethnic identity development.* Unpublished doctoral dissertation, University of Washington, Seattle.

Braxton, J. M., & Mundy, M. E. (2001). Powerful institutional levers to reduce college student departure. *Journal of College Student Retention, 3,* 91–118.

Brice-Heath, S. (1983). *Ways with words: Language, life, and work in communities and classrooms.* New York: Cambridge University Press.

Brim, S., & Whitaker, D. (2000). Motivation and students with attention deficit hyperactivity disorder. *Preventing School Failure, 44*(2), 57–60.

Bringle, R. G., Games, R., & Malloy, E. A. (Eds.). (1999). *Colleges and universities as citizens.* Needham, MA: Allyn and Bacon.

Bringle, R. G., & Hatcher, J. A. (1996). Implementing service learning in higher education. *Journal of Higher Education, 67,* 221–239.

Bringle, R. G., & Hatcher, J. A. (1999). Reflection in service-learning: Making meaning of experience. *Educational Horizons, 77,* 179–185.

Brislin, R., & Pedersen, P. (1976). *Cross-cultural orientation programs.* New York: Gardner Press.

Brown, M. (2000). Diagnosis and treatment of children and adolescents with attention-deficit/hyperactivity disorder. *Journal of Counseling and Development, 78,* 195–203.

Bruffee, K. (1993). Collaborative learning: *Higher education, interdependence, and the authority of knowledge.* Baltimore: Johns Hopkins University Press.

Bruner, J. S. (1960). *The process of education.* Cambridge: Harvard University Press.

Bryant, D., Bryant, B., & Raskind, M. (1998). Using assistive technology to enhance the skills of students with learning disabilities. *Intervention in School and Clinic, 34,* 53–58.

Burns, M., Storey, K., & Certo, N. (1999). Effect of service learning on attitudes toward students with severe disabilities. *Education and Training in Mental Retardation and Developmental Disabilities, 34*(1), 58–65.

California State University, Office of the Chancellor. (1980). *Executive order number 338: General education-breadth requirements.* Long Beach, CA: Author.

California State University, Office of the Chancellor. (1981). *Executive order number 342: Certification of general education-breadth requirements by regionally accredited institutions.* Long Beach, CA: Author.

California State University, Office of the Chancellor. (1992). *Executive order number 595: General education-breadth requirements.* Long Beach, CA: Author.

California Teachers of English to Speakers of Other Languages. *California pathways: Second language students in public high schools, colleges, and universities.* (1997). Glendale, CA: Author.

Cambridge, B. (1999, December). "The scholarship of teaching and learning: Questions and answers from the field." *AAHE Bulletin, 52*(4), 7–10. Retrieved from <http://www.aahebulletin.com/public/archive/dec99f2.asp?pf=1>

Canada, M., & Speck, B. W. (2001). *Developing and implementing service-learning programs* (New Directions for Higher Education No. 114). San Francisco: Jossey-Bass.

Carrasquillo, A. L., & Rodriguez, V. (2002). *Language minority students in the mainstream classroom* (2nd ed.). Tonawanda, NY: Multilingual Matters.

Cazden, C. B., & John, V. P. (1971). Learning in American Indian children. In M. L. Wax, S. Diamond, & F. O. Gearing (Eds.), *Anthropological Perspectives* (pp. 252–272). New York: Basic Books.

Chalmers, A. F. (1982). *What is this thing called science?* (2nd ed.). Milton Keynes, Buckinghamshire, UK: Open University Press.

Chamberlain, S. P., Guerra, P. L., & Garcia, S. B. (1999). *Intercultural Com-*

munication in the Classroom [Information analyses]. Austin, TX: Southwest Educational Development Lab.

Chang, L. S. (1998). *Hunger*. Middlesex, England: Penguin.

Chang, M. J. (1999). Does racial diversity matter?: The educational impact of a racially diverse undergraduate population. *Journal of College Student Development, 40,* 377–395.

Chang, M. J., Richards, J. S., & Jackson, A. (1996). *Accommodating students with disabilities*. Washington, DC: National Institute on Disability and Rehabilitation. (ERIC Document Reproduction Service No. 404826)

Chapin, J. R. (1999). Missing pieces in the service learning puzzle. *Educational Horizons, 77*(4), 202–207.

Chapman, P., Selvarajah, S., & Webster, J. (1999). Engagement in multimedia training systems. In *Proceedings of the Thirty-Second Hawaii International Conference on System Sciences*. Los Alamitos, CA: Institute of Electrical and Electronics Engineers Computer Society.

Ciaccoi, J. (1999, January). The community as a lab for service learning. *Education Digest, 65,* 63–66.

Claxton, C., & Murrel, P. (1987). *Learning styles: Implications for improving educational practices* (ASHE-ERIC Higher Education Report No. 4). Washington, DC: Association for the Study of Higher Education.

Clements, D. H., & Battista, M. T. (1992). Geometry and spatial reasoning. In D. A. Grouws (Ed.), *Handbook of research on mathematics teaching and learning* (pp. 420–464). New York: Macmillan.

Cliff, M. (1988). A journey into speech. In R. Simonson & S. Walker (Eds.), *Multicultural literacy: Opening the American mind* (pp. 57–62). Saint Paul, MN: Graywolf Press.

Close, F. (1990). *Too hot to handle: The story of the race for cold fusion*. London: W. H. Allen.

Code, L. (1991). *What can she know?: Feminist theory and the construction of knowledge*. Ithaca, NY: Cornell University Press.

Cohen, A. D., & Horowitz, R. (2002). What should teachers know about bilingual learners and the reading process? In J. Hammadou Sullivan (Ed.), *Literacy and the second language learner* (pp. 29–54). Greenwich, CT: Information Age.

Cohen, C., Jones, K., & Tronto, J. (Eds.) (1997). *Women transforming politics: An alternative reader*. New York: New York University Press.

Cohen, C. J. (1999). *The boundaries of blackness: AIDS and the breakdown of black politics*. Chicago: University of Chicago Press.

Cohen, E. G. (1972). Interracial interaction disability. *Human Relations, 25,* 9–24.

Cohen, E. G. (1994a). *Designing groupwork: Strategies for the heterogeneous classroom*. New York: Teachers College Press.

Cohen, E. G. (1994b). Restructuring the classroom: Conditions for productive small groups. *Review of Educational Research 64*(1), 1–35.

Cohen, E. G., Kepner, D., & Swanson, P. (1995). Dismantling status hierarchies in heterogeneous classrooms. In J. Oakes & K. H. Quartz (Eds.), *Creating new educational communities: Ninety-fourth yearbook of the national society for the study of education* (pp. 16–31). Chicago: University of Chicago Press.

Cohen, J., & Kinsey, D. (1994). "Doing good" and scholarship: A service learning study. *Journalism Educator, 48*(4), 4–14.

Cohn, D., & Fears, D. (2001, March 7). Hispanics draw even with Blacks in new census. *The Washington Post,* p. A1.

Collins, P. H. (1991). Defining Black feminist thought. In P. H. Collins (Ed.), *Black feminist thought: Knowledge, consciousness, and the politics of empowerment* (pp. 19–40). New York: Routledge, Chapman, and Hall.

Cone, R., & Harris, S. (1996). Service-learning practice: Developing a theoretical framework. *Michigan Journal of Community Service Learning, 3,* 31–43.

Conrad, D., & Hedin, D. (1982). The impact of experiential education on adolescent development. *Children and Youth Services, 4,* 57–76.

Cooper, D. (1998). *Reading, writing, and reflection. Academic service learning: A pedagogy of action and reflection* (pp. 47–56). San Francisco: Jossey-Bass.

Crenshaw, K. (1997). Beyond racism and misogyny: Black feminism and 2 Live Crew. In C. Cohen, K. Jones, & J. Tronto (Eds.), *Women transforming politics: An alternative reader* (pp. 549–568). New York: New York University Press.

Crews, Robin. (2002). *Higher education service-learning sourcebook.* Westport, CT: Oryx Press.

Cummins, J. (2000). *Language, power, and pedagogy: Bilingual children in the crossfire.* Cleveland, OH: Multilingual Matters.

Curran, P. (1989). The portfolio approach to assessing student writing: An interim report. *Composition Chronicle, 2,*(2), 6–8.

D'Ambrosio, U. (1985). Ethnomathematics and its place in the history and pedagogy of mathematics. *For the Learning of Mathematics, 5*(1), 44–48.

D'Ambrosio, U. (1999). Literacy, matheracy, and technoracy: A trivium for today. *Mathematical Thinking and Learning, 1,* 131–153.

Danek, M., & Seidman, M. (1995). Hearing disabilities. In M. Brodwin, F. Tellez, & S. Brodwin (Eds.), *Medical, psychosocial, and vocational aspects of disability* (pp. 195–216). Athens, GA: Elliot and Fitzpatrick.

Davidson, J. (1997). Experiential exercises for increasing self-awareness and an appreciation of racially and ethnically diverse populations. *Journal of Intergroup Relations, 24*(1), 22–33.

Davidson, N. (1994). Cooperative and collaborative learning: An integrative perspective. In J. S. Thousand, R. A. Villa, & A. I. Nevin (Eds.), *Creativity and collaborative learning: A practical guide to empowering students and teachers* (pp. 13–30). Baltimore: Paul H. Brookes.

Davis, B. G. (1993). *Tools for teaching.* San Francisco: Jossey-Bass.

Davis, P. J., & Hersh, R. (1986). *Descartes' dream: The world according to mathematics.* Brighton, England: Harvester.

Day, M., & Batson, T. (1995). The network-based writing classroom: The Enfi idea. In Z. L. Berge & M. P. Collins (Eds.), *Computer mediated commu-*

nication and the online classroom (Vol. 2, pp. 25–46). Cresskill, NJ: Hampton Press.

DeAngelis, T. (2001, April). Thwarting modern prejudice. *Monitor on Psychology, 32*(4), 26–30.

Deboer, G. (1991). *History of ideas in science education: Implications for practice.* New York: Teachers College Press.

Deci, E. L., & Ryan, R. M. (1985). *Intrinsic motivation and self-determination in human behavior.* New York: Plenum.

Delgado-Gaitan, C. (1994). Consejos: The power of cultural narratives. *Anthropology and Education Quarterly, 20,* 293–316.

Delong, L., & Groomes, F. (1996). A constructivist teacher education program that incorporates community service to prepare students to work with children living in poverty. *Action in Teacher Education, 5*(18), 86–95.

Delpit, L. (1988). The silenced dialogue: Power and pedagogy in educating other people's children. *Harvard Educational Review, 58,* 280–298.

Delpit, L. (1995). *Other people's children: Cultural conflict in the classroom.* New York: New Press.

Delve, C. I., Mintz, S. D., Stewart, G. M. (Eds.). (1990). *Community service as values education.* (New Directions for Teaching and Learning No. 50). San Francisco: Jossey-Bass.

Derry, S. J., Gance, S., Gance, L. L., & Schlager, M. (2000). Toward assessment of knowledge building practices in technology-mediated work group interactions. In S. P. Lajoie (Ed.), *No more walls: Theory change, paradigm shifts, and their influence on the use of computers for instructional purposes* (Vol. 2). Mahwah, NJ: Lawrence Erlbaum.

Despite gains, county slips to no. 3 in state. (2001, March 30). *San Diego Union Tribune,* pp. A1, 10.

Dewey, J. (1902). *The child and the curriculum.* Chicago: University of Chicago Press.

Dewey, J. (1916). *Democracy and education.* New York: Macmillan.

Dewey, J. (1964). The relation of theory to practice in education. In R. D. Archambault (Ed.), *John Dewey on education: Selected writings* (pp. 313–338). Chicago: University of Chicago Press. (Originally appeared in National Society for the Scientific Study of Education, *Third Yearbook,* Part 1, 1904.)

Dias, P. V. (2001, February). *Human development in history and society: Multi-perspectivity and diversity of linguistic expressions.* Paper presented at the International Conference on Science, Technology, and Mathematics Education for Human Development, Goa, India.

Duckworth, E. (1987). *"The Having of Wonderful Ideas" and other essays on teaching and learning.* New York: Teachers College Press.

Dukes, L., & Shaw, S. (1998). Not just children anymore: Personnel preparation regarding postsecondary education for adults with disabilities. *Teacher Education and Special Education, 21,* 205–213.

Duschl, R. (1990). *Restructuring science education: The importance of theories and their development.* New York: Teachers College Press.

Ebeid, W. (1999). Mathematics for all in Egypt: Adoption and adaptation. In Z. Usiskin (Ed.), *Developments in school mathematics around the world* (pp. 71–83). Reston, VA: National Council of Teachers of Mathematics.

Eddy, W. (2000, Fall). Race, gender, and faculty work lives: Data from the University of Michigan. *Diversity Digest.* Retrieved June 2002 from <http://www.diversityweb.org/digest/foo/analysis.html>

Education for All Handicapped Children Act of 1975. 20 U.S.C. § 1401 *et seq.* (1975).

Edwards, D., & Mercer, N. (1987). *Common knowledge: The development of understanding in the classroom.* London: Methuen.

Eichinger, J., & Woltman, S. (1993). Integration strategies for learners with severe multiple disabilities. *Teaching Exceptional Children, 26,* 18–21.

Elbow, P., & Belanoff, P. (1986, October). Portfolios as a substitute for proficiency examinations. *College Composition and Communication, 37,* 336–339.

Ely, R. (1989). Writing, computers, and visual impairment. *Journal of Visual Impairment and Blindness, 83,* 248–252.

Englert, C., & Mariage, T. (1991). Making students partners in the composition process: Organizing the reading "posse." *Learning Disability Quarterly, 14,* 123–138.

Englert, C., & Raphael, T. (1988). Constructing well-formed prose: Process, structure, and Metacognitive knowledge. *Exceptional Children, 54,* 513–520.

Englert, C., & Thomas, C. (1987). Sensitivity to text structure in reading and writing: A comparison of learning disabled and non–learning disabled students. *Learning Disability Quarterly, 10,* 93–105.

English, L. D. (Ed.). (2002). *Handbook of international research in mathematics education.* Mahwah, NJ: Lawrence Erlbaum.

Enos, S., & Troppe, M. (1996). Service-learning in the curriculum. In B. Jacoby & associates, *Service-learning in higher education: Concepts and practices* (pp. 156–181). San Francisco: Jossey-Bass.

Ernest, P. (1991). *The philosophy of mathematics education.* London: Falmer Press.

Er-Sheng, D. (1999). Mathematics curriculum reform facing the new century. In China. In Z. Usiskin (Ed.), *Developments in school mathematics around the world* (pp. 58–70). Reston, VA: National Council of Teachers of Mathematics.

Eyler, J., & Giles, D. E., Jr. (1999). *Where's the learning in service-learning?* San Francisco: Jossey-Bass.

Eyler, J., Giles, D. E., Jr., & Schmiede, A. (1996). *A practitioner's guide to reflection in service-learning: Student voices and reflections.* Nashville, TN: Vanderbilt University.

Fasheh, M. (1991). Mathematics in a social context: Math within education as praxis versus math within education as hegemony. In M. Harris (Ed.), *Schools, mathematics, and work* (pp. 37–61). London: Falmer Press.

Feagin, J. R., Vera, H., & Imani, N. (1996). *The agony of education: Black students at White colleges and universities.* New York: Routledge.

Fiechtner, S. B., & Davis, E. A. (1985). Why groups fail: A survey of student experiences with learning groups. *Organizational Behavior Teaching Review, 9*(4), 58–73.

Finkelstein, M. J., Seal, R. K., & Schuster, J. H. (1999). *The new academic generation: A profession in transformation.* Baltimore: Johns Hopkins University Press.

Flick-Hruska, C., & Blythe, G. (Comps.). (1992). *Disability accommodation handbook.* Kansas City, MO: Metropolitan Community Colleges. (ERIC Document Reproduction Service No. 358880)

Folkman, D., & Rai, K. (2001). Practicing action learning in a community context. *Adult Learning, 11*(3), 15–17.

Fong, R., & S. Furuto. (Eds.). (2001). *Culturally competent practice skills, interventions, and evaluations.* Boston: Allyn and Bacon.

Fordham, S. (1988). Racelessness as a factor in Black students' school success. *Harvard Educational Review, 58,* 54–84.

Forest, J. F. F. (Ed.). (1998). *University teaching: International perspectives.* New York: Coarland.

Frankenstein, M. (1989). *Relearning mathematics: A different third R—radical maths.* London: Free Association Books.

Freedman, K., & Liu, M. (1996). The importance of computer experience, learning processes, and communication patterns in multicultural networking. *Educational Technology Research and Development, 44*(1), 43–59.

Freire, P. (1970). *Pedagogy of the oppressed.* New York: Seabury.

Gadbow, N., and DuBois, D. (1998). *Adult learners with special needs.* Malabar, FL: Krieger Publishing.

Gainen, J., & Robert, B. (Eds.). 1993. *Building a diverse faculty.* San Francisco: Jossey-Bass.

Garcia, E. E. (2001). *Hispanic education in the United States: Raíces y alas.* Lanham: MD: Rowman and Littlefield.

Garcia, J., & Zea, M. (Eds.). (1997). *Psychological interventions and research with Latino populations.* Boston: Allyn and Bacon.

Garcia, M., & Smith, D. G. (1996). Reflecting inclusiveness in the college curriculum. In L. I. Rendón & R. O. Hope (Eds.), *Educating a new majority: Transforming America's educational system for diversity* (pp. 265–288). San Francisco: Jossey-Bass.

Garner, R., & Gillingham, M. G. (1996). *Internet communication in six classrooms: Conversations across time, space, and culture.* Mahwah, NJ: Lawrence Erlbaum.

Gelman, S. B. (2000). Challenges in assessing service learning. [Special issue]. *Michigan Journal of Community Service Learning,* 84–90.

Gent, P. J., & Gurecka, L. E. (1998). Service learning: A creative strategy for inclusive classrooms. *Journal of the Association for Persons with Severe Handicaps, 2*(3), 261–71.

Gerdes, P. (1999). *Geometry from Africa: Mathematical and educational explorations.* Washington, DC: Mathematical Association of America.

Glassick, C. E., Huber, M. T., & Maeroff, G. I. (1997.) *Scholarship assessed: Evaluation of the professoriate.* San Francisco: Jossey-Bass.

Goebel, B. A. (1995). Who are all these people? Some pedagogical implications of diversity in the multicultural classroom. In B. A. Goebel & J. C. Hall (Eds.), *Teaching a "new canon"? Students, teachers, and texts in the college literature classroom* (pp. 22–31). Urbana, IL: National Council of Teachers of English.

Gold, B. (2001, Winter). Diversifying the curriculum: What do students think? *Diversity Digest.* Retrieved from <http://www.diversityweb.org/digest/w01/curriculum.html>

Gold, J. (1997, January). Does CMC present individuals with disabilities opportunities or barriers? [Eighteen paragraphs]. *Computer-mediated communication magazine.* Retrieved from <http://www.december.com/cmc/mag/1997/jan/gold.html>

Gold, M. (2002). The elements of effective experiential education programs. *Journal of Career Planning and Employment, 62*(2), 20–24.

Gollnick, D. (1995). National and state initiatives for multicultural education. In J. Banks & C. Banks (Eds.), *Handbook on research on multicultural education* (pp. 44–64). New York: Macmillan.

González, K. P. (2001). Toward a Theory of Minority Student Participation in Predominantly White Colleges and Universities. *Journal of College Student Retention, 2,* 69–91.

Goodlad, J. (1984). Access to knowledge. In *A place called school: Promise for the future.* New York: McGraw-Hill.

Graham, S., & Harris, K. (2000). The role of self-regulation and transcription skills in writing and writing development. *Educational Psychologist, 35,* 3–12.

Graham, S., & Macarthur, C. (1988). Improving learning disabled students' skills at revising essays produced on a word processor: Self-instructional strategy training. *Journal of Special Education, 22,* 133–152.

Graham, S., Macarthur, C., & Schwartz, S. (1993). Knowledge of writing and the composing process, attitude toward writing, and self-efficacy for students with and without learning disabilities: A review of a program of research. *Learning Disability Quarterly, 14,* 89–114.

Greenberg, J. B. (1989). *Funds of knowledge: Historical constitution, social distribution, and transmission.* Paper presented at the meeting of the Society for Applied Anthropology, Santa Fe, NM.

Gregg, K. (1983). College learning disabled writers: Error patterns and instructional alternatives. *Journal of Learning Disabilities, 16,* 334–338.

Grusky, S. (2000). International service learning: A critical guide from an impassioned advocate. *American Behavioral Scientist, 43,* 858–865.

Guo, Y. (1989). The overseas development network. In S. W. Showalter (Ed.), *The role of service learning in international education* (pp. 105–11). Goshen, IN: Goshen College.

Gurin, P. (1999, January). *The Compelling Need for Diversity in Education.* [Expert report prepared for the lawsuits] Gratz and Hamacher v. Bollinger, Duderstadt, the University of Michigan, and the University of Michigan College of LS&A, No. 97-75231, U.S. Dist. E.D. Mi., and Grutter v. Bollinger, Lehman, Shields, the University of Michigan, and the University of Michigan Law School, No. 97-75928, U.S. Dist. E.D. Mi. Available at <http://www.umich.edu/~urel/admissions/legal/expert/gurintoc .html>. (Reprinted in *Michigan Journal of Race and Law, 5,* 1999, 363–425; *The University of Massachusetts Schools of Education Journal, 32*(2), 1999, 36–62; P. Gurin, *Supplemental Expert Report,* 2000, July.)

Haas, D. (1993). Inclusion is happening in the classroom. *Children Today, 22,* 34–35.

Hale-Benson, J. E. (1986). *Black children: Their roots, culture, and learning styles.* Baltimore: Johns Hopkins University Press.

Hall, P. A. (1992). Peanuts: A note on intercultural communication. *Journal of Academic Librarianship, 18*(4), 211–213.

Hamilton, R., & Ghatala, E. (1994). *Learning and instruction.* New York: McGraw-Hill.

Hamm, D., Dowell, D., & Houck, J. (1998). Service learning as a strategy to prepare teacher candidates for contemporary diverse classrooms. *Education, 119*(2), 196–204.

Hammond, C. (1994). Integrating service and academic study: Faculty motivation and satisfaction in Michigan higher education. *Michigan Journal of Community Service Learning, 1,* 21–28.

Hampden-Turner, C. (1974). *From poverty to dignity.* Garden City, NY: Anchor Books.

Harklau, L., Losey, K., & Siegal, M. (Eds.). (1999). *Generation 1.5 meets college composition: Issues in the teaching of writing to U.S.-educated learners.* Mahway, NJ: Lawrence Erlbaum.

Harris, M. (1987). An example of traditional women's work as a mathematics resource. *For the Learning of Mathematics, 7*(3), 26–28.

Heisenberg, W. (1933, December). *The development of quantum mechanics.* Nobel lecture presented to the Royal Swedish Academy of Sciences Ceremonies, Stockholm, Sweden.

Henson, K. T. (2000). *Curriculum planning: Integrating multiculturalism, constructivism, and educational reform.* New York: McGraw-Hill.

Hersh, R. (1997). *What is mathematics, really?* New York: Oxford University Press.

High Tech Center for the Disabled. (1999, June). *Providing access to library automation systems for students with disabilities.* Sacramento: California Community Colleges. (ERIC Document Reproduction Service No. 429636)

Hixon, A. (2002, May 20). Latinos by the numbers: A statistical sampler. *Hispanic Outlook,* 18–20.

Hohm, C. F., & Johnson, W. S. (Eds.). (2001). *Assessing student learning in sociology* (2nd ed.). Washington, DC: American Sociological Association.

Hollins, E. R. (1996). *Culture in school learning: Revealing the deep meaning.* Mahwah, NJ: Lawrence Erlbaum.

Hondagneu-Sotelo, P. (1994). Community service learning: Promises and problems. *Teaching Sociology, 22,* 248–254.

Horn, L., & Berktold, J. (1999). *Students with disabilities in postsecondary education: A profile of preparation, participation, and outcomes* (NCES Report No. 1999-187). Washington, DC: U.S. Department of Education, National Center for Education Statistics.

Howard, J. (Ed.). (1993a). Community service learning in the curriculum. In *Praxis: Vol. 1. A faculty casebook on community service learning.* Ann Arbor, MI: Office of Community Service Learning Press.

Howard, J. (Ed.). (1993b). *Praxis: Vol. 1. A faculty casebook on community service. Vol. 2. Service learning resources for university students, staff, and faculty.* Ann Arbor, MI: Office of Community Service Learning.

Howard, J. P. F. (1998). Academic service learning: A counternormative pedagogy. In R. Rhoads & J. P. F. Howard. (Eds.), *Academic service-learning: A pedagogy of action and reflection* (pp. 21–30). San Francisco: Jossey-Bass.

Huber, M. T. (1999). Disciplinary styles in the scholarship of teaching: Reflections on the Carnegie Academy for Scholarship of Teaching and Learning. Paper presented at the Seventh International Improving Student Learning Symposium, University of York, United Kingdom. Available at <www.carnegiefoundation.org/elibrary/docs/disciplinarystyles.htm>

Hughes, K. S., Frances, C., & Lombardo, B. J. (1991, August 12–14). Years of challenge: Workforce and demographic trends provide agenda for 1990s. *Nacumo Report.*

Humphreys, D. (1999, Winter). Moving beyond myths: New book examines faculty of color in the academy. *Diversity Digest.* Retrieved June 2002 from <http://www.diversityweb.org/digest/w99/myths.html>

Humphreys, D. (2000, Fall). National survey finds diversity requirements common around the country. *Diversity Digest.* Retrieved from <http:///www.diversityweb.org/digest/f00/survey.html>

Ijiri, L., & Kudzma, E. (2000). Supporting nursing students with learning disabilities: A metacognitive approach. *Journal of Professional Nursing, 16*(3), 149–157.

Irvine, J. J., & Armento, B. J. (2001). *Culturally responsive teaching: Lesson planning for elementary and middle grades.* Boston: McGraw-Hill.

Irvine, J. J., & York, D. E. (1995). Learning styles and culturally diverse students: A literature review. In J. A. Banks & C. A. M. Banks (Eds.), *Handbook of research on multicultural education* (pp. 484–497). New York: Macmillan.

Ivanič, R., & Camps, D. (2001). I am how I sound: Voice as self-representation in L2 writing. *Journal of Second Language Writing, 10,* 3–33.

Jackson, L., & Cafarella, R. (Eds.). (1994). *Experiential learning: A new approach* (New Directions for Adults and Continuing Education No. 62). San Francisco: Jossey-Bass.

Jacoby, B., & associates. (1996) *Service-learning in higher education: Concepts and practices.* San Francisco: Jossey-Bass.

Johns, A. M. (1994). Languages and cultures in the classroom. In H. Roberts (Ed.), *Teaching from a multicultural perspective* (pp. 60–76). Thousand Oaks, CA: Sage.

Johns, A. M. (1997). *Text, role, and context: Developing academic literacies.* New York: Cambridge University Press.

Johns, A. M. (2001a). ESL students and WAC programs: Varied populations and diverse needs. In S. H. Mcleod, E. Miraglia, M. Soven, & C. Thaiss (Eds.), *WAC for the new millennium: Strategies for continuing writing-across-the-curriculum programs* (pp. 141–164). Urbana, IL: National Council of Teachers of English.

Johns, A. M. (2001b). An interdisciplinary, interinstitutional learning communities program: Student involvement and student success. In I. Leki (Ed.), *Academic writing programs: Case studies in TESOL practice* (pp. 61–72). Alexandria, VA: Teachers of English to Speakers of Other Languages.

Johnson, D. W., & Johnson, R. T. (1989). *Cooperation and competition: Theory and research.* Edina, MN: Interaction.

Johnson, D. W., Johnson, R. T., & Smith, K. A. (1998). *Active learning: Cooperation in the college classroom.* Edina, MN: Interaction.

Jones, E. B. (1998a). The development of critical consciousness through a reflective literacy process. In A. Darder (Ed.), *Teaching as an act of love: Reflections on Paulo Freire and his contributions to our lives and our work* (pp. 55–58). Ontario, CA: California Association for Bilingual Education.

Jones, E. B. (1998b). *Mexican American teachers as cultural mediators: Literacy and literacy contexts through bicultural strengths.* Unpublished doctoral dissertation, Claremont Graduate University and San Diego State University, Claremont, CA.

Jones, E. B., Pang, V. O., & Rodríguez, J. L. (2001). Social studies in the elementary classroom: Culture matters. *Theory into Practice, 40*(1), 35–41.

Jones, V. C., & Clemson, R. (1996). Promoting effective teaching for diversity. In L. I. Rendón, R. O. Hope, & associates (Eds.), *Educating a new majority: Transforming America's educational system for diversity* (pp. 149–167). San Francisco: Jossey-Bass.

Joseph, G. G. (1992). *The crest of the peacock: Non-European roots of mathematics.* London: Penguin.

Kahne, J., & Westheimer, J. (1996). In the service of what? *Phi Delta Kappan, 77,* 592–599.

Katula, R., & Threnhauser, E. (1999). Experiential education in the undergraduate curriculum. *Communication Education, 48*(3), 238–255.

Katz, P. A., & Zalk, S. R. (1978). Modification of children's racial attitudes. *Developmental Psychology, 14,* 447–461.

Kay, E. J., Jensen-Osinski, B. J., Beidler, P. G., & Aronson, J. L. (1983). The graying of the college classroom. *Gerontologist, 23*(2), 196–199.

Kellner, D. (1998). Multiple literacies and critical pedagogy in a multicultural society. In G. Katsiaficas & T. Kiros (Eds.), *The promise of multiculturalism: Education and autonomy in the twenty-first century.* New York: Routledge.

Kelly, A. (1985). The construction of masculine science. *British Journal of Sociology of Education, 6,* 133–54.

Kendall, J., (Ed.). (1990). *Combining service and learning: A resource book for community and public service* (Vols. 1 and 2). Raleigh, NC: National Society for Internships and Experiential Education.

Kerka, S. (1998). *Adults with learning disabilities* (ERIC Digest No. 189). Columbus, OH: ERIC Clearinghouse on Adult Career and Vocational Education. (ERIC Document Reproduction Service No. 414434)

King, A. R., & Brownell, J. A. (1966). The disciplines as communities of discourse. In *The curriculum and the disciplines of knowledge: A theory of curriculum practice* (pp. 67–97). New York: John Wiley.

King, P. (2000). Improving access and educational success for diverse students: Steady progress but enduring problems. In C. S. Johnson & H. E. Cheatham (Eds.), *Higher education trends for the next century: A research agenda for student success.* Retrieved November 28, 2000, from <http://www.acpa.nche.edu/seniorscholars/trends/trends.html>

Kinner, J., & Coombs, N. (1995). Computer access for students with special needs. In Z. L. Berge & M. P. Collins (Eds.), *Computer mediated communication and the online classroom* (Vol. 1, pp. 53–68). Cresskill, NJ: Hampton Press.

Kintsch, W. (1998). *Comprehension: A paradigm for cognition.* New York: Cambridge University Press.

Knoblauch, B., & Sorenson, B. (1998). *Idea's definition of disabilities.* Reston, VA: ERIC Clearinghouse On Disabilities and Gifted Education. (ERIC Document Reproduction Service No. 429396)

Kolb, D. A. (1981). Learning styles and disciplinary differences. In A. W. Chickering & associates (Eds.), *The modern American college* (pp. 232–255). San Francisco: Jossey-Bass.

Kottkamp, R. (1990). Means for facilitating reflection. *Education and Urban Society, 22*(2), 182–203.

Krupnick, C. (1985). Women and men in the classroom: Inequality and its remedies. In *On teaching and learning: The journal of the Harvard-Danforth Center* (pp. 18–25). Cambridge: Harvard University Press.

Kuhn, G., Baird, L. L., & Leslie, D. W. (1992). A landmark in scholarly synthesis. *Review of Higher Education, 15*(3), 347–373.

Kuhn, T. (1970). *The structure of scientific revolutions.* (2nd ed.). Chicago: University of Chicago Press.

Ladson-Billings, G. (1994a). Culturally relevant teaching: The key to making multicultural education work. In C. A. Grant (Ed.), *Research and multicultural education: From the margins to the mainstream* (pp. 106–121). London: Falmer Press.

Ladson-Billings, G. (1994b). *The dreamkeepers: Successful teachers of African American children.* San Francisco: Jossey-Bass.

280 · *Bibliography*

Ladson-Billings, G. (1995). Toward a theory of culturally relevant pedagogy. *American Educational Research Journal, 32,* 465–491.

The landscape. (1993). The changing faces of the American college campus. *Change, 24*(5), 57–60.

Latour, B., & Woolgar, S. (1986). *Laboratory life: The construction of scientific facts.* Beverly Hills, CA: Sage.

Laurel, B. (1991). *Computers as theatre.* Reading, MA: Addison-Wesley.

Leki, I. (1992). *Understanding ESL writers.* Portsmouth, NH: Heinemann-Boynton/Cook.

Lemke, J. (1990). *Talking science: Language, learning, and values.* New York: Ablex.

Lemke, J. (2002). Multimedia semiotics: Genre for science education and scientific literacy. In M. J. Schleppegrell & M. C. Colombi (Eds.), *Advanced literacy in first and second languages: Meaning with power* (pp. 21–44). Mahwah, NJ: Lawrence Erlbaum.

Lerner, J. (1989). *Learning disabilities* (5th ed.). Boston: Houghton Mifflin.

Levine, D. (2001). Radical equations. *Rethinking Schools, 15*(4), 14–15.

Lewis, R., Ashton, T., Fielden, C., Kieley, C., & Haapa, B. (1999). Improving the writing skills of students with learning disabilities: Are word processors with spelling and grammar checkers useful? *Learning Disabilities: A Multidisciplinary Journal, 9*(3), 87–98.

Light, R. (2002.) *Making the most of college: Students speak their minds.* Boston: Harvard University Press.

Lisiecki, C. (1999). Adaptive technology equipment for the library. *Computers in Libraries, 19*(6), 18–20, 22.

Lissner, L. (1997). Legal issues concerning all faculty in higher education. In B. Hodge & J. Preston-Sabin (Eds.), *Accommodations, or just good teaching? Strategies for teaching college students with disabilities* (pp. 5–22). Westport, CT: Praeger.

Loewen, J. W. (1995). *Lies my teacher told me: Everything your American history textbook got wrong.* New York: Touchstone.

Lum, D. (1999). *Culturally competent practice: A framework for growth and action.* Pacific Grove, CA: Brooks/Cole.

Lyons, N. (Ed.). (1998). *With portfolio in hand: Validating the new teacher professionalism.* New York: Teachers College Press.

Mabrito, M. (1991). Electronic mail as a vehicle for peer response. *Written Communication, 8,* 509–532.

MacArthur, C., Graham, S., & Schwartz, S. (1991). Knowledge of revision and revising behavior among learning disabled students. *Learning Disabilities Quarterly, 14,* 61–73.

Machado, A. (1982). *Selected poems; translated and with an introduction by Alan S. Trueblood.* Cambridge, MA: Harvard University Press.

Mahan, J., Fortney, M., & Garcia, J. (1983). Linking the community to teacher education: Toward a more analytical approach. *Action in Teacher Education, 5*(1–2), 1–10.

Maimon, E. P., & García, M. (1997, Fall). Transforming institutions: The Importance of faculty diversity. *Diversity Digest*. Retrieved June 2002 from <http://www.diversityweb.org/digest/f97/transforming.html>

Marin, P. (2000). The educational possibility of multi-racial/multi-ethnic college classrooms. In *Does diversity make a difference? Three research studies on diversity in college classrooms*. Retrieved November 2, 2002, from <http://www.acenet.edu/program/omhe/diversity-report.pdf>

Markus, G. B., Howard, J., & King, D. (1993). Integrating community service and classroom instruction enhances learning: Results from an experiment. *Educational Evaluation and Policy Analysis, 15*(4), 410–419.

Martin, D. B. (2001). *Mathematics success and failure among African-American youth*. Mahwah, NJ: Lawrence Erlbaum.

Martinez, E. (1998). *De colores means all of us: Latina views for a multi-colored century*. Cambridge, MA: South End Press.

Marullo, S. (1998). Bringing home diversity: A service-learning approach to teaching race/ethnic relations. *Teaching Sociology, 26*(4), 259–275.

Maruyama, G., & Moreno, J. F. (2000). University faculty views about the value of diversity on campus and in the classroom. In *Does diversity make a difference: Three research studies on diversity in college classrooms*. Retrieved November 2, 2002, from <http://www.acenet.edu/program/omhe/diversity-report.pdf>

Matalene, C. (1985). Contrastive rhetoric: An American writing teacher in China. *College English, 47,* 789–808.

Mattel. (1999, February 7). *Barbie doll gala kicks off year-long celebration* [Company press release]. El Segundo, CA: Author.

Maybach, C. W. (1996). Investigating urban community needs. *Education and Urban Society, 28,* 224–236.

McCown, R., Driscoll, M., & Roop, P. G. (1996). *Educational psychology: A learning-centered approach to classroom practice* (2nd ed.). Boston: Allyn and Bacon.

McCue, M. (1993). Clinical diagnostic and functional assessment of adults with learning disabilities. In P. Gerber & H. Reiff (Eds.), *Learning disabilities in adulthood: Persisting problems and evolving issues* (pp. 55–71). Boston: Andover Medical Publishers.

McCutchen, D. (2000). Knowledge, processing, and working memory: Implications for a theory of writing. *Educational Psychologist, 35,* 13–23.

McDermott, L. C., Shaffer, P. S., & Rosenquist, M. L. (1996). *Physics by inquiry: An introduction to physics and physical science*. New York: John Wiley.

McGoldrick, K. M., & Ziegert, A. (2002). *Putting the invisible hand to work: Concepts and models for service learning in economics*. Ann Arbor: University of Michigan Press.

McLeod, S. H., Miraglia, E., Soven, M., & Thaiss, C. (Eds.). (2001). *WAC for the new millennium: Strategies for continuing writing-across-the-curriculum programs*. Urbana, IL: National Council of Teachers of English.

McNeil, L. (1986). *Contradictions of control: School structure and school knowledge.* New York: Routledge and Kegan Paul.

McTighe, J., & Wiggins, G. P. (2000). *Understanding by design.* Englewood Cliffs, NJ: Prentice-Hall.

Merbler, J., Haladian, A., & Ulman, J. (1999). Using assistive technology in the inclusive classroom. *Preventing School Failure, 43*(3), 113–117.

Mercer, N. (1995). *The guided construction of knowledge: Talk amongst teachers and learners.* Philadelphia, PA: Multilingual Matters.

Merta, R. J., Stringham, E. M., & Ponterotto, J. G. (1988). Simulating cultural shock in counselor trainees: An experiential exercise for cross-cultural training. *Journal of Counseling and Development, 66,* 242–245.

Michaels, S., & O'Connor, M. C. (1990, July). *Literacy as reasoning within multiple discourses: Implications for policy and educational reform.* Paper presented at the Council of Chief State School Officers 1990 Summer Institute, Cambridge, MA.

Michaelsen, L. K. (1992). Team learning: A comprehensive approach for harnessing the power of small groups in higher education. *To Improve the Academy, 11,* 107–121.

Michigan Journal of Community Service Learning, 3. (1996). Available at <http://www.umich.edu/~mjcsl/>

Miles, M. B., & Huberman, A. M. (1994). *Qualitative data analysis: An expanded sourcebook* (2nd ed.). Thousand Oaks, CA: Sage.

Millar, R. (1989). *Doing science: Images of science in science education.* London: Falmer Press.

Millis, B. J., & Cottell, P G. (1998). *Cooperative learning for higher education faculty.* Phoenix, AZ: American Council on Education; Westport, CT: Oryx Press.

Mink, L. O. (1987) *Historical understanding.* Ithaca, NY: Cornell University Press, 1–88.

Moll, L. C., & Greenberg, J. B. (1990). Creating zones of possibilities: Combining social contexts for instruction. In L. C. Moll (Ed.), *Vygotsky and education: Instructional implications and applications of sociohistorical pyschology* (pp. 319–348). New York: Cambridge University Press.

Moody, V. R. (2001). The social constructs of the mathematical experiences of African-American students. In B. Atweh, H. Forgasz, & B. Nebres (Eds.), *Sociocultural research on mathematics education* (pp. 255–276). Mahwah, NJ: Lawrence Erlbaum.

Moses, R. P., & Cobb, C. E. (2001). *Radical equations: Math literacy and civil rights.* Boston: Beacon Press.

Moses, R. P., Kamii, M., Swap, S. M., & Howard, J. (1989). The algebra project: Organizing in the spirit of Ella. *Harvard Educational Review, 59,* 423–443.

Muffo, J. A., & Bunda, M. A. (1993). Attitude and opinion data. In T. W. Banta (Ed.), *Making a difference: Outcomes of a decade of assessment in higher education* (pp. 168–178). San Francisco: Jossey-Bass.

Mukhopadhyay, S. (1998). When Barbie goes to classrooms: Mathematics in creating a social discourse. In C. Keitel (Ed.), *Social justice and mathematics education: Gender, class, ethnicity, and the politics of schooling* (pp. 150–161). Berlin: Freie Universität.

Mulkay, M. (1975). Norms and ideology in science. *Social Science Information, 15,* 637–656. (Reprinted in *Sociology of Science,* pp. 62–78, by M. Mulkay, Ed., 1991, Bloomington: Indiana University Press)

Myers-Lipton, S. (1998). Effect of a comprehensive service learning program in college students' civic responsibility. *Teaching Sociology 26,* 243–258.

Nash, G. B., Crabtree, C., & Dunn, R. E. (1997). *History on trial: Culture wars and teaching of the past.* New York: Vintage Books.

Nasir, N. S., & Cobb, P. (Eds.). (2002). Diversity, equity, and mathematical learning [Special issue]. *Mathematical Thinking and Learning, 4,* 2 & 3.

National Association of Scholars. (1996). *The dissolution of general education: 1914–1993.* Princeton, NJ: Author.

National Center for Education Statistics. (1994). *National education longitudinal study of 1988: Third follow-up survey* (NELS Publication No. 88/94). Washington, DC: U.S. Department of Education.

National Center for Education Statistics. (1998). *1995–96 National postsecondary student aid study* (NPSAS Publication No. 96). Washington, DC: U.S. Department of Education.

National Council for Accreditation of Teacher Education. (1977). *Standards for the accreditation of teacher education programs.* Washington, DC: Author.

National Council for Black Studies. (n.d.). *Promoting academic excellence and social responsibility.* Retrieved from <http://www.nationalcouncilforblack-studies.com>

National Council for Teachers of Mathematics (2000). *Principles and standards for school mathematics.* Reston, VA: Author.

National Organization on Disability. (2000). Americans with disabilities trail non-disabled in key life areas, benchmark NOD/Harris Survey finds [Eight paragraphs]. In *Survey program on participation and attitudes: The 2000 NOD/Harris Survey press conference.* Retrieved from <http://nod.org/hs2000.html#findings>

National Spinal Cord Injury Statistical Center. (2001). Spinal cord injury [Fifteen paragraphs]. In *Facts and figures at a glance.* Retrieved from <http://www.spinalcord.uab.edu>

National Survey of Student Engagement (2002). *Improving the college experience: National benchmarks of effective educational practice* (NSSE 2001 Report). Bloomington, IN: Author.

Newcomer, P., & Barenbaum, E. (1991). The written composing ability of children with learning disabilities: A review of the literature from 1980 to 1990. *Journal of Learning Disabilities, 24,* 578–593.

Newman, B., & Newman, P. (1999). *Development through life: A psychosocial approach.* Belmont, CA: Wadsworth.

Nichols, J. O. (1995a). *Assessment case studies: Common issues in implementation with various campus approaches to resolution.* New York: Agathon Press.

Nichols, J. O. (1995b). *The departmental guide and record book for student outcomes assessment and institutional effectiveness.* New York: Agathon Press.

Nichols, J. O. (1995c). *A practitioner's handbook for institutional effectiveness and student outcomes assessment implementation* (3rd ed.). New York: Agathon Press.

Noddings, N. (1984). *Caring: A feminine approach to ethics and moral education.* Berkeley: University of California Press.

Norment, N. (1997). Some effects of culture-referenced topics on the writing performance of African American students. *Journal of Basic Writing, 16*(2), 17–45.

Norris, P. (Ed.). (1997). *Women, media, and politics.* New York: Oxford University Press.

Novak, J., & Gowin, B. (1984). *Learning how to learn.* Cambridge: Cambridge University Press.

Oakes, J. (1985). *Keeping track: How schools structure inequality.* New Haven, CT: Yale University Press.

Oakes, J. (1990). *Multiplying inequalities: The effects of race, social class, and tracking on opportunities to learn mathematics and science.* Santa Monica, CA: Rand Corporation.

Oakes, J., & Guiton, G. (1995). Matchmaking: The dynamics of high school tracking decisions. *American Educational Research Journal, 32,* 3–33.

O'Brien, J., & Kollock, P. (2001). *The production of reality: Essays and readings on social interaction.* Thousand Oaks, CA: Pine Forge Press.

Ochoa, A. (1986). *Reforming preservice education: An international dimension* [Executive summary]. Bloomington: Indiana University. (ERIC Document Reproduction Service No. ED298130)

Office for Civil Rights. (1998). *Auxiliary aids and services for postsecondary students with disabilities: Higher education's obligations under section 504 and title II of the ADA.* Washington, DC: Author. (ERIC Document Reproduction Service No. 425687)

Ogbu, J. (1978). *Minority education and caste: The American system in cross-cultural perspective.* New York: Academic Press.

Ogbu, J. (1986). The consequences of the American caste system. In U. Neisser (Ed.), *The School Achievement of Minority Children: New Perspectives* (pp. 19–56). Hillsdale, N.J.: Lawrence Erlbaum Associates.

Ortiz-Franco, L., & Flores, W. V. (2001). Sociocultural considerations and Latino mathematics achievement: A critical review. In B. Atweh, H. Forgasz, & B. Nebres (Eds.), *Sociocultural research on mathematics education* (pp. 233–253). Mahwah, NJ: Lawrence Erlbaum.

Osborne, R., & Freyberg, P. (1985). *Learning in science: The implications of children's science.* Portsmouth, NH: Heinemann.

Ostermeier, T. (1992). *An experiential approach to an upper division course in inter-*

cultural communication. Paper presented at the annual meeting of the Central States Communication Association, Cleveland, OH.

Paciello, M. G. (2000). *Web accessibility for people with disabilities.* Lawrence, KS: CMP Books.

Pacifici, T, & McKinney, K. (1997). *Disability support services for community college students.* Los Angeles: ERIC Clearinghouse for Community Colleges. (ERIC Document Reproduction Service No. 409972)

Panek, W. (1995). Visual disabilities. In M. Brodwin, F. Tellez, & S. Brodwin (Eds.), *Medical, psychosocial, and vocational aspects of disability* (pp. 217–231). Athens, GA: Elliot and Fitzpatrick.

Paulson, F. L., Paulson, P. R, Meyer, C. A. (1991). What makes a portfolio a portfolio? *Educational Leadership, 48*(5), 60–63.

Pennycook, A. (1996). Borrowing other's words: Text, ownership, memory, and plagiarism. *Tesol Quarterly, 30,* 201–230.

Phinney, Jean S., & Rotherham, M. J. (Eds.). (1987). *Children's ethnic socialization.* Newbury Park, CA: Sage.

Popper, K. R. (1963). *Conjectures and refutations: The growth of scientific knowledge* (Vols. 7–9). London: Routledge and Kegan Paul.

Powell, A. B., & Frankenstein, M. (Eds.). (1997). *Ethnomathematics: Challenging Eurocentrism in mathematics.* Albany: State University of New York Press.

Raimes, A. (2001). *Keys for writers: A brief handbook* (3rd ed.). Boston: Houghton Mifflin.

Ramírez, M., & Castañeda, A. (1974). *Cultural democracy, bicognitive development, and education.* New York: Academic Press.

Raskind, M., Higgins, E., Shaw, T., & Slaff, N. (1998). Assistive technology in the homes of children with learning disabilities: An exploratory study. *Learning Disabilities: A Multidisciplinary Journal, 9*(2), 47–56.

Rendón, L. I., & Garza, H. (1996). Closing the gap between two- and four-year institutions. In L. Rendón & R. O. Hope (Eds.), *Educating a new majority: Transforming America's system for diversity.* San Francisco: Jossey-Bass.

Rendón, L. I., & Hope, R. O. (1996). An educational system in crisis. In L. I. Rendón & R. O. Hope (Eds.), *Educating a new majority: Transforming America's educational system for diversity* (pp. 1–32). San Francisco: Jossey-Bass.

Rhoads, R. A., & Howard, J. P. F. (Eds.). (1998). *Academic service learning: A pedagogy of action and reflection* (New Directions for Teaching and Learning No. 73). San Francisco: Jossey-Bass.

Richards, T., Rosen, L., & Ramirez, C. (1999). Psychological functioning differences among college students with confirmed ADHD, ADHD by Self-Report Only, and without ADHD. *Journal of College Student Development, 40,* 299–304.

Riess, R. D., & Muffo, J. A. 1996. Exit interviews in mathematics. In T. W. Banta, J. P. Lund, K. E. Black, & F. W. Oblander (Eds.), *Assessment in practice: Putting principles to work on college campuses,* (pp. 129–131). San Francisco: Jossey-Bass.

Roberge, M. (2002, March). *Working with generation 1.5 immigrant ESL students*. Paper presented at the California Teachers of English to Speakers of Other Languages (CATESOL) Conference, San Francisco, CA.

Roberts, H. (Ed.). (1994). *Teaching from a multi-cultural perspective*. Thousand Oaks, CA: Sage.

Rodriguez, R. (1982). *Hunger of memory: The education of Richard Rodriguez*. New York: Bantam Books.

Roffman, A. (2000). *Meeting the challenge of learning disabilities in adulthood*. Baltimore: Paul H. Brookes.

Sadow, S. A. (1987). Experiential techniques that promote cross-cultural awareness. *Foreign Language Annals, 20*(1), 25–30.

San Diego State University. (1981). *1981–1982 general catalog, San Diego State University*. San Diego, CA: Author.

San Diego State University. (1992a). *1992–1993 general catalog, San Diego State University*. San Diego, CA: Author.

San Diego State University. (1992b). *SDSU curriculum guide*. San Diego, CA: Author.

San Diego State University. Department of Africana Studies. (1994). Mission statement and philosophy statement of Africana Studies. *Africana Studies Self Study* (pp. 2–3). San Diego, CA: Author.

San Diego State University. (2000a). *SDSU curriculum guide*. San Diego, CA: Author.

San Diego State University. (2000b). *2000–2001 general catalog, San Diego State University*. San Diego, CA: Author.

San Diego State University, Office of Institutional Research. (1993, Fall). Enrollment by Ethnicity. San Diego, CA: Author.

San Diego's melting pot: City heights area has most racial diversity of any place in county. (2001, April 6). *San Diego Union Tribune,* pp. B1–2.

Saunders, M. (1998). The service learner as researcher: A case study. *Journal on Excellence in College Teaching, 9*(2), 55–67.

Scarcella, R. (1996). Secondary education in California and second language research: Instructing ESL students in the 1990s. *CATESOL Journal, 9,* 129–52.

Schleppegrell, M. (2002). Challenges of the science register for ESL students: Errors and meaning-making. In M. L. Schleppegrell & M. C. Colombi (Eds.), *Developing advanced literacy in first and second languages: Meaning with power* (pp. 119–142.). Mahwah, NJ: Lawrence Erlbaum.

Schleppegrell, M. J., & Colombi, M. C. (Eds.). (2002). *Developing advanced literacy in first and second languages: Meaning with power*. Mahwah, NJ: Lawrence Erlbaum.

Schneider, C. G. (2001, Winter). Diversity requirements: Part of a renewed civic education. *Diversity Digest*. Retrieved from <http://www.diversity web.org/digest/w01/civic.html>

Schoem, D., Frankel, L., Zuniga, X., & Lewis, E. A. (Eds.). (1993). *Multicultural teaching in the university*. Westport, CT: Praeger.

Schofield, J. W. (1997). Causes and consequences of the colorblind perspective. In J. A. Banks & C. A. M. Banks (Eds.), *Multicultural education: Issues and perspectives* (3rd ed., pp. 251–271). Boston: Allyn and Bacon.

Schon, D. (1983). *The reflective practitioner: How professionals think in action.* Washington, DC: Basic Books.

Schroeder, F. (1989). Literacy: The key to opportunity. *Journal of Visual Impairment and Blindness, 83,* 290–293.

Schulz, A. R. (1998). *Supporting intermediate and secondary readers.* Costa Mesa, CA: California Reading Association.

Schwab, J. J. (1962). Education and the structure of the disciplines. In I. Westbury & N. J. Wilkof (Eds.), *Science, curriculum, and liberal education* (pp. 229–273). Chicago: University of Chicago Press.

Schwab, J. J. (1978). Eros and education: A discussion of one aspect of discussion. In I. Westbury & N. J. Wilkof (Eds.), *Science, curriculum, and liberal education* (pp. 105–132). Chicago: University of Chicago Press.

Schwartz, C., Foley, F., Rao, S., Bernardin, L., Lee, H., & Genderson, M. (1999). Stress and the course of disease in multiple sclerosis. *Behavioral Medicine, 25*(3), 110–116.

Secada, W. G. (1992). Race, ethnicity, social class, language, and achievement in mathematics. In D. A. Grouws (Ed.), *Handbook of research on mathematics teaching and learning* (pp. 623–660). New York: Macmillan.

Selfe, C. (1990). Technology in the English classroom: Computers through the lens of feminist theory. In C. Handa (Ed.), *Computers and community: Teaching composition in the twenty-first century* (pp. 118–139). Portsmouth, NH: Boynton/Cook.

Shade, B., Kelly, C., & Oberg, M. (1997). *Creating culturally responsive classrooms.* Washington, DC: American Psychological Association.

Shapiro, B., & Capute, A. (1994). Cerebral palsy. In F. A. Oski, C. D. DeAngelis, R. D. Feign, J. A. McMillan, & J. B. Warshaw (Eds.), *Principles and practice of pediatrics* (2nd ed., pp. 679–686). Philadelphia: J. B. Lippincott.

Sheets, R. H. (1999). Student self-empowerment: A dimension of multicultural education. *Multicultural Education, 6*(4), 2–8.

Shor, I. (1992). *Empowering education: Critical teaching for social change.* Chicago: University of Chicago Press.

Shulman, L. S. (2000.) From Minsk to Pinsk: Why a scholarship of teaching and learning? *Journal of Scholarship of Teaching and Learning, 1*(1), 48–52. Available at <http://titans.iusb.edu/josotl/VOL_1/NO_1/shulman_vol_1_no_1.htm>

Sigsbee, D. L., Speck, B. W., & Maylath, B. (Eds.). (1997). *Approaches to teaching non-native English speakers across the curriculum* (New Directions for Teaching and Learning No. 70). San Francisco: Jossey-Bass.

Simon, J. (1999). *California Community Colleges AHEAD training: Executive summary.* Sacramento: California Community Colleges, Chancellor's Office.

Simon, S., & Schatz, M. (1998). The portfolio approach for BSW generalist social work students. *The New Social Worker, 5,* 12–14.

Singer, B., & Bashir, A. (2000). What are executive functions and self-regulation and what do they have to do with language-learning disorders? *Language, Speech, and Hearing Services in Schools, 30,* 265–273.

Skovsmose, O., & Valero, P. (2001). Breaking political neutrality: The critical engagement of mathematics education with democracy. In B. Atweh, H. Forgasz, & B. Nebres (Eds.), *Sociocultural research on mathematics education* (pp. 37–56). Mahwah, NJ: Lawrence Erlbaum.

Skovsmose, O., & Valero, P. (2002). Democratic access to powerful mathematical ideas. In L. D. English (Ed.), *Handbook of international research in mathematics education: Directions for the twenty-first century* (pp. 383–408). Mahwah, NJ: Lawrence Erlbaum.

Slavin, R. E. (1979). Effects of biracial learning teams on cross-racial friendships. *Journal of Educational Psychology, 71,* 381–387.

Slavin, R. E. (1990). *Cooperative learning.* Englewood Cliffs, NJ: Prentice-Hall.

Smith, B. L., & MacGregor, J. T. (1992). What is collaborative learning? In A. S. Goodsell, M. R. Maher, V. Tinto, B. L. Smith, & J. MacGregor (Eds.), *Collaborative learning: A sourcebook for higher education* (pp. 9–22). University Park, PA: National Center, Teaching, Learning, and Assessment.

Smith, D. G. (1996). *Achieving faculty diversity: Debunking the myths.* Washington, DC: Association of American Colleges and Universities.

Smith, D. M., & Kolb, D. A. (1986). *User's guide for the learning style inventory: A manual for teachers and trainers.* Boston: McBer.

Smith, S., & Jones, E. (1999). The obligation to provide assistive technology: Enhancing the general curriculum access. *Journal of Law and Education, 28*(2), 247–265.

Staik, Irene M., & Rogers, J. S. (1996). Listening to your student. In T. W. Banta, J. P. Lund, K. E. Black, & F. W. Oblander (Eds.), *Assessment in practice: Putting principles to work on college campuses* (pp. 132–135). San Francisco: Jossey-Bass.

Stanton, T. K., Giles, D. E., Jr., & Cruz, N. I. (1999). *Service-learning: A movement's pioneers reflect on its origins, practice, and future.* San Francisco: Jossey-Bass.

State's Latino, Asian populations soar. (2001, March 30). *San Diego Union Tribune,* pp. A1, 10.

Stephens, O. (1989). Braille: Implications for living. *Journal of Visual Impairment and Blindness, 83,* 288–289.

Stewart, G. M. (1990). Learning styles as a filter for developing service-learning interventions. In C. I. Delve, S. D. Mintz, and G. M. Stewart (Eds.), *Community service as values education* (New Directions for Teaching and Learning No. 50, pp. 31–42). San Francisco: Jossey-Bass.

Sue, D., & David, S. (1999). *Counseling the culturally different: Theory and practice.* New York: John Wiley.

Sue, D. W., & Sue, D. (1990). *Counseling the culturally different: Theory and practice* (2nd ed.). New York: Wiley.

Svinicki, M. D., & Dixon, N. M. (1987). The Kolb model modified for classroom activities. *College Teaching, 35*(4), 141–146.

Swenson, A. (1988). Using an integrated literacy curriculum with beginning Braille readers. *Journal of Visual Impairment and Blindness, 82,* 336–338.

Swisher, K., & Deyhle, D. (1989, August). The styles of learning are different, but the teaching is just the same. [Special issue]. *Journal of American Indian Education,* 1–13.

Takaki, R. (1993). *A different mirror: A history of multicultural America.* Boston: Little, Brown, and Company.

Takaki, R. (Ed.). (1994). *From different shorts: Perspectives on race and ethnicity in America.* New York: Oxford University Press.

Tate, W. F. (1995). Returning to the root: A culturally relevant approach to mathematics pedagogy. *Theory into practice, 34*(3), 166–173.

Thomas, C., Englert, C., & Gregg, S. (1987). An analysis of errors and strategies in the expository writing of learning disabled students. *Remedial and Special Education, 8,* 21–30, 46.

Thomas, J. (2001). Globalization and politics of mathematics education. In B. Atweh, H. Forgasz, & B. Nebres (Eds.), *Sociocultural research on mathematics education* (pp. 95–112). Mahwah, NJ: Lawrence Erlbaum.

Thompson, A., Bethea, L., Rizer, H., & Hutto, M. (1997). *College students with disabilities and assistive technology: A desk reference guide.* Washington, DC: U.S. Department of Education, Office of Special Education and Rehabilitation Technology. (ERIC Document Reproduction Service No. ED407810)

Tolley, K. (1996). Science for ladies, classics for gentlemen: A comparative analysis of scientific subjects in the curricula of boys' and girls' secondary schools in the United States, 1794–1850. *History of Education Quarterly, 36,* 129–153.

Tomlinson, L. M. (1996). *Applying banks' typology of ethnic identity development and curriculum goals to story content, classroom discussion, and the ecology of classroom and community: Phase one* (Instructional Resource No. 24). Athens, GA: Universities of Georgia and Maryland College Park, National Reading Research Center.

Townsend, D. (2001). An unfair graduation requirement: Why Hispanics are at a disadvantage in passing the TAAS test. In R. A. Horn & J. L. Kincheloe (Eds.), *American standards: Quality education in a complex world* (pp. 149–158). New York: Peter Lang.

Traweek, S. (1988). *Beamtimes and lifetimes: The world of high energy physicists.* Cambridge: Harvard University Press.

Turnock, P., Rosen, L., & Kaminski, P. (1998). Differences in academic coping strategies of college students who self-report high and low symptoms of attention deficit hyperactive disorder. *Journal of College Student Development, 39,* 484–493.

Tyler, J., & Colson, S. (1994). Common pediatric disabilities: Medical aspects and educational implications. *Focus on Exceptional Children, 27*(4), 1–16.

Tymoczko, T. (1986). *New directions in the philosophy of mathematics.* Boston: Birkhauser.

United Cerebral Palsy. (2000). Cerebral palsy—Facts and figures. *UCPnet: Who Is UCP?* Retrieved from <http://www.ucp.org/ ucp_generaldoc .cfm/45/3/43/43-43/4477. Updated 2001 version at <http://www.ucp .org/ucp_generaldoc.cfm/1/3/43/43-43/447>. Updated 2001.

U.S. Census Bureau. (1997). Table 2. Prevalence of types of disability among individuals fifteen years old and over: 1997. *Americans with disabilities: 1997.* Retrieved from <http://www.census.gov/hhes/www/disable/sipp/ disab97/ds97t2.html>

Usiskin, Z. (1999a). *Developments in school mathematics around the world.* Reston, VA: National Council of Teachers of Mathematics.

Usiskin, Z. (1999b). Is there a worldwide mathematics curriculum? In Z. Usiskin (Ed.), *Developments in school mathematics around the world* (pp. 213–227). Reston, VA: National Council of Teachers of Mathematics.

Vacca, R. T., & Vacca, J. L. (2002). *Content area reading: Literacy and learning across the curriculum* (7th ed.). Boston: Allyn and Bacon.

Vallecorsa, A., & Debettencourt, L. (1997). Using a mapping procedure to teach reading and writing skills to middle grade students with learning disabilities. *Education and Treatment of Children, 20*(2), 173–188.

Vann, R. D., Myer, E., & Lorenz, F. O. (1984). Error gravity: A study of faculty opinion of ESL errors. *TESOL Quarterly, 18,* 427–440.

Van Voorhis, R. M. (1998). Culturally relevant practice: A framework for teaching the psychodynamics of oppression. *Journal of Social Work Education, 34*(1), 121–133.

Varlotta, L. (2000). Service as text: Making the metaphor meaningful. *Michigan Journal of Community Service Learning, 7,* 76–84.

Vélez-Ibáñez, C. (1983). *Bonds of mutual trust: The cultural systems of rotating credit associations among urban Mexicans and Chicanos.* New Brunswick, NJ: Rutgers University Press.

Vélez-Ibáñez, C. (1996). *Border visions: Mexican cultures of the southwest United States.* Tucson: University of Arizona Press.

Vogel, S. (1998). Adults with learning disabilities. In S. Vogel & S. Reder (Eds.), *Learning disabilities, literacy, and adult education* (pp. 5–28). Baltimore: Paul H. Brookes.

Vogel, S., & Konrad, D. (1988). Characteristic written expressive language deficits of the learning disabled: Some general and specific intervention strategies. *Reading, Writing, and Learning Disabilities, 4,* 89–99.

Volmink, J. D. (1999). School mathematics and outcome-based education: A view from South Africa. In Z. Usiskin (Ed.), *Developments in school mathematics around the world* (pp. 84–95). Reston, VA: National Council of Teachers of Mathematics.

Von Daniken, E. (1970). *Chariots of the gods?* New York: Bantam Books.

Vygotsky, L. S. (1978). *Thought and Language.* Cambridge: MIT Press.

Wade, R. C., & Saxe, D. W. (1996). Community service learning in social studies: Historical roots, empirical evidence, and critical issues. *Theory and Research in Social Education, 24,* 331–360.

Wagener, U. E. (1989). Quality and equity: The necessity for imagination. *Harvard Educational Review, 59,* 240–250.

Walker, R. D., & Muffo, J. A. 1996. Alumni involvement in civil engineering. In T. W. Banta, J. P. Lund, K. E. Black, & F. W. Oblander (Eds.), *Assessment in practice: Putting principles to work on college campuses* (pp. 147–149). San Francisco: Jossey-Bass.

Walsh, C. E. (1991). *Pedagogy and the struggle for voice: Issues of language, power, and schooling for Puerto Ricans.* New York: Bergin and Garvey.

Waluconis, C. J. (1993). Student self-evaluation. In T. W. Banta, *Making a difference: Outcomes of a decade of assessment in higher education* (pp. 244–255). San Francisco: Jossey-Bass.

Walvoord, B. E., & Anderson, V. J. 1998. *Effective grading: A tool for learning and assessment.* San Francisco: Jossey-Bass.

Wang, M. J., & Folger, T. (in progress). *An exploration of diversity, communication, and learning outcomes in college classrooms.* An award entry submitted to the 2001 National Education Association Art of Teaching Prize.

Wang, M. J., Rossett, A., & Wangemann, P. (2002). An exploration of engagement and mentoring in online problem solving. In C. Sleezer, R. Cude, & T. Wentling (Eds.), *Human resource development in a networked world: Building competitive advantage.* Boston: Kluwer Academic Publishers.

Warschauer, M., Turbee, L., & Roberts, B. (1996). Computer learning networks and student empowerment. *System, 24,* 1–14.

Washburn, D. K., & Crowe, D. W. (1988). *Symmetries of cultures: Theory and practice of plane pattern analysis.* Seattle: University of Washington Press.

Washington, P. (2000a). From college classroom to community action. *Feminist teacher, 13*(1), 12–34.

Washington, P. (2000b). Women's studies and community-based service learning: A natural affinity. In B. Balliet and K. Heffernan (Eds.), *The practice of change: Concepts and models for service learning in women's studies* (pp. 103–116). Washington, DC. American Association for Higher Education.

Washington, P. (2002). The individual and collective rewards of community-based service learning. In N. Naples & K. Bojar (Eds.), *Teaching feminist activism* (pp. 166–182). New York: Routledge.

Weah, W., Simmons, V. C., & Hall, M. (2000). Service-learning and multicultural/multi-ethnic perspectives. *Phi Delta Kappan, 81,* 673–675.

Wilgoren, J. (2001, June 6). Repetition + rap = charter school success. *New York Times,* pp. A1, B7.

Williams, T. (1990). *Portfolio design: A handbook for faculty.* San Diego: San Diego State University Teacher Scholar Program.

Williford, A. M., & Moden, G. O. (1996). Assessing student involvement. In

T. W. Banta, J. P. Lund, K. E. Black, & F. W. Oblander (Eds.), *Assessment in practice: Putting principles to work on college campuses* (pp. 256–258). San Francisco: Jossey-Bass.

Wilson, A. (1982). Cross-cultural experiential learning for teachers. *Theory into Practice, 21*(3), 184–192.

Wittrock, M. (1986). Students' thought processes. In M. Wittrock (Ed.), *Handbook of Research on Teaching* (pp. 297–314). New York: Macmillan.

Wlodkowski, R. J., & Ginsberg, M. B. (1995). *Diversity and motivation: Culturally responsive teaching.* San Francisco: Jossey-Bass.

Wolfram, W., Adger, C. T., & Christian, D. (1999). *Dialects in schools and communities.* Mahwah, NJ: Lawrence Erlbaum.

Wolsk, D. (1974). *An experience centered curriculum: Exercises in personal and social reality.* Paris, France: United Nations Educational, Scientific, and Cultural Organization. (ERIC Document Reproduction Service No. ED099269)

Wong, B. (2000). Writing strategies instruction for expository essays for adolescents with and without learning disabilities. *Topics in Language Disorders, 20*(4), 29–44.

Wong, B., Wong, R., & Blenkinsop, J. (1989). Cognitive and metacognitive aspects of learning disabled adolescents' composing problems. *Learning Disability Quarterly, 12,* 300–322.

Woody, T. (1929). *A history of women's education in the United States.* New York: Science Press. Reprint, New York: Octagon Books, 1966.

Woolgar, S. (1988). *Science: The very idea.* Chichester: Ellis Horwood.

World Federation of the Deaf. (2000, February 4). Resolution of the XIII world congress of the world federation of the deaf [Ten paragraphs]. *WFD News.* Retrieved from <http://www.wfdnews.org/news/news3.asp>

Yerrick, R., Doster, E., Parke, H., & Nugent, J. (2003). Social interaction and the use of analogy: An analysis of pre-service teachers. *Journal of Research in Science Teaching, 40,* 443–463.

Ylvisaker, M., & Debonis, D. (2000). Executive function impairment in adolescence: TBI and ADHD. *Topics in Language Disorders, 20*(2), 29–57.

York, Darlene. (1994). *Cross-cultural training programs.* Westport, CT: Bergin and Garvey.

Young, R. (1993). Cross-cultural experiential learning for teacher trainees. *Teacher Education Quarterly, 20*(3), 67–76.

Zaslavsky, C. (1973). *Africa counts: Number and pattern in African culture.* Brooklyn, NY: Lawrence Hill Books.

Zinn, H. (1995). *A people's history of the United States, 1492 to present.* New York: Harper Collins.

Zlotkowski, E. (Ed.). (1998). *Successful service-learning programs: New models of excellence in higher education.* Boston: Anker.

Zlotkowski, E. (1999). Pedagogy and engagement. In R. Bringle, Richard Games, & Edward A. Malloy (Eds.), *Colleges and universities as citizens* (pp. 96–120). Boston: Allyn and Bacon.

About the Authors

André J. Branch is an assistant professor in the School of Teacher Education at San Diego State University. He teaches courses in multicultural education, foundations of education, and ethnic identity development. His research interests include multicultural curriculum development, teacher-facilitated ethnic identity development, and the recruitment and retention of African American faculty members in higher education and of teachers of color in K–12 schools. His recent publications include *How to Retain African-American Faculty during Times of Challenge for Higher Education* (2001), *Increasing the Numbers of Teachers of Color in K–12 Public Schools* (2001), and *Creating Effective Urban Schools: The Impact of School Climate* (2001). Dr. Branch earned a Ph.D. in curriculum and instruction at the University of Washington, Seattle, and is a former principal of Cultural Diversity Associates. This national consulting firm provided workshops in cultural diversity to educators in K–12 schools, to teachers and students in colleges and universities, and to businesses in the public and private sectors.

Carl Fielden was the founder and, for eleven years, the coordinator of San Diego State University's High Tech Center for Students with Disabilities. He also serves as a lecturer in the Department of Rhetoric and Writing Studies (formerly the Academic Skills Center), where he currently teaches courses in developmental writing and study skills for students with disabilities and serves as the proficiency test coordinator for the Developmental Writing Program. Mr. Fielden holds M.A. degrees in linguistics and special education and is a student in the Claremont Graduate University/San Diego State University Ph.D. program in education.

Terre Folger is presently a Ph.D. candidate in elementary education at the University of Missouri–Columbia. Her teaching career includes eighteen years in elementary education, with classroom experiences from preschool through fifth grade in central Missouri schools. While pursuing her Ph.D., Ms. Folger has taught several literacy courses in the Teacher Development Program at the University of Missouri. Her research interests include literacy development and assessment issues, ranging from emergent literacy to literacy education preparation of preservice teachers and continuing literacy education for in-service teachers. Ms. Folger is also interested in multicultural issues and the use of technology in preservice teacher education. She has copublished in the *Journal of Research and Development in Education* (1996, 1999) and in *Reading, Research, and Instruction* (in progress).

Brian Greer is a professor of mathematics in the Department of Mathematics and Statistics at San Diego State University and a fellow at SDSU's Center for Research in Mathematics and Science Education. His teaching and research interests center on sociocultural and political aspects of mathematics education. In addition to publishing a number of journal articles, Professor Greer is associate editor of the journal *Mathematical Thinking* and coauthor of the volume *Making Sense of Word Problems*. He is also completing an introductory statistics textbook, *Making Sense of Data in Psychology*.

Charles F. Hohm received his Ph.D. in sociology from the University of Southern California and is a professor of sociology and the associate dean of the Division of Undergraduate Studies at San Diego State University. He served as editor of *Sociological Perspectives* (the official journal of the Pacific Sociological Association) and has published widely in the area of demography and social problems. His most recent books are *Population: Opposing Viewpoints* (2000) and *California's Social Problems* (2002). As associate dean of the Division of Undergraduate Studies, his primary responsibility is the advancement of assessment of student learning outcomes on campus. As such, he has conducted numerous assessment studies on campus. Dr. Hohm also administers the Summer AVID Program on campus. Professor Hohm also serves on the advisory board for the Center for Community Based Service-Learning at SDSU. He utilizes community service learning in his classes and has recently finished the production of a seventeen-minute video entitled *The Road to Community Service Learning*.

Ann M. Johns is a professor of linguistics and writing studies at San Diego State University and past director of the university's Writing-across-the-Curriculum and Center for Teaching and Learning programs. In addition to more than fifty articles and book chapters on academic reading and writing, she has published two recent volumes, *Text, Role, and Context: Developing Academic Literacies* (Cambridge, 1997) and *Genre in the Classroom: Multiple Perspectives* (Lawrence Erlbaum, 2002).

Evangelina Bustamante Jones, a third-generation Latina, was born and educated in Phoenix, Arizona. After completing a B.A. in liberal arts and an M.A. in English education at Arizona State University, she began her teaching career in California secondary and elementary classrooms that were comprised of mostly Mexican, Mexican American, and Latino students. In 1998, she completed the Claremont Graduate University and San Diego State University joint Ph.D. program. Her dissertation, *Mexican American Teachers as Cultural Mediators: Literacy and Literacy Contexts through Bicultural Strengths,* explored the relationship between teachers' biculturalism and the teaching ideology developed through bicultural consciousness. Previously teaching at SDSU's Imperial Valley Campus, she is now a professor in the College of Education's Policy Studies department.

Swapna Mukhopadhyay, currently an assistant professor of curriculum and instruction at Portland State University, is a critical math educator. Within her frame of reference of mathematics as a human construction, her teaching and research focus on the social, cultural, and political aspects of social organization as they influence human cognition. With Barbara Waxman and Nancy M. Robinson, she has published two monographs, *Parents Nurturing Math-Talented Young Children* and *Teachers Nurturing Math-Talented Young Children,* both for the National Center on the Gifted and Talented, University of Connecticut, 1996. Her current research interests are ethnomathematics, equity and social justice issues, informal and formal learning, and bridging formal learning to out-of-school practice.

Maureen Kelley Sipp is a lecturer in the Department of Rhetoric and Writing Studies as well as the Department of English and Comparative Literature. She has been teaching lower and upper division writing courses since 1996. She is the Learning Communities Co-coordinator of approximately forty integrated course packages for the Thomas B. Day Freshman Success program, a program offering personal and academic growth opportunities for incoming freshmen. She also serves on the Lower Division Writing Committee, which is responsible for developing curriculum, course descriptions, and all matters relating to lower division courses in the Department of Rhetoric and Writing Studies. In addition, she assists incoming graduate teaching associates by providing office hours and classroom consultations and participating in a series of weekly meetings entitled "Issues in Teaching Composition." She is also the editor of *Instructors' Resource Guide,* a comprehensive online guide including course descriptions and material important to instructors for all courses taught by the Department of Rhetoric and Writing Studies. She was one of six SDSU faculty members who in spring 1999 participated in a pilot program for Blackboard, a widely used course management software program, and she participates yearly as a presenter at the fall conference of the Department of Rhetoric and Writing Studies.

Carol F. Venable is on the faculty of the School of Accountancy at San Diego State University. She teaches courses in auditing/systems, professional responsibility and ethics, regulatory controls, and reporting for accountants. Her interests include experiential learning, collaborative pedagogy, and the use of technology. She designed and developed a collaborative-learning technology classroom that is being used for various business communication and accounting classes. She is the current curriculum fellow for the Center for Community Based Service-Learning at SDSU and serves on its advisory board. She is a member of the University Assessment Committee and was on the General Education Committee for nine years, serving as its chair for five of those years. She serves on the editorial board of *Advances in Accounting Education.*

Minjuan Wang is assistant professor of educational technology at San Diego State University. Her primary areas of interest include computer-supported collaborative learning, technology and teacher education, and design of instructional systems and materials. She currently teaches "Technologies for Teaching," "Procedures of Investigation and Report," and "Instructional Design." Dr. Wang completed her Ph.D. work in the School of Information Science and Learning Technologies at the University of Missouri–Columbia. She was a research coordinator for the Center for Technology Innovations in Education (CTIE) at the University of Missouri. She worked as an instructional design consultant for PricewaterhouseCoopers and collaborated with Motorola University in conducting research and evaluation on the Internet-based Expeditions (iExpeditions) program. She has published a book and several articles in international journals.

Pat Washington is an assistant professor of women's studies at San Diego State University. A sociologist by training, she uses a gendered lens to examine social stratification in the United States and abroad, with an emphasis on social inequalities and efforts to eradicate those inequalities. Her current research focuses on the use of community-based service learning to advance feminist pedagogy, enhance student learning outcomes, and foster civic and intellectual engagement. Dr. Washington has written and consulted nationally and internationally on the efficacy of community-based service learning for promoting positive social change. A second major area of Dr. Washington's research is hate- and bias-motivated violence and the revictimization of lesbian and gay sexual assault survivors, with particular emphasis on the revictimization of lesbian and gay sexual assault survivors of color.

Shirley N. Weber is an associate professor of Africana Studies at San Diego State University. As one of the original members of the Africana Studies Department she has served as chairperson of the department and curriculum chair. She considers herself an "activist scholar." Her publications are in the areas of nationalism, movement studies, and Black language. Currently, she is vice president of the National Council for Black Studies. She is also a founder of the W. E. B. Du Bois Young Black Scholars, which is supported by the N.A.A.C.P. and Africana students. She holds a B.A., an M.A., and a Ph.D. from UCLA in speech communication. Dr. Weber has received hundreds of awards from academic and community associations. She lectures widely throughout the nation and West Africa.

Randy Yerrick is a science teacher educator at San Diego State University. His research interests include lower-track high school science students within the context of current science education reform. Dr. Yerrick has studied his own efforts to invoke shifts in lower-track science classroom discourse in a variety of multicultural contexts, most recently in the rural South. Currently recognized as an Apple Distinguished Educator, he continues his efforts in San Diego to bring majority teacher education candidates to an understanding of their own culture and its relevance to teaching science for diversity and equity.

Russell L. Young is a professor of education in the Department of Policy Studies in Language and Cross-Cultural Education at San Diego State University. He teaches courses in multicultural education, language policy, and educational research. His current research interests include ethnic identity, multicultural strategies toward teaching, and education of Asians. He has published in the diverse fields of public health, multicultural education, counseling, sociolinguistics, and teacher education. He has lived in Hong Kong and Taiwan. He has also published award-winning children's stories, including *Dragonsong,* recipient of the 2000 National Association of Multicultural Education Children's Book Award.

Maria Zuniga has been a professor of social work at San Diego State University for the past sixteen years. Prior to her teaching career, she worked as a psychiatric social worker in a mental health clinic, as a public welfare worker in a child protective services unit, and as a medical social worker in a hospital. As a member of the board of directors of the Council of Social Work Education, she cochaired the First Task Force on Cultural Competency, held at the University of Michigan School of Social Work, and is editing a text based on this conference. She has published numerous articles and chapters on how to intervene competently with Latino families and individuals, with a special focus on immigrant Latino populations. She is an editor for the *Journal of Multicultural Social Work.*

Index

Page numbers in *italics* refer to figures and tables.

mathematics (*continued*)
geometry of cultural artifacts, 197–198
inclusive view of diversity, 201–203
knowledge construction process, 195–201
NCTM (National Council for Teachers of Mathematics) principles, 190–191
pedagogical alternatives ("mathematics of all"), 191–203
pedagogical homogeneity ("mathematics for all"), 188–193
tax and discount problem, 200–201
traditional vs. modern views of, 187–188
value of diversity for, 193–194
meaning enhancement, 55, 66–68
men. *See* gender
mobility/orthopedic disabilities, 117–119, 127–128
Montevallo, University of, 8
Moses, Bob, 53–54
Mukhopadhyay, Swapna, 2, 3, 53, 63, 187–206
multicultural curricula. *See* cross-cultural curricula
multiple sclerosis, 118

National Association of Scholars, 7
National Center for Education Statistics, 117, 124
National Council for Accreditation of Teacher Education (NCATE), 232–233
National Council for Black Studies, 249
National Council for Social Studies (NCSS), 232
National Council for Teachers of Mathematics (NCTM) principles, 190–191

National Council of Teachers of English (NCTE), 232
National Educational Longitudinal Study, 124
National Organization on Disability, 114
National Postsecondary Student Aid Study, 117
National Study of Postsecondary Faculty, 152
National Survey of Student Engagement, x
National Urban League, 254
New York at Stony Brook, State University of, 78

Office of Diversity and Equity (ODE), San Diego State University, xii, 1
Ohio University, 8
Operation Breadbasket, 250
organizations and associations, xi. *See also specific titles*
orthopedic/mobility disabilities, 117–119, 127–128

partnerships, community-based service learning (CBSL), 223–227
Peace and Freedom Party, 226–227
Pittsburgh school district, 77
plagiarism and linguistically diverse students, 145
Plato, 29, 187, 188
portfolios, 72–95
advantages and disadvantages, 78–79
challenges involved in using, 79–81
defining, 75–77
diversity as central focus of class, 82–86
diversity content and, 79–80
integrated diversity content, classes with, 86–91